Becoming a Reflective English Teacher

Becoming a Reflective English Teacher

Edited by Andrew Green

Open University Press

Open University Press
McGraw-Hill Education
McGraw-Hill House
Shoppenhangers Road
Maidenhead
Berkshire
England
SL6 2QL

email: enquiries@openup.co.uk
world wide web: www.openup.co.uk

and Two Penn Plaza, New York, NY 10121-2289, USA

First published 2011

A catalogue record of this book is available from the British Library

ISBN-13: 978 0 335 24289 4 (pb)   978 0 335 24290 0 (hb)
ISBN-10: 0 0335 24289 8 (pb)   0335 24290 1 (hb)
eISBN 978 0 335 24291 7

Library of Congress Cataloging-in-Publication Data
CIP data applied for

Typesetting and e-book compilation by
RefineCatch Limited, Bungay, Suffolk
Printed in the UK by CPI Antony Rowe, Chippenham

The **McGraw·Hill** Companies

Contents

Figures

Tables

Contributors

Angella Cooze is Senior Lecturer in the School of Education at Swansea Metropolitan University. She is Subject Leader for the PGCE English course and Strand Manager for the MA(Ed) EAL strand. Angella is also module leader for both the Language and Learning and ESDGC MA(Ed) modules. She also contributes to a number of other courses, primarily in the areas of literacy, language acquisition and development, English as an additional language, diversity, and research methods. Prior to this, she enjoyed teaching English at schools in South Wales. Her research interests include English as an additional language, literacy, and philosophy for children. She is the author of *100 Tips for Teaching English*, *100+ Ideas for Teaching English* and *100 Ideas for Trainee Teachers*.

Robert Fisher taught for more than twenty years in schools in the UK, Africa and Hong Kong and was head of a primary school in Richmond. He has published more than thirty books on education, including *Teaching Children to Think*, *Teaching Children to Learn*, *Teaching Thinking*, the *Stories for Thinking* series, and *Creative Dialogue*. His books have been translated into thirteen languages. He was awarded a PhD for research into philosophy for children. He was a professor of education at Brunel University, and since retiring is a conference speaker and educational consultant on teaching thinking, dialogic learning and creativity. He also cultivates his own creativity through art, sculpture, poetry, music and Argentinian tango. He has a website at www.teachingthinking. net and a blog featuring his art and poetry.

Jenny Grahame taught media in London comprehensives for many years. She is Media Consultant at the English and Media Centre, London, where she delivers continuing professional development, writes teaching resources, and edits *MediaMagazine* for 16+ media and film students. She has developed continuing professional development and initial teacher education courses in media education from Key Stage 3 to MA level for local authorities and higher education institutions, including a National Strategy training package for media in English at Key Stage 3. She has devised classroom publications from Key Stage 2 to A level including work on advertising, news, TV drama, reality TV and short film, and has collaborated on many cross-curricular research projects in partnership with TDA, QCA, Gulbenkian, Esmee Fairbairn and CSCYM. She is a founder member of the Media Education Association.

Andrew Green is Senior Lecturer in English Education at Brunel University, where he leads the PGCert in Secondary English Education. He also teaches on Masters and PhD programmes. Recent books are *Starting an English Literature Degree, Transition and Acculturation, Frankenstein* and *Wuthering Heights*. He is also the author of numerous literary articles, A level student text guides and A level resources, as well as academic papers on the subject of English A level and higher education English. Prior to commencing his role at Brunel, he taught in a range of secondary schools in Oxfordshire and South London.

Joanna McIntyre is Lecturer in English Education at the University of Nottingham where she is a member of the Centre for Research in Schools and Communities (CRSC). At the University of Nottingham, and in her previous position at Nottingham Trent University, Jo has taught on a range of initial teacher education programmes, including PGCE, GTP and Teach First. She also teaches on the Masters in Education programme. Previously, as a teacher of English, a head of department and an Advanced Skills Teacher, she developed a strong philosophy about the importance of English to students as a means of personal expression, developing cultural values, critical enquiry and fostering creativity. This has led to an interest in research which focuses on narrative. Jo has worked on a range of funded research projects and is particularly interested in research on the discourses surrounding schools and the teachers that work in them, the lives of both long-serving and beginner teachers, and approaches to mentoring.

Bethan Marshall is Senior Lecturer in the Department of Education and Professional Studies at King's College, London. One of her major areas of interest is in the competing philosophies or models of English as a subject and how these impact on policy. She is currently researching the way in which English teachers' philosophies of their subject change over time. She is also concerned with the relationship between assessment and learning, with particular reference to English, a subject on which she has published widely, as well as the relationship between film and television and pupils' developing literacy.

Debra Myhill is Professor of Education at the University of Exeter, and is Acting Dean for the College of Social Sciences and International Studies. She leads the PGCE Secondary English programme and her research interests focus principally on aspects of language and literacy teaching, particularly writing and grammar, and talk in the classroom. She has led three ESRC-funded research projects; one on talk for learning and two on writing (Patterns and Processes, and Grammar for Writing) and one funded by Esmee Fairbairn (From Talk to Text); co-convened an ESRC Research Seminar series 'Reconceptualising Writing'; and given research presentations at numerous conferences, national and international, for both professional and research communities. She is the author of *Better Writers*, and co-editor of *Talking, Listening, Learning: Effective Talk in the Primary Classroom, Using Talk to Support Writing* and the *Handbook of Writing Development*.

Vicky Obied is Lecturer in Secondary English with Media and Drama on the PGCE programme at Goldsmiths. She also works on the Masters in Education: Culture,

Language and Identity and the MPhil/PhD programme in the Educational Studies Department. She is a committee member of the Centre for Language, Culture and Learning at Goldsmiths. Her expertise is in language development, and her doctorate research was in the area of language and literacy and applied linguistics. Vicky's research interests lie in biliteracy and biculturalism, and poetry. A key area of her research is an analysis of cultural perspectives in relation to literacy, and the conflicts which might arise from contrasting cultural and social practices. Her research interests also include the literacy development of bi- and multi-lingual students in mainstream classes.

Maggie Pitfield is Lecturer in Secondary English with Media and Drama on the PGCE programme at Goldsmiths. Maggie jointly co-ordinates the Flexible PGCE programme and is also Deputy Head of the Department of Educational Studies. She is a committee member of the Centre for Arts and Learning at Goldsmiths. A key area of research interest is drama in the English curriculum, although she has also published on flexible learning models in initial teacher education. Prior to joining Goldsmiths in 2002, Maggie taught drama and English, and latterly media studies, in London secondary schools, a career spanning twenty-four years. She has had considerable experience as a Head of English. She was Chair of Harrow Teachers' Consultative Committee for a number of years, and was a member of the now disbanded BBC English Education Consultative Group.

Richard Quarshie is Programme Leader for Secondary PGCE and GTP English at the Cass School of Education, University of East London. He taught English for twenty-two years in London comprehensive schools, and for eight years was Head of the Department of English and Media Studies at Stoke Newington School, Hackney. He first moved into initial teacher education at the University of London Institute of Education, where he taught for five years before taking up his present post. He is a former Chair of the Multicultural Committee of the National Association for the Teaching of English. His research interests include autobiography, learner autonomy, and linguistic and cultural diversity in English.

Gary Snapper was Head of English at Impington Village College, Cambridge. He is currently a Research Associate in the School of Education at Brunel University, the editor of NATE's professional journal *English Drama Media*, a teacher of A level English at the Cheney School in Oxford, a member of NATE's Post-16 Committee, and a freelance consultant. He recently completed doctoral research into the transition between sixth form and university English, and is planning further research into and writing about the history, theory and practice of post-16 English.

Linda Varley taught and examined A level English and language before joining the University of Manchester in 2002 as a PGCE tutor and course director for an MEd course on the teaching of English. She is currently Joint Programme Manager for the Teach First North West PGCE programme, which she combines with her role as Professional and English Subject Tutor. She is Lead Subject Studies Tutor for English, co-ordinating the English Subject Studies programme nationally. She took a lead role within Teach First in implementing the transition of QTS ITT to PGCE and moving mentors and tutors to M level. Her research interest is the 1944 Normandy Campaign, and she has designed and resourced a website for Normandy veterans, recording their first-hand experiences.

Annabel Watson is a PhD candidate at the University of Exeter, UK, working on a large-scale ESRC-funded project investigating the impact of contextualised grammar teaching on the development of students' writing at Key Stage 3. Her particular area of study is the relationship between teachers' beliefs and pedagogic practices. Her wider research interests include multi-modal literacy and the teaching of writing. She teaches on various courses in the Graduate School of Education at Exeter, and is responsible for the media element of the English with Media Secondary PGCE.

Paula Zwozdiak-Myers is Lecturer in Education at Brunel University. She is an experienced teacher, teacher educator, researcher and writer of educational materials. She has worked in urban and rural secondary schools in England. She has a particular interest in inclusion and special educational needs (SEN), and leads a specialist SEN strand at Masters level, focusing on difference and diversity, the promotion of individual potential and entitlement, and the meanings of inclusion as a philosophical, socio-cultural, political and educational agenda. Her current major research focuses on reflective practice for professional development in teacher education. Other areas of interest include qualitative approaches to research, partnership working in initial teacher education, interpersonal relationships and communication skills, and dance and movement studies.

Abbreviations

AF	assessment focuses
AFL	Assessment for Learning
APP	Assessing Pupils' Progress
CR	collaborative reasoning
EAL	English as an additional language
ERA	Education Reform Act
ESRC	Economic and Social Research Council
ETUCE	European Trade Union Committee for Education
FHEQ	Framework for Higher Education Qualifications
HE	higher education
IB	International Baccalaureate
ICT	Information and Communications Technology
ITE	Initial Teacher Education
JMB	Joint Matriculation Board
KAL	knowledge about language
KS	Key Stage
LATE	London Association for the Teaching of English
LEA	Local Education Authority
LINC	Language in the National Curriculum
LSA	learning support assistant
MFL	modern foreign language
NAGTY	National Academy of Gifted and Talented Youth
NATE	National Association for the Teaching of English
NCC	National Curriculum Council
NEAB	Northern Examination Association Board
NLS	National Literacy Strategy
NQT	newly qualified teacher
OECD	Organisation for Economic Co-operation and Development
PIRLS	Progress in International Reading Literacy Study
PNI	positive, negative, informative
POS	programmes of study

QTS	Qualified Teacher Status
S&L	speaking and listening
SEN	special educational needs
TDA	Training and Development Agency
VLE	virtual learning environments

1

ANDREW GREEN
Getting started

Introduction

Welcome to the exciting and challenging world of teaching English. Whatever else they may be, the course of teacher education you are about to enter and your future career as a teacher of English in secondary school will never be dull. Every lesson you teach, every student you come into contact with, every new concept you try to impart will throw up new challenges for you. It is in working through and reflecting upon these events and challenges that you will develop as a teacher, and it is in this very process that the greatest rewards of teaching are to be found.

This book is built on the principle that the practice of teaching is more rewarding and robust when it is founded on sound academic foundations. Theory and practice interconnect, and it is the purpose of this book to help you understand how. Theory that does not relate to practice is empty content, but by the same token practice that takes no account of theory is like shooting in the dark. With this principle in mind, reflection is a major focus of this book, as it is through reflection that you will be able to develop your sense of how theory feeds into practice. It has a central role to play in the cycle of teaching and learning (see Figure 1.1).

This diagram illustrates the cyclical nature of the teaching and learning process. Planning takes place in preparation for teaching. Once teaching has taken place (or while it is taking place), teachers reflect on their practice and evaluate its impact on learning. Evaluation feeds further cycles of planning to inform teaching and learning, and so on. The reflection required will be of different types depending upon the situations you are facing:

- Personal – think about the relationships you are developing with students and a variety of colleagues
- Professional – consider the meaning of professionalism and what this constitutes within the school environment
- Academic – seek to develop your understanding of your subject
- Pedagogic – explore the wide range of ways in which learning can be mediated and enhanced.

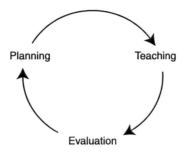

Figure 1.1 The cycle of teaching and learning

Throughout this book you will find activities designed to help you in this process. Each chapter addresses a significant aspect of your work as a teacher of English. These are varied in their focus to reflect the diverse and continually developing nature of English in schools. Since 2009 there have been significant political and curricular changes to English – the abolition of the Key Stage (KS) 3 SATs, new specifications for GCSE and A level, the inauguration of a new National Curriculum, and so on – and the nature of English as a discipline is also changing to take account of new literacies, developments in Information and Communications Technology (ICT), changes in the ways in which readers consume and relate to text, and so forth. With this in mind, the need for teachers to be critically reflective has, perhaps, never been more pronounced.

The structuring of the chapters in this book is designed to reflect the constantly changing nature of the subject and the demands this places on those training to teach it. Some are based on enduring subject matter for teaching (e.g. Chapter 9, 'Drama in English'; Chapter 10, 'Media in English'; Chapter 11, 'Knowledge about language and multi-literacies'; and Chapter 13, 'Teaching post-16 English'); others are based on the modalities of language, the issues we face when teaching processes in these areas, and the ways in which they may operate in the classroom (e.g. Chapter 5, 'Teaching writing'; Chapter 6, 'Teaching reading'; and Chapter 7, 'Dialogic teaching'); a third set consider broader aspects of teaching (e.g. Chapter 4, 'Planning the curriculum'; Chapter 8, 'Assessing English'; and Chapter 12, 'English and student diversity'); a final group of chapters looks at other aspects of your career experience (e.g. Chapter 2, 'What is English?'; Chapter 3, 'Reflective practice for professional development'; Chapter 4, 'Planning the curriculum'; and Chapter 14, 'Academic writing at M level').

Through a close consideration of these and other issues, you will be introduced to the theories and concepts underpinning the practice of English within the contemporary classroom. Practice is always more robust, and reflection more thorough when theoretically informed. By engaging with a range of relevant policy and theoretical perspectives, your ability to locate, rationalise and understand your own practice will be enhanced.

Masters level

The nature of Initial Teacher Education (ITE) has undergone a change. In response to the Bologna Agreement (1999), the National Framework for Higher Education

Qualifications (FHEQ) in 2001 made it clear that 'postgraduate' must be postgraduate not only in terms of time (i.e. completed after graduation from a first degree), but also postgraduate in terms of content (i.e. study must be at a level beyond undergraduate study in the relevant discipline). In the case of PGCE qualifications, therefore, students should engage with the discipline of education at Masters level. Most ITE courses now provide at least the option for students to gain Masters level credits in the course of their studies, and in most cases this is now the expectation. Students opting not to or failing effectively to complete the Masters level components of courses in ITE can no longer be awarded a postgraduate certificate, but will receive instead a professional certificate, assuming they meet the requirements of the Standards for Qualified Teacher Status (QTS).

Along with changing political agendas with regard to higher education (HE), school and training agendas have also developed. There is now a general thrust towards teaching becoming a Masters level profession. This is reflected not only in the provision of ITE courses in HE, but also in the Standards for QTS with their focus on knowledge and understanding, and in the ongoing Standards for Professional Development, against which all teachers now work. These embody a substantial component of professional reflection and require demonstrable criticality in developing practice. It is the purpose of this book to help introduce you to the process and to provide constructive ways of building bridges between academic and practical elements of your ITE through a sequence of Masters level activities related to elements of practice and through the development of robust models of reflective practice.

Sound academic practice and reflective criticality are, of course, foundational for effective teaching. The QTS Standards engage with reflective practice as a model for professional and personal development, and in that sense these Standards also embody the Masters level agenda. Teachers have to demonstrate engagement with their subject and its pedagogy in a sustained and critical way as part of their everyday role. The Standards state that teachers must have 'a creative and constructively critical approach towards innovation, being prepared to adapt their practice where benefits and improvements are identified'. This takes us beyond a model based simply on professional competence and into the realms opened up by Masters level study. Such engagement with education as a discipline is mirrored in the FHEQ descriptor for Masters level, which calls for teachers to have 'a critical awareness of current problems and/or new insights, much of which is at, or informed by, the forefront of their academic discipline, field of study, or area of professional practice'.

Standards for QTS

The successful achievement of QTS depends upon the fulfilment of a set of 33 Standards. These are divided into three sub-sections: Professional Attributes (Q1–Q9), Professional Knowledge and Understanding (Q10–Q21) and Professional Skills (Q22–Q33). These subdivisions reflect the complex inter-relationship between differing components of the teacher's role. The first section covers the personal and professional qualities that underpin effective teaching and learning, the second deals with more numinous issues of knowledge and understanding and looks at a range of

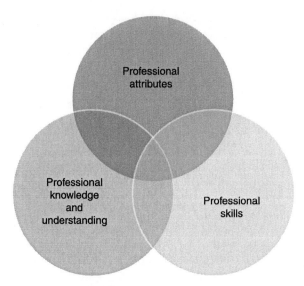

Figure 1.2 Interaction of standards

factors underpinning effective work within the classroom, and the third focuses on the practical operation of the classroom and the processes this entails.

While in one sense these professional Standards need to be considered discreetly – each Standard is a unit for assessment in its own right – the bigger picture is, of course, far more complex, and the three areas of the Standards frequently overlap, as Figure 1.2 illustrates. It is impossible, for example, to implement effective processes for assessment (a professional skill) without having a detailed knowledge and understanding of the philosophies and the processes that underpin assessment (professional knowledge and understanding) and without having a clear commitment to developing students' experience as learners of English and developing appropriate contexts within which this can occur (a professional attribute). The most powerful practice, and therefore the best teaching and learning, resides in the central section of the diagram, where all three aspects of the teacher's work coincide. The Standards cannot all be evidenced in the same way, however. It is important from early in your thinking about the Standards that you are aware of the explicit differences between them.

Key features

In order to help you develop your own reflection and to further your thinking about the issues covered in each chapter, the following key features can be found throughout the book:

1. Introductory boxes: outlining the major issues that will be covered in order to begin your thinking processes and to indicate the range of coverage for easy reference.

2. Summary boxes: a summary of key points; these will provide final thoughts on the issues that have been covered.

3. Recommended reading lists: a selection of relevant books, journal articles, websites and other sources relating to the matter covered in the chapter; these lists will focus on texts at Masters level to assist you in targeting your wider reading and in preparing for both the practical and the academic elements of your work.

4. Professional reflection: targeted reflective activities (e.g. reflection on practice or practical scenarios, auditing activities, self- and peer-assessment, observation and evaluation activities, and readings to feed into thinking about practice).

5. Masters level tasks: designed to help you develop strong and meaningful connections between academic and practical components of your studies (e.g. summaries of key concepts, digests about key thinkers, application of theory to practical teaching contexts).

6. Into practice: opportunities to think about the practical application of what you have read (e.g. planning exercises, devising assessment tasks, developing a range of resources, trying out certain activities personally).

There are certain issues in teaching that are of general professional significance and underpin your work as a teacher. These are often known as cross-curricular issues. In order to reflect this, there are feature boxes addressing these issues in most chapters to allow you to think about how these matters affect your practice in a range of areas and ways:

1. Inclusion (special educational needs [SEN]/inclusion/gifted education): These features will guide your thinking in relation to a range of student needs, from the most to the least able. They will focus your attention specifically on the issues underlying students' particular needs and the practicalities of meeting these (e.g. What are the particular issues in working with gifted students on writing?)

2. English as an additional language (EAL): It is difficult to deal generically with issues of EAL, as the needs of EAL learners vary very specifically from one language to another. There are, however, some general principles, and these boxes will focus your thinking – what, for instance, may be the particular difficulties an EAL learner may face with drama?

3. ICT: ICT has a binary role in the English classroom. It is a pedagogic tool that opens up a wealth of opportunities in the classroom, but it is also an area of cognitive content for teaching. This feature provides activities and ideas relating to both.

4. Creativity: This is designed to develop creative thinking about how to teach English, providing you with a range of innovative ways of thinking about doing English in the classroom. More general issues about the role of creativity within learning and of ways of understanding creativity will also be addressed.

Happy reading and reflection.

2

ANDREW GREEN AND JOANNA MCINTYRE
What is English?

> In this chapter you will consider
>
> - the background of English as an academic discipline;
> - personal experiences of English teaching;
> - the role of the English teacher; and
> - what constitutes subject knowledge for teaching.

Introduction

What is English? It may seem a simple question, but the answer is in fact far from straightforward. Is it a language, a subject or a people? A noun or an adjective? If we accept it is a subject for study, does its content deal solely with language or does it also incorporate literature, media, spoken text, ICTs and so on? If it incorporates literature, who decides which books are considered of sufficient literary merit? Issues of nationhood and the legacy of Empire are also encoded in the subject in ongoing debates about whether English literature means works written solely by authors from England, or by any author writing in English (e.g. Canadians, Australians, New Zealanders, Americans, South Africans, Caribbean writers and so forth). And what about literature in translation or studied in its original language? Why the presence of the troublesome adjective 'English', which implies a certain distinction from the rest of the world?

The idea of what constitutes English, then, is not as simple as it may at first appear. Nor is the history of the subject. The subject's place in the curriculum was hard won, due in part to the subject's awkward status as medium as well as object of study, a debate that is still rife in the battle between subject skills and subject content. In short, English has always been and continues to be something of a political football, and as such it is a subject fraught with social, national, religious, philosophical and political ideology. And every day the subject is developing and mutating, taking on new words, new media and associated methods of textual production and reception, shaping itself to new social and political forces, stretching to incorporate new works of literature and cinema. The list could go on. Suffice it to say that great challenges and great rewards await those engaged in teaching this most vibrant, dynamic and troublesome of subjects.

With all this in mind, it is very important for you to spend some time coming to an understanding of where your subject comes from, what it involves, and how you as a practitioner respond to these shaping forces. Perhaps it is useful to begin by considering how you and others around you view teachers in general and English teachers in particular.

Creativity: anatomy of an English teacher

Speak to as many non-teachers as you can about the kind of person they think of when they imagine an English teacher. On the basis of their replies, draw a caricature of the archetypal English teacher and label it. What are their characteristics? What do they wear? What do they look like? Is this caricature a fair representation? Is this what you want people to think of you?

Now jot down the characteristics you would like to display to your students.

History of English as a subject

It is sometimes a revelation to beginning teachers that there was a time *before* a statutory prescribed curriculum for English. Simply because the English language (in some form) has been around for over 1,400 years, and because there is an extensive body of literature covering the language's entire history, it is easy to assume that English as a subject has also existed for a long time. The history of English as a subject, however, has been short and turbulent. Debates and battles about what should constitute a curriculum for English are as old as the subject itself.

Professional reflection: your experiences of English

Think back to your own study of English in school. Make a list of any significant events or issues that had an impact upon how you were taught. How did these influence your experience of English? Can you link these to wider social, historical or political changes that were going on at the time?

One of the first key markers in the development of the subject was the 1835 English Education Act. Set against the background of Victorian colonial expansion, this Act officially required Indians to study in English and to study works of English literature. English was seen as 'civilising'. Member of the Supreme Council of India T.B. Macaulay in a political Minute of 2 February 1835 perfectly captures the tone of the age, its pride, arrogance and missionary zeal:

> We have to educate a people who cannot at present be educated by means of their mother-tongue. We must teach them some foreign language. The claims of

our own language it is hardly necessary to recapitulate. It stands pre-eminent even among the languages of the West. It abounds with works of imagination not inferior to the noblest which Greece has bequeathed to us, with models of every species of eloquence, with historical composition, which, considered merely as narratives, have seldom been surpassed, and which, considered as vehicles of ethical and political instruction, have never been equalled, with just and lively representations of human life and human nature, with the most profound speculations on metaphysics, morals, government, jurisprudence, trade, with full and correct information respecting every experimental science which tends to preserve the health, to increase the comfort, or to expand the intellect of man. Whoever knows that language has ready access to all the vast intellectual wealth which all the wisest nations of the earth have created and hoarded in the course of ninety generations. It may safely be said that the literature now extant in that language is of greater value than all the literature which three hundred years ago was extant in all the languages of the world together.

(Macaulay 1835, in Bureau of Education 1920)

Having established the principle in the colonial context, English (and specifically literature) was introduced as a mechanism of social cohesion in the English context when it was felt that religion no longer fulfilled this function; it was 'literally the poor man's Classics' and was introduced in 'the Mechanic's Institutes, working men's colleges and extension lecturing circuits' (Eagleton 1983: 23). So, from its inception, the subject English has had a social and political purpose. Over time, these social and political purposes have shifted in response to differing claims on the place of English within the curriculum.

In 1851, the poet Matthew Arnold, one of the first of Her Majesty's Inspectorate for schools, campaigned for the place of English within the curriculum (and particularly the study of literature) of the new state education system. Again, it was thought that literature could be used as a mechanism for bringing civilising influences and culture to the masses. However, Arnold railed against the emphasis on examination skills, which he believed stifled creativity. Marshall argues that 'Arnold's legacy, his desire to use culture to oppose the mechanistic, is the progenitor of competing traditions in the fight to establish English on the curriculum' (2000: 22).

Towards the end of the century, the debate over English surfaced once more. The study of English was by now entering the universities, but was largely confined to the study of linguistics and philology. Literature was still not seriously considered as a subject for study. In 1887 Henry Nettleship published *The Study of Modern European Languages and Literatures in the University of Oxford* in which he argued the inferiority of English literature compared to the classics. Writing in 1891, however, J.C. Collins in *The Study of English Literature* offered the view that literature provided 'moral and aesthetic' education.

The Newbolt Report (1921), produced in response to questions about the function of state education in a country recovering from the First World War, again promoted the role of English as a driver for social unity and claimed that literature and art had the potential to develop the human character and to help lead 'the bulk of our people' who 'are unconsciously living starved existences' (1921: 157). A model of English emerged from Newbolt which emphasised the subject's responsibility to communicate particular systems of culture and values alongside encouraging personal growth. The report recognised the levels of professional knowledge and understanding required to teach English and made some surprisingly modern recommendations concerning student voice and peer-assessment.

Simultaneously, English was emerging as a serious subject to study at university. It had progressed from Professor Sandy's dismissive observation in 1893 that 'English is a subject suitable for women and the second- and third-rate men who are to become schoolmasters' (cited in Davison and Dowson 2003: 18) to being championed in the 1930s at the University of Cambridge as 'not only a subject worth studying, but *the* supremely civilising pursuit, the spiritual essence of the social formation' (Eagleton 1983: 27). The debate about the validity of English literature as a subject for study had reached a nexus in 1919 when F.R. Leavis, Q.D. Leavis, E.M.W. Tillyard and I.A. Richards taught the first English literature course at Cambridge.

M level task: further reading

For a fuller understanding of the genesis of English as a subject, the following are recommended:

- Moran, J. (2002) 'F.R. Leavis, English and the university', *English* 51: 1–13.
- Palmer, D.J. (1965) *The Rise of English Studies.* London: Oxford University Press.
- Sarbu, A. (2005) 'English as an academic discipline: some history', *Neohelicon* 32:2: 443–56.

In developing their course, Leavis and his colleagues were obliged to make the aesthetic and academic case for English, which they did in terms that are a curious mixture of the scientific (objective, context-free consideration of text) and the aesthetic (canon of texts to admire and appreciate). Figure 2.1 outlines the major features of Leavis' model of English and encapsulates this dichotomy. The Leavisite-influenced Cambridge journal *Scrutiny* (first published in 1932) continued to develop 'the map of English literature' by promoting texts and authors as constituent parts of what 'was English Literature' (Eagleton 1983: 28). According to Eagleton, Leavis and his contemporaries used the journal *Scrutiny* as 'moral and cultural crusade' which took the message of what was worthy of study out to schools and universities. Although the varying pushes and pulls of what constitutes English at university initially had limited impact on what was actually happening in the classroom, such an influence soon became apparent as graduates of university English courses began to enter the teaching profession. This influence can be neatly illustrated by comparing the authors promoted by the Cambridge journal (listed in Eagleton 1983: 28) with those found in the prescribed list of authors to be studied in the National Curriculum today.

Into practice: literature in the curriculum

Look at the list of authors in the Programme of Study for English who make up the
English literary heritage. Ask yourself these questions:

· Who is missing from this list of authors?
· What is the relationship between notions of literary heritage and assumptions
  about shared cultural identity?
· What counts as literature?

While literature was promoted by Leavisites as the humanising force of the curriculum, there were other schools of thought regarding the role of English in the curriculum. According to Burgess (2002: 26 – our emphasis), after the Second World War
'there were major gains in understanding the importance of audience and of the functions of written language' with an emphasis on real texts and a deepening understanding of the different types of literacies encountered by students in the world beyond the
school gates: significantly, 'such understandings derived not just from research but
also from *initiatives by teachers*'.

The Bullock Report (DES 1975) was a major influence on how English was re-
shaped. It endorsed curriculum approaches which valued the language of the home,
replaced notions of correctness with those of appropriateness, and promoted the
importance of language.

Throughout this period, decisions about appropriate curriculum 'models' of
English were largely left to the teachers themselves. This was partly because of the
introduction in 1964 of the Schools Council, which was dominated by representatives
of teachers. Classroom practitioners had a fair amount of autonomy and in the main
worked with models of English which conformed to notions of progressive education.
Learning was seen as a collaborative endeavour between student and teacher. English
departments were fairly free to develop or follow their own understandings of the subject, and individual teachers' professional identities were formed or evolved in relation
to their own identifications with the models and discourses of English followed in a
particular school or Local Education Authority (LEA).

In spite of the flexibility and freedom enjoyed by English departments at this time,
outside the classroom there were conflicting views. Jones (2003: 72) explains that by
the end of the 1970s discourses about schooling had changed: 'less areas of consensus
than battlegrounds where a defensive left and an ascendant right fought over educators'
meaning, methods and purposes'. In 1976 the Schools Council was abolished after the
findings of a report, known as the 'Yellow Book' (commissioned by the Prime Minister,
James Callaghan), were disseminated. The report which had examined education over
three decades challenged the authority of teachers in deciding curriculum matters. In
a speech at Ruskin College, Oxford, Callaghan stated that 'Education policy should be
guided by economic imperatives; students should be prepared for the "world of work";
existing classroom practice should be subject to critical scrutiny, central influence
over educational change asserted' (Jones 2003: 73). Education subsequently became
subject to what Ball (1990: 22) has described as 'discourses of derision' where media

(and governmental) portrayals of teachers, teaching and the curriculum made them the object of scorn and ridicule. There was perceived to be a link between progressive models of education and the economic decline that characterised the late 1970s. This translated into a wider debate about how youth was associated with images of social decline (this was the age of punk) and became part of a wider debate about the decline in standards. Slips in educational standards particularly those related to English were linked with slips in standards of behaviour, morality and even cleanliness. The argument was taken to its extreme logical conclusion in the mid-1980s. Marshall draws attention to the most obvious example of this in an interview with the Conservative minister Norman Tebbit on the *Today* programme in 1985:

> If you allow standards to slip to the stage where good English is no better than bad English, where people can just turn up filthy and nobody takes any notice of them in school ... all those things tend to cause people to have no standards at all, and once you lose your standards then there's no imperative to stay out of crime.
>
> (Norman Tebbit, as cited in Marshall 1997: 111)

The autonomy that teachers had enjoyed was shortly to reach a crisis point in the imposition of a statutory National Curriculum for all state schools. The government now had control over the content and assessment standards of the education system. This would enshrine the content of English once and for all.

Professional reflection: response

- Jot down your immediate response to the outline given above.
- What surprises you?
- How does this alter or confirm your initial view of English as a subject?

Constructing views of subject

It is important as you begin your career as an English teacher to think carefully about your own relationship with the subject. Before you go on to consider all of the issues surrounding curriculum, pedagogy and content that will be central to your work, you need to consider your own experiences. These are powerful formative influences upon you as a teacher. The ways in which you were taught will have encoded philosophies and perspectives on English favoured by your teachers and lecturers, and these will in their turn have shaped your own preferences and views of the subject you are preparing to teach. As Grossman *et al.* (1989: 35) observe, '[t]eacher education begins long before students enter formal programs for teacher preparation'.

Formative experiences (both positive and negative) have already played a part in shaping your sense of the kind of teacher you wish to be and the methods you feel comfortable employing. In many cases these experiences underpin the very reasons why you have chosen to become a teacher. Some of these influences may not be obvious, taking the form of tacit assumptions about the subject and how it should be taught.

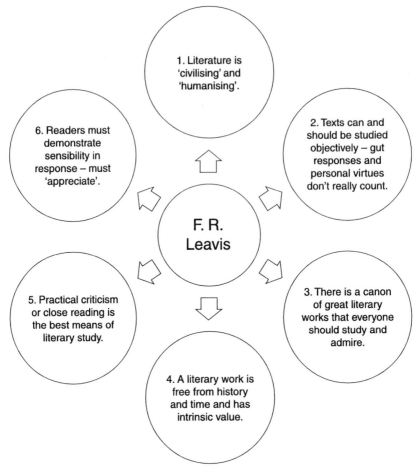

Figure 2.1 Key ideas from Leavis

One of the most powerful thinkers and shaping influences on English (and upon school English still), as discussed above, is F.R. Leavis. It is interesting, therefore, to take Leavis' ideas as a starting point when considering our own views of the subject.

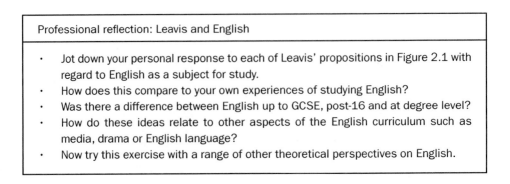

Professional reflection: Leavis and English

- Jot down your personal response to each of Leavis' propositions in Figure 2.1 with regard to English as a subject for study.
- How does this compare to your own experiences of studying English?
- Was there a difference between English up to GCSE, post-16 and at degree level?
- How do these ideas relate to other aspects of the English curriculum such as media, drama or English language?
- Now try this exercise with a range of other theoretical perspectives on English.

It is very important to spend some time unpicking these questions, so that you are aware of the motivations, assumptions and even prejudices that inform your views of English. Once you have done so, try to set out your own philosophy of what English is about.

Professional reflection: personal philosophy

Think carefully about what you hope to achieve through your teaching of English.

- How do you value the different component parts of your subject and how do they relate to each other?
- What aspects of the subject are you particularly interested in teaching?
- What aspects of the subject do you find it more difficult to accommodate and what are you less comfortable about teaching?
- What do you wish students to learn – content, skills, process, personal – from their study of English?

This initial philosophy is central to your understanding of yourself as a beginning teacher, as it is your first attempt at defining your beliefs about what you want to do. It will form the building blocks that will shape your initial forays into the classroom, and will also be the means you will use to measure these. It will also provide the basis of knowledge you believe it is necessary to have in order to function effectively within the classroom. Keep this philosophy and return to it from time to time throughout your training year and, indeed, throughout your career. Look critically at any changes to this philosophy, considering what caused them, and whether you are happy with them. This will ensure that you always remain thoughtful about your practice and how it relates to your personal intentions and values.

Subject knowledge for teaching

Subject knowledge for teaching is a complex issue. What do you need to know to be an effective teacher? How do you relate degree level knowledge to the school curriculum? What about language and grammar? Is it more than content alone? How do you develop subject knowledge for teaching? These and many other questions require careful thought.

It is important to realise that all academic subjects are constructs, comprising a number of components (see Figure 2.2), all of which feed into your overall relationship with the subject. Out of issues such as these, Banks *et al.* (1999) suggest, every teacher develops a personal subject construct, a set of philosophical and educational views about the nature of their subject and what they wish to achieve through their teaching of it.

Evans (1993) suggests that English is a subject which constantly operates at boundaries – it is a subject about transactions and transitions on many different levels. Green (2010) takes this idea and develops it into a model exploring the many classroom transactions that emerge at the boundaries Evans identifies (see Figure 2.3).

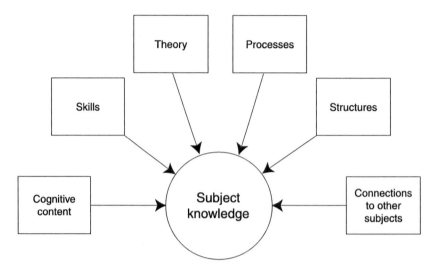

Figure 2.2 Subject knowledge

(These ideas also relate interestingly to Robert Fisher's discussion of the importance of 'dialogue' and 'dialogism' in Chapter 12.)

M level
Look at the transactions identified in Figure 2.3. What different elements of subject knowledge do these transactions deal with? What kinds of transaction take place in each case?

Transitions are also important. In the course if their secondary schooling, students have to negotiate a set of potentially difficult transitions in English: from KS2 to KS3, KS3 to GCSE, GCSE to A level, and A level to higher education. It is often assumed that there is a seamless connection between one phase and the next, whereas in reality the connections may be far from straightforward. Each phase of English education enshrines (often implicitly) its own paradigms of subject – its own particular political agendas, assumptions, priorities, pedagogic practices, assessment imperatives, desired outcomes, and so on. It is important to think about these changes in the nature of English and the developing relationship these imply between teachers and learners (McInnis and James 1995; Knights 2005).

Professional reflection: a joined-up curriculum?
• Look at the National Curriculum at KS2, KS3 and KS4. How effectively do these connect to each other?

- Look at exam specifications for GCSE and A level (all easily available through the exam board websites). Does GCSE prepare students effectively for the demands of A level?
- Does A level prepare students well for the demands of either higher education or the world of work?
- Does English look the same, or does it change?
- Consider your own experience of each of these transitions in your study of English. What difficulties did these transition points cause you?
- How will you help students as they manage the transition from one phase to the next?

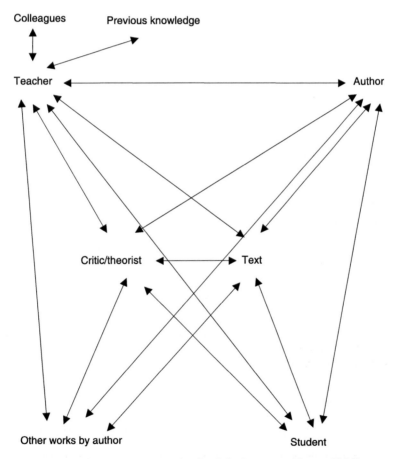

Figure 2.3 Transactions in the English classroom (Green 2010)

From university to school: using your subject knowledge

You are also going through a difficult transition as you move from university back into school (Daly 2004; Burley 2005; Turvey 2005; Green 2006). This move is not simple. Research suggests that academic experience of a subject is, in itself, inadequate preparation for understanding the complexities of teaching that subject (Holmes Group 1986; Grossman *et al.* 1989). As a beginning teacher of English, you need to re-evaluate your understanding of subject knowledge to meet the demands of the school environment. The successful negotiation of this process requires a refinement and redefinition of the knowledge you have obtained through your degree in order to shape this into a workable classroom model. Central in this process is the interrogation of innate assumptions about what you teach, why you teach it, and how you teach it.

How, for example, do you use your degree level knowledge? Maybe you studied George Gissing, the films of Alfred Hitchcock or socio-linguistics in depth. None of these is specifically present on the curriculum. Are they for that reason irrelevant? Or does the learning you have developed relate to your teaching of the subject in other ways? The contextual and critical understanding of Victorian fiction gained through studying the works of Gissing can certainly feed into your teaching of other Victorian literature, such as Dickens or Tennyson. The same is likely to be true of many other authors you may have studied. Likewise, the detailed content of linguistics, drama or media studies courses will probably be most useful for its general rather than its specific application. Even knowledge of universally taught figures such as Shakespeare – the only obligatory author for study in the National Curriculum – can present challenges, as what constitutes effective working knowledge of Shakespeare at degree level is substantially different from practical classroom knowledge of use with students at KS3, GCSE or A level. As one student-teacher (in Green 2006: 113) put it:

> The transformation from graduate in English to teacher of English primarily concerns the ability to devise appropriate teaching strategies to modify my knowledge and understanding into accessible and motivating experience.

This student recognises that scholarship and pedagogy must interact. Good practice at any stage of education must be based around what Knights (2005: 33) calls 'the mutually constitutive relations of pedagogic and scholarly practice'. As a teacher, your relationship with subject changes. You remain on one level a student, but you also need to think about how enthusiasm and understanding can be evoked in your students, and how you can introduce them to the processes and practices of the subject in increasingly complex ways. The teacher needs a multi-faceted knowledge of the subject.

Into practice: using your degree

- Think back over the content of your degree.
- Choose two or three specific topics, authors or modules you studied.
- How might you use the knowledge you gained within your teaching at KS3, GCSE and A level?

- Which aspects will be useful and which will not?
- How will your knowledge need to be adapted?
- How will you introduce students to steadily more complex issues and concepts in these areas?

Early in their courses, beginning teachers tend to focus heavily upon the 'content' dimension of their subject knowledge, measuring themselves against lists of authors, or technical knowledge relating to language, or drama or media as set out in the National Curriculum, GCSE or A level syllabuses. As Turvey (2005: 6) observes:

> Literature – what constitutes its 'objects of study' and the processes of engagement in classrooms – is ... for many (but not all) PGCE students central to how they define themselves as English teachers.

This is understandable. The point at which beginning teachers (and many more experienced teachers) feel most exposed is at the point of knowledge of *what* they are going to teach – the content. Turvey, however, also identifies a particular tendency to place too heavy an emphasis upon knowledge of literature. Blake and Shortis (2010) also identify this, noting interestingly that many graduates of English language, linguistics, drama and media courses find themselves marginalised. Such marginalisation is certainly not justifiable on the basis of the curriculum. English as a school subject is much more than the study of literature, although many schools and many teachers give this an unduly high prominence. Language, non-fiction and non-literary writing, drama, a proliferation of media, and the spoken word, to identify but a few, also have a central role to play in the English curriculum. English teachers need, therefore, not only to expand their knowledge of the literary canon, but also to develop themselves across the whole spectrum of knowledge required.

Effective subject knowledge for teaching, however, is more complex than knowledge of academic content alone. As Dewey (1903: 285–6) remarks:

> Every study or subject thus has two aspects: one for the scientist as a scientist; the other for the teacher as a teacher. These two aspects are in no sense opposed or conflicting. But neither are they immediately identical.

The interface between these two linked but separate knowledges is the business of teaching and learning. Effective teachers have a mastery of their subject (in the case of English, a very rich and varied range of knowledge), but also recognise that this encompasses more than solely the academic content of the subject. Metacognitive and reflexive engagement with subject content knowledge and the processes of learning in English is also necessary.

Models of subject knowledge for teaching

Let us briefly consider two models.

Banks *et al.* (1999)

Banks *et al.* (1999) propose a tripartite division of inter-related subject knowledges (see Figure 2.4).

Subject knowledge

This is the teacher's content knowledge. It provides a straightforward way of measuring what a teacher knows. There is a natural tendency to see this as the key indicator of likely effectiveness as a teacher. While it is important to remember that prior knowledge of a topic or even a specific text does not stand on its own, the National Curriculum and exam specifications are, at least in part, content-based, and so this provides a useful starting point for thinking about what you are and are not confident to teach.

Professional reflection: auditing subject knowledge

Look at the National Curriculum (http://curriculum.qcda.gov.uk/key-stages-3-and-4) focusing on the 'Range' and 'Content' sections for KS3 and KS4. Audit your knowledge against the content outlined here. On the basis of this, set yourself some initial targets for developing the range of your content knowledge.

School knowledge

This dimension of knowledge relates to curricular issues. It covers the range and content of the National Curriculum, the requirements of GCSE and A level courses,

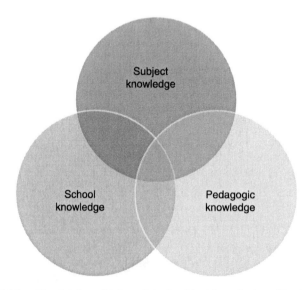

Figure 2.4 A tripartite division of inter-related subject knowledges (Banks *et al.* 1999)

or the materials of the Secondary Strategy. It also covers current modes of assessment and their influence upon the forms the subject takes. Other issues it encompasses are:

- The historical development of the subject and its academic roots.
- The forces that shape educational policy, both locally and nationally.
- School and departmental policies and procedures.
- 'Live' developments in subject material (e.g. trends in children's and teenagers' literature; ICT developments).

In the course of your studies, you will have the opportunity to explore these issues in a range of school and/or other educational settings. In this dimension of subject knowledge, you will begin to confront key questions such as:

- How does the curriculum balance content and skills?
- What is 'in' and what is 'out' of the curriculum and why?
- What is obligatory and what is recommended?
- How do the four modalities of speaking, listening, reading and writing inter-relate both cognitively and functionally in school?

Thinking about such questions will help you see how English is constructed within a range of school contexts. It will also help you to understand how these constructions encode socio-political, cultural and ideological principles. These principles and the messages they convey are central in shaping the choices teachers are faced with, and you should consider them critically as you develop the kind of English teacher you wish to be. This is why it is so important to reflect upon your personal beliefs and philosophy for teaching English (which Banks *et al.* (1990) term the 'personal subject construct').

School knowledge also encompasses assessment. With the trend for ever-increasing burdens of assessment (Barnes 2000; Hodgson and Spours 2003; Daly 2004; Green 2005) and the high profile of league tables, the practice of English in schools has changed. It is important here to consider the purposes and role of assessment and to weigh up your responsibility to enable your students as learners in English and to balance this with parental expectations and the need to ensure students gain the best grades they can. While in school you should evaluate school practices in this respect and establish your personal views of effective and ethical practice.

Professional reflection: comparing school environments

As you go through your course, keep notes on the way English is approached in the contrasting educational environments you encounter. Compare and contrast these. What elements of school knowledge do you need to expand or acquire?

Pedagogic knowledge

This is the body of skills and approaches you will develop for teaching English through-out the school. It involves developing strategies for gaining and sustaining the interest of students, for encouraging the disaffected, and for personalising learning to ensure that students across the full ability range are enabled to learn effectively.

Inclusion

Read 'London' by William Blake, 'Death of a Naturalist' by Seamus Heaney and 'The Thought-Fox' by Ted Hughes. What particular difficulties does each poem raise for less able learners? How might you plan to address these? What issues could the most able learners be encouraged to approach, and how would you enable this?

Conveying information effectively and creating suitable conditions and activities for students to process and learn are complex and demanding tasks. Daly (2004: 194) highlights the importance of recognising 'learner readiness'. This requires creative empathy to understand students' particular and varied needs. Teachers need to locate where students are in their understanding so that they can appropriately mediate further learning. This is practical classroom knowledge.

M level

Using the Venn diagram outline shown in Figure 2.4, draft out your initial ideas about the inter-relation of subject knowledge, school knowledge and pedagogic knowledge in English. Be as specific as you can. Can you think of aspects of these knowledges which cross over between two of the categories or even all three? Use the diagram to explore your developing thoughts.

Grossman et al. (1989)

Grossman et al. (1989) identify four categories within what they term 'subject matter knowledge', or subject knowledge for teaching. The first, content knowledge, equates with what Banks et al. (1990) term subject knowledge, but they go on to identify three new areas for consideration (see Figure 2.5).

Substantive knowledge

This focuses on the nature of inquiry within the subject and takes multiple forms within English (e.g. models of literary criticism, literary theory or linguistic frameworks), each having its own modes of interrogating text or language, according to its rationale. Metacognitive engagement with these varied substantive manifestations of subject is essential for the teacher. Different 'versions' of English imply different

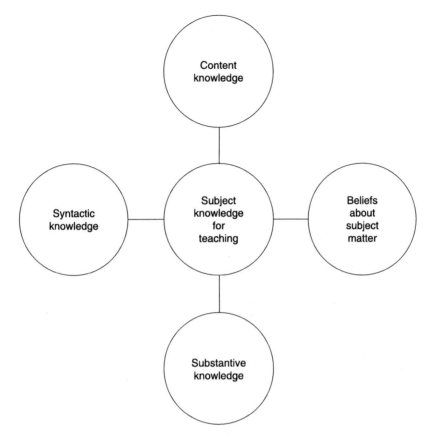

Figure 2.5 The four categories of subject knowledge for teaching (Grossman *et al.* 1989)

relationships between teacher and learner (Knights 2005) as well as between the reader and the material studied. The role of the teacher, here, is frequently synthetic, providing students with the tools to engage with a range of substantive forms of the subject. In order for a fruitful dialogue to emerge, a focus on substantive knowledge is important. It must not remain tacit. Think back to the earlier task where you compared Leavis' view of English with a range of other approaches to the subject – there you were engaged in precisely this dimension of the subject. The NATE post-16 committee (2005) urge the importance of such substantive frameworks within the curricular formation of English, bemoaning the lack of coherent theoretical underpinning of the curriculum, and the attendant lack of any holistic view of the relationship between language, linguistics, literature and media in current formations of the subject in the UK.

Syntactic knowledge

This relates to methods of inquiry within the subject, to the formation of canons of knowledge, the types of evidence and proof accepted within the discipline, and the ways in which new knowledge is brought into the field. This is subject not as content,

but as process. Learners need gradually to be introduced to the conventions and processes by which the subject operates if they are to become more effective and more
autonomous. Engagement with these processes needs to be explicit and detailed to
allow learners to function independently. Good teachers steadily do themselves out of
a job. If a student still needs you in the same ways at the end of a year as they did at the
beginning, you should ask yourself some serious questions. It is, of course, essential
that teachers remain abreast of developments in the syntactic structures of the subject
if they are effectively to deal with this aspect of English.

ICT: using ICT

Information and Communications Technology is constantly developing, and students
now engage with a very wide range of technologies both inside and outside the
classroom. What demands does the proliferation of ICTs place on teachers of English?
How does this change the shape and nature of the subject? What are the particular
advantages and disadvantages of using ICT as a tool within the classroom? How will you
teach students to use ICT responsibly? What issues of e-safety need to be considered?
Look into school and other policies. How will you teach students to use ICT fairly in their
work? Think around issues such as plagiarism, collusion and research. What 'content'
needs to be taught around ICT? How do reading, writing and speaking and listening
need to be reconceived?

Beliefs about subject matter

This takes into account individual teachers' values and assumptions about their subject. Early in this chapter you began to consider such issues, and your locus in any
given area of the subject is very important. For example, some adhere firmly to the
notion that language and grammar should be taught discretely and the skills thus
learned applied to reading and writing; others hold strongly to the view that they
should only be taught integrally and in context; others (e.g. Gregory 2003) argue
for a balance of both. Some prioritise great literature, while others hold a wider and
more utilitarian view. Political, philosophical, theoretical and religious views – as well
as personal experiences of the subject at school, at university and elsewhere – will also
play an important role in shaping teachers' views. Such differences, provided they are
not too idiosyncratic, are to be celebrated and result in rich and varied learning experiences. Personal beliefs and constructs of subject, however, should not be exclusive,
nor should interpretations and values impinge on learners' freedom to form their own
views and to develop their own interactions with the subject.

Think back now to the personal philosophy you defined earlier in this chapter.
Consider this in the light of Grossman *et al.*'s ideas. Is there anything you feel the need
to change or develop?

Deliverable subject models

Having considered the above dimensions of subject knowledge and established how
these can fit together practically and theoretically in the classroom, it is important to

establish the version of English you are able and happy to teach. Green (2006) terms this the 'personal deliverable model'. This is a personal version of the subject, combining academic, educational and pragmatic components, which together create the area of functioning subject within which individual teachers operate. This will, of course, be more a successful subject system in some cases than others, and constantly needs to be re-evaluated in the light of such issues as individual and whole-class needs or the purposes of particular teaching sessions or sequences of sessions. The personal deliverable model represents the interface between the teacher, the student and the curriculum, and is the outcome of a negotiation of the needs of all three, undertaken by the teacher and applied to the class. The success of work undertaken in the classroom context is dependent upon the sensitivity and practicality with which the teacher conducts this negotiation.

Conclusions

The development of effective teacherly knowledge is a complex and interactive process. According to Grossman *et al.* (1989: 32), it is 'by drawing on a number of different types of knowledge and skill [that] teachers translate their knowledge of subject matter into instructional representations'. As you read this book, you will become aware of some of the interventions and thinking necessary to assist you in the process of developing your subject knowledge for teaching. Feiman-Nemser and Buchman (1985: 29) observe, '[i]n learning to teach, neither firsthand experience nor university instruction can be left to work themselves out by themselves'.

English as a subject and the subject knowledge required to teach it are fluid. Calderhead and Miller (1985) explore the relationship between teachers' subject content knowledge and class-specific knowledge – for example, knowledge of the individuals within the class, whole-group needs and preferences, and the dynamics these establish. In bringing these knowledges to bear on each other, they suggest, teachers create 'action-relevant' knowledge. Similarly, Feiman-Nemser and Buchman (1985) advocate 'pedagogical thinking', whereby teachers locate their subject knowledge within the individual needs of students and their beliefs about the subject they are being taught in order to create optimum conditions for learning.

Into practice

What information do you as a teacher need in order to prepare for the teaching of your classes so that you can most effectively address individual students' needs within the whole-class context?

In order to give yourself the best start to your teaching career, and in order to keep yourself fresh as you grow in experience, it is important to keep alive a critical relationship with English. The best teachers of English see themselves as ongoing students of the subject, using their developing understanding of familiar areas of the subject (e.g. literature, film, drama, language) and their engagement with new areas of it (e.g.

multi-modal texts, emerging ICTs, text language) explicitly to inform engagement with forms and processes and pedagogy. This is the excitement of teaching.

In summary

- Your own experiences of English, your views of what English is as a subject and how it should be taught are an essential foundation for your work as a teacher and need to be carefully considered.
- Subject knowledge for teaching is complex and multi-faceted.
- English is more than English literature.
- It is essential to develop a rounded knowledge of English and to plan carefully for programmes of the development of subject-content knowledge.
- If teachers are to develop students' autonomy as learners, it is essential to teach the processes and pedagogy of English explicitly.

References

Ball, S. J. (1990) *Politics and Policy Making in Education: Explorations in Policy Sociology*. London: Routledge.

Banks, F., Leach, J. and Moon, B. (1999) 'New understandings of teachers' pedagogic knowledge', in J. Leach and B. Moon (eds), *Learners and Pedagogy*. London: Paul Chapman Publishing: 89–110.

Barnes, D. (2000) *Becoming an English Teacher*. Sheffield: NATE.

Blake, J. and Shortis, T. (2010) *Who's Prepared to Teach School English?* London: Committee for Linguistics in Education, King's College, London.

Bureau of Education (1920) *Selections from Educational Records, Part I (1781–1839)*, ed. H. Sharp. Calcutta: Superintendent, Government Printing. Reprint: Delhi: National Archives of India, 1956, 107–17.

Burgess, T. (2002) *Writing, English Teachers and the New Professionalism*. Sheffield: NATE.

Burley, S. (2005) 'The impact of a language education programme on the development of PGCE English student teachers' perceptions of subject identity', *Changing English* 12(1): 137–46.

Calderhead, J. and Miller, E. (1985) 'The integration of subject matter knowledge in student teachers' classroom practice'. Paper presented to the annual meeting of the British Educational Research Association: Sheffield.

Daly, C. (2004) 'Trainee English teachers and the struggle for knowledge', *Changing English* 11(2): 189–204.

Davison, J. and Dowson, J. (2003) *Learning to Teach in the Secondary School*. London: RoutledgeFalmer.

DES (1975) *A Language for Life (Bullock Report)*. London: HMSO.

Dewey, J. (1903) 'The child and the curriculum', in *John Dewey: The Middle Works, 1899–1924, Volume 2: 1902–1903*. Carbondale, IL: Southern Illinois University Press: 285–6.

Eagleton, T. (1983) *Literary Theory*. Oxford: Blackwell.

Evans, C. (1993) *English People: The Experience of Teaching and Learning English in British Universities*. Buckingham: Open University Press.

Feiman-Nemser, S. and Buchman, M. (1985) 'The first year of teacher preparation: transition to pedagogical thinking?' Research Series No. 156. East Lansing, MI: Michigan State University, Institute for Research on Teaching.

Green, A. (2005) *Four Perspectives on Transition: English Literature from Sixth Form to University*. London: Higher Education Academy English Subject Centre, Royal Holloway, University of London.

Green, A. (2006) 'University to school: challenging assumptions in subject knowledge development', *Changing English* 13(1): 111–23.

Green, A. (2010) *Transition and Acculturation*. London: Lambert Academic Publishing.

Gregory, G. (2003) 'They shall not parse! Or shall they?', *Changing English* 10(1): 13–33.

Grossman, P.L., Wilson, S.M. and Shulman, L.S. (1989) 'Teachers of substance: subject matter knowledge for teaching', in M.C. Reynolds (ed.), *Knowledge Base for the Beginning Teacher*. Oxford: Pergamon Press.

Hodgson, A. and Spours, K. (2003) *Beyond A Levels: Curriculum 2000 and the Reform of 14–19 Qualifications*. London: Kogan Page.

Holmes Group (1986) *Tomorrow's Teachers*. East Lansing, MI: Holmes Group.

Jones, K. (2003) *Education in Britain: 1944 to the Present*. Cambridge: Polity.

Knights, B. (2005) 'Intelligence and interrogation: the identity of the English student', *Arts and Humanities in Higher Education* 4(1): 33–52.

Marshall, B. (1997) 'Education: the great education debate?', *Critical Quarterly* 39(1): 112–18.

Marshall, B. (2000) *English Teachers: The Unofficial Guide*. London: Routledge.

McInnis, C. and James, R. (1995) 'First year on campus: diversity in the initial experience of Australian undergraduates', *Journal of the Freshman Year Experience* 9(2): 33–51.

NATE (2005) *Text: Message – The Future of A Level English*. Sheffield: NATE.

Newbolt, H. (1921) *The Teaching of English in England (The Newbolt Report)*. London: HMSO.

Turvey, A. (2005) 'Who'd be an English teacher?', *Changing English* 12(1): 3–18.

3

PAULA ZWOZDIAK-MYERS
Reflective practice for
professional development

In this chapter you will consider

- the key characteristics of extended professionals;
- the complex multi-dimensional nature of reflective practice; and
- qualitative distinctions in reflective practice.

Introduction

Reflective practice for professional development is in the foreground of attempts to raise educational standards and maximise the learning potential of all students, with an increasing emphasis placed on professional accountability through evidence-based outcomes. The broad consensus arising from recent national and international large-scale surveys is that teacher quality is the 'single most important school variable influencing student achievement' (OECD 2005: 2), and that effective teaching is built 'on a concept of teaching as praxis in which theory, practice and the ability to reflect critically on one's own and others' practice illuminate each other' (ETUCE 2008: 26). Teachers need to become very active agents in analysing both their own practice 'in the light of professional standards and their own students' progress in the light of standards for student learning' (OECD 2005: 11).

Complex phenomena lie at the heart of reflective practice. This chapter presents a new framework to capture dimensions of reflective practice in which teachers can provide evidence to inform their own teaching. Reflective practice is defined as:

> a disposition to enquiry incorporating the process through which ... teachers structure or restructure actions, beliefs, knowledge and theories that inform teaching for the purpose of professional development.
>
> (Zwozdiak-Myers 2010: 83)

Key attributes of extended professionals

Reflective practice as a disposition to enquiry has, at its roots, the early work of Dewey (1933), particularly in relation to the attitudes of open-mindedness, responsibility and wholeheartedness, which he argues are integral to reflective action. Open-mindedness refers to the willingness to consider more than one side of an argument and fully embrace and attend to alternative possibilities. This may require recognition that formerly held views and beliefs could be misconceived. Responsibility refers to the disposition to consider carefully the consequences of actions and the willingness to accept those consequences. Dewey (1933: 32) argues that misconceptions and confusion can arise when individuals 'profess certain beliefs (yet) are unwilling to commit themselves to the consequences that flow from them'. Wholeheartedness refers to the way in which open-mindedness and responsibility come together in response to a particular situation or event. As Dewey (1933: 30) writes:

> a genuine enthusiasm is an attitude that operates as an intellectual force. When a person is absorbed, the subject carries him on. Questions occur to him spontaneously; a flood of suggestions ... further inquiries and readings are indicated and followed ... the material holds and buoys his mind up and gives an onward impetus to thinking.

The work of several theorists in the 1970s into the nature of the teacher as a professional extends Dewey's discourse. Hoyle (1974), for example, distinguishes between *restricted* and *extended* professionals, and, in building upon this work with a particular focus on the teacher as researcher, Stenhouse (1975: 143–4) claims that the outstanding hallmark of extended professionals is their capacity and commitment to engage in autonomous self-development through systematic self-study. Extended professionals, he states, need to:

- reflect critically and systematically on their practice;
- have a commitment to question their practice as the basis for teacher development;
- have the commitment and skills to study their own teaching and in so doing develop the art of self-study;
- appreciate the benefit of having their teaching observed by others and discussing their teaching with others in an open and honest manner; and
- have a concern to question and to test theory in practice.

Dimensions of reflective practice

Reflective practice as a process embraces numerous concepts, particularly in relation to the nature of reflective activity and its translation into professional practice. These have been captured within nine discrete, yet inter-related dimensions, as shown in Figure 3.1. Although they are presented in a sequential manner it is important to note that any dimension can provide the initial catalyst for reflective practice.

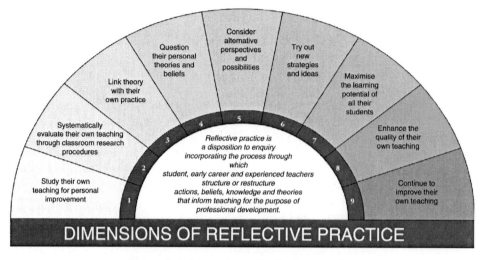

Figure 3.1 Dimensions of reflective practice

1) Study their own teaching for personal improvement

An understanding of reflection, how it can be structured and used to guide practice, underpins self-study for personal improvement. Dewey (1933) associates reflection with thinking that involves turning a subject over in the mind to give it serious consideration and thought, incorporating five stages – problem, suggestions, reasoning, hypothesis and testing. When pieced together, the stages form a process of reflective thinking which involves 'a state of doubt, hesitation, perplexity, mental difficulty, in which thinking originates, and an act of searching, hunting, inquiring, to find material that will resolve the doubt, settle and dispose of the perplexity' (Dewey, 1933: 12). To engage effectively in this process requires the development of specific skills such as keen observation, logical reasoning, analysis, synthesis and evaluation (Bloom 1956). Teachers must be able to:

> describe and analyse the structural features of an educational situation, issue, or problem – *problem definition*; gather and evaluate information as to the possible sources of the dilemma under consideration and to generate multiple alternative solutions and their potential implications – *means/ends analysis*; and, integrate all of the information into a tempered conclusion about or solution for the problem identified – *generalisation*.
>
> (LaBoskey 1993: 30)

Reflection is an integral part of Kolb's (1984) model of experiential learning, in which immediate or concrete experiences provide the basis for observations and reflections. These are distilled and assimilated into abstract concepts, which produce new possibilities for action that can be actively tested through experimentation, which in turn create new experiences, as shown in Figure 3.2.

Kolb describes this process as 'self-perpetuating' in that the learner shifts from actor to observer, from direct involvement to analytical detachment, which creates a

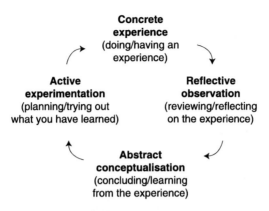

Figure 3.2 Kolb's (1984) model of experiential learning

new form of experience to reflect on and conceptualise. Boud *et al.* (1985: 19) integrate feelings and emotions within their approach to reflection, as teachers are required to 'recapture their experience, think about it, mull it over and evaluate it' through:

- *Association* – relating new data to that which is already known, making links between feelings and ideas about teaching
- *Integration* – seeking relationships among the data, making sense of associations in some way
- *Validation* – determining the authenticity of the ideas and feelings which have resulted, trying out new ways of viewing and understanding teaching
- *Appropriation* – making knowledge one's own, by taking ownership of new insights and learning to inform teaching.

These approaches illuminate how reflection becomes a powerful agent for understanding 'self', as teachers not only recount what they observed and thought about a specific context but also their feelings, emotions and ideas as to 'future possibilities' (Pollard 2002: 314).

Professional reflection

- Observe two or three teachers teaching a range of lessons, and during each lesson track your emotional response.
- Reflect upon how your emotional responses might inform your own future teaching.

---

2) Systematically evaluate their own teaching through classroom research procedures

Central to the concept of teacher as researcher is 'systematic reflection on one's classroom experience, to understand it and to create meaning out of that understanding'

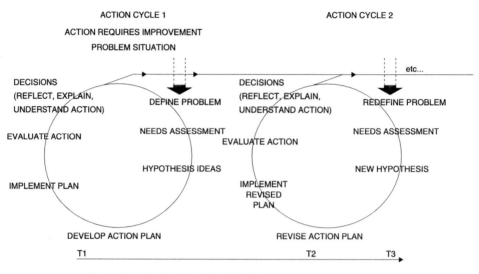

Figure 3.3 McKernan's (1996: 29) model of action research

(Hopkins 2002: 5). Systematically reflecting on data gathered lesson-by-lesson to examine why particular outcomes were achieved in relation to a particular strategy is the hallmark of action research, which Carr and Kemmis (1986: 162) describe as a 'self-reflective spiral of cycles of planning, acting, observing, reflecting then re-planning, further action, further observation and further reflection'. Figure 3.3 illustrates the cyclical nature of action research.

Formative evaluation through classroom research enables teachers to translate feedback into 'modifications, adjustments, directional changes, redefinitions as necessary' (Cohen *et al.* 2007: 192) as they retain and build upon successful elements of their teaching and modify or discard less successful elements in light of their reflections.

M level: action research

Use the following prompts drawn from McKernan's (1996) action research model to design an intervention strategy to improve a particular aspect of your teaching:

- Clarify and define the problem or area of interest.
- Conduct a literature search to establish current theories and relevant research.
- Devise an action plan outlining the teaching and learning approaches you might use.
- Identify what type/s of data you need to collect.
- Design appropriate research instruments to gather these data.
- Plan the first lesson and teach it.
- Gather data which capture student response/s to your teaching.
- Analyse and evaluate the data.

- Reflect upon the data.
- In light of these reflections plan the second lesson and teach it ... continue this cycle over a series of lessons.

Critically evaluate how this process has impacted on your wider approach to teaching.

3) Link theory with their own practice

The pursuit of linking theory with practice implies that teachers should be research minded and encouraged to value and undertake research within professional contexts, as they need to be able 'to analyse critically the research evidence they read as part of their professional role, and to judge its findings and conclusions from a well-informed point of view' (Campbell *et al.* 2003: 2). This builds on Stenhouse's (1983) view that the purpose of educational research is to develop thoughtful reflection so as to strengthen the professional judgement of teachers.

Theories associated with learning to teach emerge from at least two perspectives: *espoused theories* – those which encompass the formal philosophy of the profession (e.g. Leavisite models of English), and *theories-in-use* – patterns of behaviour learned and developed in day-to-day work (Argyris and Schon 1974). Schon (1987) claims it is the latter type which characterises professional behaviour, as effective teachers develop artistry and skilfulness in learning to work with particular groups of students in particular environments.

Although Schon acknowledges that professionals must acquire a body of specialised knowledge, he argues that such knowledge cannot be applied in a rule-governed way to guide practice. He posits that professionals generate personal epistemologies of practice (i.e. the repertoire of teaching approaches and strategies they gain from experience provides exemplars, images and metaphors they draw upon to frame each new teaching situation). Intelligent action becomes evident when professionals respond effectively in particular situations, displaying knowing in action. He associates knowing in action with reflection in action (1987: 28), which occurs when professionals encounter and have to overcome unknown situations in the learning environment. The expressions 'thinking on your feet' and 'keeping your wits about you' aptly portray reflection in action.

Although verbal (re)constructions of experience might seem inadequate, it is important to move from knowing in action to reflection on action (Schon 1987), making the implicit explicit. Reflection on action involves looking back on action some time after the event has taken place and provides a frame for recognising how teachers make sense of, and gain control over, their situated knowledge. It acknowledges that teachers' personal reflection must be subject to systematic questioning so that their professional practice can be justified. For example, teachers should question:

- what action/s they might have taken in a particular situation and why (*reflection in action*);
- possible reasons to suggest how student learning opportunities might be maximised or inhibited (*reflection on action*); and

- what problems they encountered in their teaching and how they overcame them, or what they need to do to overcome them in future (*reflection on experience*).

The purpose behind such questions is for teachers to ensure they are doing all that they can to improve the quality of their teaching so as to enhance student learning and development. By looking back at an incident that happened in a given lesson and reflecting on their own experience, teachers question what happens in classrooms and develop their professional understanding. Although the focus is on the teaching, this process starts with the consideration of student learning. This enables teachers to 'ground' (McKernan 1996), 'craft' (Schon 1987) and 'validate' (Elliott 1991) curriculum theory through their own experience as they provide reasons for judgements made from an informed evidence base.

4) Question their personal theories and beliefs

All teachers have personal theories and beliefs about the nature of knowledge, their roles and responsibilities within the classroom, and how learning takes place (see Chapter 2). Personal theories and beliefs become more articulate when teachers engage in the process of reflection (Zeichner and Liston 1996: 35). Biases, preconceived judgements or opinions and problem areas can be detected, challenged and appropriately modified. Failure to re-examine personal theories and beliefs for their validity in light of new information can lead to mindless teaching or habitual practice (Mezirow 1990). The importance of questioning personal theories and beliefs is highlighted by Palmer (1998: 2):

> When I do not know myself, I cannot know who my students are. I will see them through a glass darkly, in the shadows of my unexamined life – and when I cannot see them clearly, I cannot teach them well.

Into practice

Write a short narrative in response to the following sentence stems:

- The purpose of education is to ...
- English teaching should aim to ...
- My approach to teaching English is ... because ...

Discuss your responses with a peer or colleague and then answer the following:

- To what extent are your views similar and/or different?
- What personal dispositions, background and/or experiences might have shaped your own theories and beliefs?
- Is it important that teachers reflect upon personal theories and beliefs? If yes, why? If no, why not?

---

5) Consider alternative perspectives and possibilities

From a social constructivist perspective, interpretation is a meaning-making process, which requires teachers to recognise that

> a problem is seen as a human construct which arises out of a particular perception or interpretation formed about a unique educational context with its values and ends; the values, interests and actions of its inhabitants; and crucially, the particular relation of these features to a theoretical perspective which describes and explains them and their interrelations.
>
> (Parker 1997: 40)

Freire (1972) argues the need for teachers to adopt a reflective posture, one that enters the public arena and examines personal experience through conversations with others.

Within her three-stage approach, Pendlebury (1995) explores how conversations between student teachers and mentors can be structured in order to allow exploration of classroom situations from the perspective of the student with the guidance of an experienced practitioner, and how they might frame problems of practice. Open-mindedness (Dewey 1933) lies at the core of this.

Valli's (1992) 'deliberative reflection', which involves consolidating several sources of information from a range of perceived experts to weigh up competing claims and give sound reason for decisions made, is also relevant here.

Professional reflection: professional conversations

Think back over your ITE course. Make a list of times when you had opportunities to engage in conversations with others, and against this describe the nature and purpose of each discourse.

---

6) Try out new strategies and ideas

When teachers ask searching questions that arise from their own circumstances and interests they demonstrate an active approach to professional learning by seeking new strategies and ideas. This approach is particularly vital if teachers are to stay abreast of major trends which can influence aspects of the curriculum and classroom contexts (e.g. awareness of global issues, living in multi-cultural societies, issues of gender and sexuality, rapid advances in ICT).

Moon (1999) suggests that learners approach their studies with a cognitive structure, a flexible network of ideas and knowledge, shaped by prior learning. This provides the framework within which teachers locate new ideas, and may, if deep learning is to occur, be challenged and modified (transformed) in the process. Moon associates the development of new understandings, insights and increased awareness with deep as opposed to surface learning. Transformative learning describes situations where learners are prepared to abandon preconceptions and re-examine fundamental assumptions they may have about subject matter, themselves, teaching and the nature of knowledge.

Through integrating new strategies and ideas into their own practice, teachers take ownership of their teaching as they 'appropriate' (Boud *et al.* 1985) new knowledge, which gives them the degree of autonomy needed to make professional judgements in response to classroom situations. In turn, this has potential to generate knowledge, be transformative, and build the capacity 'to assess progress and effectiveness' (Phillips 2007: 395). Failure to experiment with alternative strategies and/or viewpoints and thoughtless acceptance of 'received wisdom' characterise what Dewey (1933) terms routine action.

ICT
• What major developments in ICT are likely to impact on teaching English? What new ways of thinking do these demand?   • How can we teach reading and writing in online texts?   • What measures can/should you take to stay abreast of cutting-edge developments in education generally and in English more specifically?

7) Maximise the learning potential of all their students

The principles of entitlement and inclusion are at the core of this dimension. This can be particularly challenging within twenty-first-century schools as teachers are called upon to deal with 'an increasingly diverse cohort of students with different needs, different learning styles and different aspirations' (AGQTP 2007: 4).

The current emphasis in England on 'personalised learning' (DfES 2007) requires teachers to tailor learning to accommodate individual aptitudes, needs and interests to ensure that all students realise their full potential, irrespective of background and personal circumstances. Differentiated strategies which aim to target individual achievement might include accelerated learning, Assessment for Learning, booster classes or goal-setting, and those which aim to target achievement for all students might incorporate active learning, collaborative learning, interventions through questioning, learning to learn or literacy across the curriculum (QCA 2008). These approaches also aim to give students greater autonomy over their own learning and prepare them 'for a society and an economy in which they will be expected to be self-directed learners, able and motivated to keep learning over a lifetime' (OECD 2005: 2).

Teachers must take a number of factors into account when planning for progression in student learning:

- their knowledge of students;
- theoretical perspectives on how learning happens (e.g. cognitive development, concept development, constructivism, information-processing theories, social constructivism) within the teaching process;

- what constitutes progression in their subject area; and
- what demands are placed on specific students in relation to specific tasks.

Having designed a range of learning experiences that enable all students to access the curriculum, teachers must then reflect upon and evaluate their effectiveness in maximising the learning potential of all their students to inform future planning.

Inclusion: policy and practice
Read the inclusion policy in the school you are working in, and the policy of the English department. How far do these policy documents adequately deal with the issue of inclusion? Do you see these policies in action in the classroom? What is their impact on student learning? What challenges do teachers face in implementing them?

8) Enhance the quality of their own teaching

This dimension is inextricably linked to the previous one and is based on the premise that 'what teachers teach' is as important as 'how they teach' (Shulman 1987). Teachers must acquire a range of knowledge bases and models for teaching and explore ways in which they can transform this knowledge into meaningful learning experiences for all their students. Pedagogic expertise (TLRP/ESRC 2010: 5) comprises:

- *The art of teaching* – responsive, creative and intuitive capacities
- *The craft of teaching* – mastery of a full repertoire of skills and practices
- *The science of teaching* – research-informed decision-making.

The *Professional Standards for Teachers* (TDA 2007a) coupled with the *Professional Values and Practice* (GTCE 2006) set out specific criteria that teachers in England must acquire and evidence to demonstrate personal effectiveness.

Reflecting on lesson outcomes and how effectively these have been met, by examining the minutiae of teaching and assessment evidence, enables teachers to make informed professional judgements to guide their future teaching, which should enhance their pedagogic expertise.

9) Continue to improve their own teaching

ITE provides an essential basis for teaching, but ongoing professional development is required to equip teachers with knowledge and understanding of the ever-changing demands of educational reform (Barber and Mourshed 2007; AGQTP 2008; ETUCE 2008). Learning to teach is viewed as a gradual process, which means that 'teacher education must be seen as a career-long process placed within the context of life-long learning' (OECD 2005: 44). Day (1999: 4) suggests that continuing professional development is the process by which, alone and with others, teachers review, renew and extend their commitment as change agents to the moral purposes of teaching; and by which they acquire and develop critically the knowledge, skills and emotional intelligence essential to good professional thinking, planning and practice with children, young people and colleagues throughout each phase of their professional lives.

In England, the Career Entry Development Profile (TDA 2007b) provides an important bridge between ITE and the years as a newly qualified teacher (NQT), and forms the basis for ongoing professional development. Teachers are expected to reflect upon their strengths, areas of interest and those in need of further work, and to devise an action plan and set personal targets.

Qualitative distinctions in reflective practice

The types of discourse or reflective conversations teachers engage in can be indicative of their development from *surface to deep to transformative learning* (Moon 1999), progressive stages of *epistemological cognition* (Baxter Magolda 1999; Moon 2005) and *reflective reasoning* (King and Kitchener 1994). Three broad types of reflective conversation can be related to the dimensions of reflective practice framework in Figure 3.4.

It is important to note that within any discourse more than one type of reflective conversation might be evident as the conversation unfolds: moving from descriptive through comparative towards critical. Thus, although each type has been separated out for the purpose of clarification they should not be viewed as mutually exclusive, as reflective conversations can be 'dynamic and fluid' (Ghaye and Ghaye 1998: 25).

Descriptive reflective conversations

This type of discourse can be characterised as a personal retrospective account of teaching, which involves 'returning to experience' (Boud *et al.* 1985) and providing a context-rich description of that experience. Different types of question involve

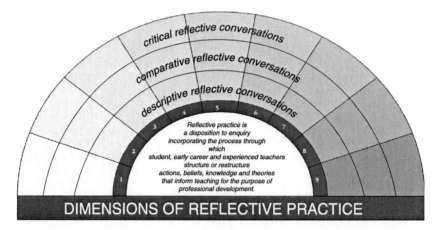

Figure 3.4 Qualitative distinctions between reflective conversations

different patterns of thinking. 'How did I teach the lesson?' requires a reflective process-analysis of the approach that has been followed. 'How might I do things differently next time?' requires a reflective self-evaluation of a particular type of performance using criteria against which judgements can be made. 'How does this make me feel?' appeals to the affective nature of teaching, and discourse arising from this question can reveal insights into the teacher's disposition to enquiry. Descriptive reflective conversations provide an important foundation for the generation of *living educational theory* (Whitehead 1993) and personal *epistemology of practice* (Schon 1987).

Comparative reflective conversations

This type of discourse requires teachers to reframe the focus of their reflection in the light of alternative views and possibilities, drawing on their own prior experiences and research findings from literature. Comparative reflective conversations are evident when teachers relate personal theories, beliefs, assumptions, conceptions of teaching and values to those of others. It is a meaning-making process, which moves the teacher from one experience into the next 'with deeper understanding of its relationships with and connections to other experiences and ideas' (Rodgers 2002: 845). Essentially this type of discourse is 'a deliberation among choices of competing versions of good teaching' (Grimmett *et al.* 1990) and involves ethical, moral and value commitments as well as questions concerning aspects of teaching such as 'how students learn' and 'the nature of pedagogy' (Furlong and Maynard 1995). Teachers come to recognise that knowledge claims contain elements of uncertainty. Teachers need to think through opinions and issues, and express themselves in a valid manner, recognising that colleagues have useful contributions to make. This type of discourse has resonance with *transitional knowing* (Baxter Magolda 1999; Moon 2005) and *quasi-reflective reasoning* (King and Kitchener 1994).

Critical reflective conversations

Critical thinking is situated at the core of this type of discourse, which Moon (2005: 12) defines as the capacity

> to work with complex ideas whereby a person can make effective provision of evidence to justify a reasonable judgment. The evidence, and therefore the judgment, will pay appropriate attention to the context of the judgment.

Further, the fully developed capacity to think critically

> relies on an understanding of knowledge as constructed and related to its context (relativistic) and is not possible if knowledge is viewed only in an absolute manner (knowledge as a series of facts).
>
> (Moon, 2005: 12)

Thus, critical reflective conversations are characterised by the acceptance that knowledge claims cannot be made with certainty, and that teachers make judgements that are 'most reasonable' and about which they are 'relatively certain', based upon the evaluation of available data. They believe they must actively construct their decisions, and that knowledge claims must be evaluated in relation to the context in which they were generated to determine their validity. Teachers are also willing to re-evaluate the adequacy of their judgements as new data become available.

Critical reflective conversations require teachers to analyse the wider cultural, social and political contexts, challenge their assumptions, and question their practice in relation to ideological and equity issues. If teachers are to engage meaningfully in this type of discourse, complex issues associated with power and politics as they relate to schools need to be understood (Ghaye and Ghaye 1998). This can be exemplified when teachers engage in conversations that address questions concerned with 'why' the educational, ideological, political and professional systems of which they are an integral part serve either to constrain or to empower them (Carr and Kemmis 1986; Barnett 1997; Moon 2005). In turn, critical reflective conversations can give rise to new understandings of previously taken-for-granted assumptions about practice (Grimmett *et al.* 1990) and lead to 'a renewed perspective' (Jay and Johnson 2002: 77).

M level
Select a specific lesson you have recently taught and conduct an in-depth analysis of your experiences by drawing upon the descriptive, comparative and critical types of question shown in Table 3.1.

Table 3.1 Types of question related to specific types of qualitative discourse

Types of discourse	Types of question
Descriptive reflective conversations	• What did I teach in the lesson? • How did I teach it? • Did all students achieve the intended learning outcomes? • What teaching and learning strategies were effective, or ineffective? • How do I know? • What does this mean? • How does this make me feel?
Comparative reflective conversations	• What different strategies might I use in my teaching? • What are the advantages or disadvantages of using particular strategies for diverse learners? • How might colleagues and/or students explain what is happening in my classroom? • What research enables me to gain further insights into this matter? • In what ways can I improve the ineffective elements of my teaching?

Table 3.1 *(continued)*

Types of discourse	Types of question
	• Having identified learning objectives, in what ways can they be achieved? • How do colleagues accomplish these same objectives? • For each alternative perspective, whose learning needs are addressed and whose are not?
Critical reflective conversations	• What are the implications of using particular strategies in my teaching when viewed from alternative perspectives? • On the basis of these perspectives and their implications, what strategies would be the most effective in helping students to achieve the intended learning outcomes within a specific context? • Are these learning outcomes appropriate for the whole range of diverse learners within the class – where is the evidence? • Why select this particular strategy for this particular group of students rather than an alternative – what evidence base have I drawn upon and why? • Why do I teach what I teach in the way that I teach it to a particular group of students? • How does my choice of objectives, learning outcomes and teaching strategies reflect the cultural, ethical, ideological, moral, political and social purposes of schooling?

In summary

- Complex phenomena reside at the heart of reflective practice for professional development, which need to be unpacked so that essential ingredients can be recognised and fully understood.
- When viewed as a disposition to enquiry, reflective practice incorporates the key attributes used to characterise extended professionals.
- When conceptualised as a process, reflective practice can be captured within nine discrete yet inter-related dimensions within which teachers can demonstrate capacity and commitment as they assume the role of teacher as researcher to study their own teaching and provide evidence of or for improved practice.
- Qualitative distinctions in reflective practice can be discerned through the different types of discourse and questions teachers engage in and raise about aspects of their own and others' teaching.
- Learning to teach is a gradual process, and with experience reflective practice can become internalised as professionals adopt the stance of a *critical being* (Barnett 1997) – one who thinks critically as a way of life and is willing to act upon personal insights and new understandings to continuously enhance their pedagogic expertise.

References

AGQTP (Australian Government Quality Teacher Programme) (2007) *Quality Teachers, Collaborative Communities, Effective Learning.* Canberra: Department of Education, Employment and Workplace Relations, Commonwealth of Australia.

AGQTP (Australian Government Quality Teacher Programme) (2008) *Innovative and Effective Professional Learning.* Canberra: Department of Education, Employment and Workplace Relations, Commonwealth of Australia.

Argyris, C. and Schon, D. (1974) *Theory into Practice: Increasing Professional Effectiveness.* San Francisco, CA: Jossey-Bass.

Barber, M. and Mourshed, M. (2007) *How the World's Best-performing School Systems Come Out on Top.* London: McKinsey and Company.

Barnett, R. (1997) *Higher Education: A Critical Business.* Buckingham: Open University Press.

Baxter Magolda, M. (1999) *Creating Contexts for Learning and Self-Authorship.* San Francisco, CA: Jossey-Bass.

Bloom, B. (1956) *Taxonomy of Educational Objectives, Handbook 1: Cognitive Domain.* London: Longman.

Boud, D., Keogh, R. and Walker, D. (1985) 'Promoting reflection in learning: a model', in D. Boud, R. Keogh and D. Walker (eds), *Reflection: Turning Experience into Learning.* London: Kogan Page, 18–40.

Campbell, S., Freedman, E., Boulter, C. and Kirkwood, M. (2003) *Issues and Principles in Educational Research for Teachers.* Southwell: British Educational Research Association.

Carr, W. and Kemmis, S. (1986) *Becoming Critical: Education, Knowledge and Action Research.* Lewes, Sussex: Falmer Press.

Cohen, L., Manion, L. and Morrison, K. (2007) *Research Methods in Education*, 6th edition. London: RoutledgeFalmer.

Day, C. (1999) *Developing Teachers: The Challenges of Lifelong Learning.* London: Falmer Press.

Dewey, J. (1933) *How we Think: A Restatement of the Relation of Reflective Thinking to the Educative Process.* Boston, MA: DC Heath and Company.

DfES (2007) *Pedagogy and Personalisation.* London: DfES.

Elliott, J. (1991) *Action Research for Educational Change.* Milton Keynes: Open University Press.

ETUCE (European Trade Union Committee for Education) (2008) *Teacher Education in Europe: An ETUCE Policy Paper.* Brussels: ETUCE.

Freire, P. (1972) *Pedagogy of the Oppressed.* Harmondsworth: Penguin.

Furlong, J. and Maynard, T. (1995) *Mentoring Student Teachers: The Growth of Professional Knowledge.* London: Routledge.

Ghaye, A. and Ghaye, K. (1998) *Teaching and Learning through Critical Reflective Practice.* London: David Fulton.

Grimmett, P., Mackinnon, A., Erickson, G. and Riecken, T. (1990) 'Reflective practice in teacher education', in R. Clift, W. Houston and M. Pugach (eds), *Encouraging Reflective Practice in Education: An Analysis of Issues and Programs.* New York: Teachers College Press.

GTCE (General Teaching Council for England) (2006) *The Statement of Professional Values and Practice for Teachers.* Available online at www.gtce.org.uk (accessed 12 September 2008).

Hopkins, J. (2002) *A Teachers' Guide to Classroom Research*, 3rd edition. Buckingham: Open University Press.

Hoyle, E. (1974) 'Professionality, professionalism and control in teaching', *London Education Review* 3(2): 13–19.

Jay, J. and Johnson, K. (2002) 'Capturing complexity: a typology of reflective practice for teacher education', *Teaching and Teacher Education* 18: 73–85.

King, P. and Kitchener, K. (1994) *Developing Reflective Judgement*. San Francisco, CA: Jossey-Bass.

Kolb, D. (1984) *Experiential Learning as the Science of Learning and Development*. Englewood Cliffs, NJ: Prentice Hall.

LaBoskey, V. (1993) 'A conceptual framework for reflection in preservice teacher education', in J. Calderhead and P. Gates (eds), *Conceptualising Reflection in Teacher Development*. Lewes: Falmer Press.

McKernan, J. (1996) *Curriculum Action Research: A Handbook of Methods and Resources for the Reflective Practitioner*, 2nd edition. London: Kogan Page.

Mezirow, J. (1990) *Fostering Critical Reflection in Adulthood: A Guide to Transformative and Emancipatory Learning*. San Francisco, CA: Jossey-Bass.

Moon, J. (1999) *Reflection in Learning and Professional Development*. London: Kogan Page.

Moon, J. (2005) *We Seek it Here: A New Perspective on the Elusive Activity of Critical Thinking: A Theoretical and Practical Approach*. Bristol: Higher Education Academy, University of Bristol.

OECD (Organisation for Economic Co-operation and Development) (2005) *Teachers Matter: Attracting, Developing and Retaining Effective Teachers, An Overview*. Paris: OECD. Available online at www.oecd.org (accessed April 2010).

Palmer, J. (1998) *The Courage to Teach*. San Francisco, CA: Jossey-Bass.

Parker, S. (1997) *Reflective Teaching in the Postmodern World: A Manifesto for Education in Postmodernity*. Buckingham: Open University Press.

Pendlebury, S. (1995) 'Reason and story in wise practice', in H. McEwan and K. Egan (eds), *Narrative in Teaching, Learning and Research*. New York: Teachers College Press.

Phillips, D. (2007) 'Adding complexity: philosophical perspectives on the relationship between evidence and policy', in P. Moss (ed.), *Evidence and Decision Making: The 106th Yearbook of the National Society for the Study of Education*. Malden, MA: Blackwell: 376–402.

Pollard, A. (2002) *Reflective Teaching: Effective and Evidence-informed Professional Practice*. London: Continuum.

QCA (2008) *A Big Picture of the Curriculum*. London: Crown.

Rodgers, C. (2002) 'Defining reflection: another look at John Dewey and Reflective Thinking', *Teachers College Record* 104(4): 842–66.

Schon, D. (1987) *Educating the Reflective Practitioner*. San Francisco, CA: Jossey-Bass.

Shulman, L. (1987) 'Knowledge and teaching: foundations of the new reform', *Harvard Educational Review* 57: 1–22.

Stenhouse, L. (1975) *An Introduction to Curriculum Research and Development*. London: Heinemann Education.

Stenhouse, L. (ed.) (1983) *Authority, Education and Emancipation: A Collection of Papers*. London: Heinemann Education.

TDA (Training and Development Agency for Schools) (2007a) *Professional Standards for Teachers: Qualified Teacher Status*. Available online at www.tda.gov.uk (accessed 6 August 2008).

TDA (Training and Development Agency for Schools) (2007b) *Supporting the Induction Process: TDA Guidance for Newly Qualified Teachers*. Available online at www.tda.gov.uk (accessed 20 October 2008).

TLRP and ESRC (Teaching and Learning Research Project and Economic and Social Research Council) (2010) *Professionalism and Pedagogy: A Contemporary Opportunity*. Available online at www.tlrp.org.uk (accessed 15 September 2010).

Valli, L. (ed.) (1992) *Reflective Teacher Education: Cases and Critiques*. Albany, NY: SUNY Press.

Whitehead, J. (1993) *The Growth of Educational Knowledge: Creating your own Living Educational Theories.* Bournemouth: Hyde Publications.

Zeichner, K. and Liston, D. (1996) *Reflective Teaching: An Introduction.* Mahwah, NJ: Lawrence Erlbaum Associates.

Zwozdiak-Myers, P. (2010) *An Analysis of the Concept Reflective Practice and an Investigation into the Development of Student Teachers' Reflective Practice within the Context of Action Research.* PhD thesis, Brunel University, London.

4

JOANNA MCINTYRE AND ANDREW GREEN
Planning the curriculum

In this chapter you will consider

- the narrative of the development of a National Curriculum for English;
- the National Strategy;
- the new National Curriculum;
- how these relate to your own philosophies about English teaching;
- a range of personal responses to issues emerging from the revised programme of study for English (2007); and
- lesson planning.

Introduction

As you begin to think about planning schemes of work, inevitably you will be required to consult the National Curriculum. The main premise for this chapter is that, in order to do this well, you will need to have an informed understanding of the developments that led up to its introduction.

A common narrative emerges from the literature tracing the origins of English as a school subject. English emerges as a subject which refuses to be pinned down as well as being value-laden and politically driven. As Jones reminds us, any version of English is a reaction to the version that has gone previously, 'each significant policy actor in education seems compelled to go over past ground, and to justify their current preferences in terms of a history which they will continue, recover or redeem' (Jones 2003: 7). So you, as a beginning teacher of English, have your own role to play within the ongoing narrative of the English curriculum. To be able to fulfil this, you need a sense of the history of the subject to better understand your own experiences and those of the young people you will be encountering as your part in the narrative unfolds. The account found in Chapter 2 will help you with this.

The National Curriculum years

In 1988, the educational landscape within England, Scotland and Wales changed with the introduction of the Education Reform Act (ERA; UK Parliament 1988). Through this, the power of LEAs was marginalised as financial budgets were delegated to schools, and schools entered a climate of marketisation whereby they could opt out of the state system and parents could choose which school to send their children to. This apparent freedom of choice was matched by increased powers of government (e.g. Ofsted) and 'pervasive and often draconian structures of surveillance, under the guise of improving quality' (Wrigley 2009: 63).

M level

The development of English as a school subject has been controversial. Dixon (2003) provides a useful chronological account of the 'battles for English', while Marshall presents a history of English as a 'series of competing traditions' (2000: 18), and no review of the social, political and historical influences on the evolution of English would be complete without reference to Eagleton's overview of approaches to teaching English literature (1983).

Present a narrative of the ways in which English as a subject has developed over time which draws on the readings recommended below and incorporates your own philosophies about the teaching of English. How will this affect the ways in which you plan to teach English?

Key readings
- Dixon, J. (2003) 'The battle for English', in J. Davison and J. Dowson (eds), *Learning to Teach English in the Secondary School*. London: RoutledgeFalmer.
- Eagleton, T. (1983) *Literary Theory*. Oxford: Blackwell.
- Jones, K. (2003) *Education in Britain 1944 to the Present*. Cambridge: Polity.
- Marshall, B. (2000) *English Teachers: The Unofficial Guide*. London: Routledge.

The 1988 ERA also brought specific changes to the English teaching community as a result of two government-sponsored reports: the Kingman Report (DES 1988) and the Cox Report (DES 1989). The Kingman committee was charged with recommending 'a model of the English language as a basis for teacher training and professional discussion, and to consider how far and in what ways that model should be made explicit to students' (DES 1988: 1). The report recommended teaching knowledge about language in a descriptive rather than prescriptive way. Its recommendations found favour with socio-linguists and with teachers but not with the traditional views of the government and their advisors.

Brian Cox was chosen to lead a project which would form the thinking behind the first National Curriculum for English. Cox had contributed to a series of right-wing publications known as the 'Black Papers' which advocated traditionalist approaches to English teaching. However, rather than promoting a traditional model, Cox and his working party based their recommendations on what they identified as five views of English teaching. As Marshall (2000: 4) explains:

The choice of the word view is significant in that Cox and his working party were not necessarily attributing these views to English teachers themselves. Rather, they were suggesting that these views needed to be identified before they got on with the complicated task of writing an English curriculum.

In acknowledging different ways of viewing the English curriculum that were not mutually exclusive, Cox found broad consensus with the English teaching community.

M level: the notion of curriculum

Curriculum is a complicated notion. Ivor Goodson examines curriculum from a historical and sociological perspective and argues that curriculum is a social construction:

> A curriculum ... is at once political theory, curriculum history, curriculum theory, and sociology. In short ... curriculum ... is a remarkably complex construction rooted in the past, active in the present, and often creative of the future. Most importantly ... the curriculum is a social construction made in a variety of arenas and at a variety of levels ... If we are to understand schooling, we must recognise that curriculum often sets the parameters of practice and of possibility, and therefore deserves our attention.
>
> (Harvard Education Review 1998)

In 1987, the government published a consultation document which summarised the arguments for introducing a National Curriculum (DES 1987). The main premise was to improve standards and to provide a common assessment framework. It was argued that:

> A national curriculum backed by clear assessment arrangements will help to raise standards of attainment by:
>
> (i) ensuring that all students study a broad and balanced range of subjects ...
> (ii) setting clear objectives for what children ... should be able to achieve ...
> (iii) ensuring that all students ... have access to ... the same ... programmes of study which include the key content, skills and processes which they need to learn ...
> (iv) checking on progress towards those objectives and performance at various stages ...
>
> (DES 1987: 3–4, cited in Torrance 2002)

However, Protherough and King (1995: 14) state that

> A rigid mandatory curriculum for English is a nonsense because consensus is impossible to achieve; there will be endless wrangling by groups wanting change because their particular views seem unrepresented and by Secretaries of State

with different priorities. Instead we need a framework for the curriculum that is flexible enough not to rule out any sensible interpretation of English for ages 5–16.

More recently, Marshall has suggested that the implementation of a range of mandated curriculum strategies and initiatives can only lead at best to 'satisfactory teaching' (2006a: 75).

What do you believe to be the advantages and disadvantages of a National Curriculum for the Teaching of English?

Suggested reading

- Cox, B. (1991) *Cox on Cox: An English Curriculum for the 1990s.* London: Hodder and Stoughton.
- DES (1987) *The National Curriculum 5–16: A Consultation Document.* London: DES.
- Goodson, I. (1997) *The Changing Curriculum: Studies in Social Construction.* New York: Peter Lang.
- Harvard Education Review (1998) *The Changing Curriculum* (summer). Available online at www.hepg.org/her/booknote/176 (accessed 12 September 2010).
- Marshall, B. (2000) 'The battle for the Curriculum', in *English Teachers: The Unofficial Guide.* London: Routledge.
- Marshall, B. (2006a) 'The future of English', *FORUM* 40:1: 69–79.
- Protherough, R. and King, P. (eds) (1995) *The Challenge of English in the National Curriculum.* London: Routledge.

The first English National Curriculum (DES 1990) was based on the recommendations of the National Curriculum English Working Group, led by Cox (1988–89). The National Curriculum was a statutory document which detailed the content of the subject. Its five attainment targets (speaking and listening; reading; writing; spelling; handwriting) and the accompanying programmes of study (POS) separated elements of the curriculum into discrete elements for assessment but allowed for integrated teaching. Teachers were provided with detailed statutory POS and non-statutory guidance about curriculum coverage.

Professional reflection

Look at the outline of the five views articulated by Cox's working group below. Are there particular ones that you recognise from your own experiences of teaching? Are you drawn to any when thinking about your own approaches to teaching? What are the benefits for the child? What are the implications for teaching?

A *personal growth view* focuses on the child: it emphasises the relationship between language and learning in the individual child, and the role of literature in developing children's imaginative and aesthetic lives.

A *cross-curricular view* focuses on the school: it emphasises that all teachers (of English and of other subjects) have a responsibility to help children with the language demands of different subjects on the school curriculum; otherwise, areas of the curriculum may be closed to them. In England, English is different from other school subjects, in that it is both a subject and a medium of instruction for other subjects.

An *adult needs view* focuses on communication outside the school: it emphasises the responsibility of English teachers to prepare children for the language demands of adult life, including the workplace, in a fast-changing world. Children need to learn to deal with the day-to-day demands of spoken language and of print; they also need to be able to write clearly, appropriately and effectively.

A *cultural heritage view* emphasises the responsibility of schools to lead children to an appreciation of those works of literature that have been widely regarded as among the finest in the language.

A *cultural analysis view* emphasises the role of English in helping children towards a critical understanding of the world and cultural environment in which they live. Children should know about the processes by which meanings are conveyed, and know about the ways in which print and other media carry values.

The document was generally well received by the English teaching community (Clark 1994). Despite the many objectives detailing what students should achieve, there was a welcome lack of detail in terms of what should be studied; for example, rather than listing particular authors (with the exception of Shakespeare) teachers were able to apply critical judgement in response to the requirement to read some 'of the works which have been most influential in shaping and defining the English language' (DES 1990: 31). In terms of grammar and Standard English (topics which were close to the Conservative rhetoric of raising standards), the report recommended that these be taught as part of an approach to knowledge about language that allowed for a discussion of appropriateness and context. In addition, drama, media studies and ICT were seen as important components of the English curriculum.

Creativity

What would your ideal National Curriculum for English include? Make sure that you can justify your decisions. Share your ideas with your peers and with experienced teachers within your placement school. Can you reach a consensus?

However, less than two years after the implementation of the English Subject Order, there were calls from the government to review the National Curriculum. The original version was perceived as too liberal (Protherough and King 1995: 12), and questions were asked about the relationship between curriculum content and the ways in which this could be tested. When the National Curriculum Council (NCC) recommended revising the Order, it purported to draw upon the findings of an evaluation project commissioned by the NCC and carried out by a team at Warwick University.

Inclusion: planning for diversity

In order to fulfil the requirement of the revised National Curriculum to 'establish an entitlement for all children', teachers need to ensure that diversity is at the heart of the curriculum. Within English, cultural understanding makes up one of the key concepts.

Look at the explanatory notes which accompany the range and content sections for reading. Review the schemes of work in your placement schools and talk to the teachers in your department about the ways in which current provision in schools allows teachers to fulfil National Curriculum requirements. Are there any resources within the school stock cupboard which seem particularly well suited to dealing with issues of diversity and inclusion? In what ways are the challenges different in predominantly white schools compared to ethnically diverse schools?

Key reading
- Quarshie, Richard, *English for Students with Diverse Backgrounds*, pages 9–10. Available online at www.ite.org.uk/ite_readings/english_for_pupils_with_diverse_ backgrounds_20080326.pdf (accessed on 21 February 2010).
- www.naldic.org.uk.

The struggles of the research team, working 'in a dark, ever-receding tunnel' and negotiating the 'mystery and secrecy' that characterised any communications between the team and the NCC, have been eloquently articulated by Urszula Clark in 'Bringing English to order' (1994: 33), which records the different stages of shock, dismay and guilt the researchers felt as they saw their work being leaked to the media and mis-quoted as apparently endorsing the decision to support the review. Consequently, we endorse Protherough and King's observation that 'we cannot now read any document … as an innocent set of pedagogic guidelines' (1995: 2).

The National Curriculum for English was revised with a new version published in 1995, following the recommendations of the Dearing Review in 1993. This was a slimmed down version of the earlier Order with three attainment targets of speaking and listening, reading and writing. Detailed non-statutory guidance was removed and the assessment elements of the attainment targets (rather than the programmes of study) were foregrounded. The literary canon was also introduced. There were further revisions in 2000 and more recently in 2007.

English teachers have become adept at managing and negotiating changes to their daily work which, post-1988, has become increasingly driven by top-down initiatives. Alongside the changes to the statutory elements of content taught to children aged 5–16, there have been accompanying changes in assessment regulations and require-ments as well as the introduction of a National Literacy Strategy (NLS). This has led Jones (2003: 137) to argue that the professional identity of English teachers is under threat:

The authoritative status of the National Curriculum tended to foreclose argu-ments about educational purpose: especially as the testing system developed, questions of purpose and process became less a centre of debate, initiative and controversy than a set of matters that had been pre-decided outside the school.

Professional reflection

Should the teaching community have debates about the curriculum and its assessment and question the processes and purposes of the subject they have elected to teach?

The strategy years

The NLS was introduced in primary schools in 1998 and extended to secondary schools in 2001. The strategy provided a framework for teaching in secondary English lessons which echoed the model of the literacy hour in primary schools by advocating the four-part lesson structure: it has been described as 'this country's most ambitious and radical programme of teacher and curriculum development since the introduction of the National Curriculum' (Goddard 2009: 30). For the first time teachers of English were told not just what to teach but how to teach it.

Although a non-statutory document, the strategy re-shaped the ways in which English was taught, first in the primary schools (where 'English' became replaced by 'literacy') and subsequently in the secondary schools. As well as bringing about changes to the ways in which English was viewed within schools, there was a significant change in the ways in which teachers experienced professional development. This took the form of training delivered by LEA-appointed consultants. This top-down training was, according to Barnes *et al.* (2003: 5), 'authoritarian and patronising, making any sort of discussion or open exploration of issues impossible'; it smacked of 'professional distrust' and did not allow critical professional engagement (Goddard 2009).

While the NLS remained non-statutory, teachers were forced to adapt their teaching to ensure that their students were demonstrably making good progress within the 'continuing pressure of testing, targets and performance tables'; this led to a 'creeping hegemonisation of the curriculum' (Alexander 2004: 15). Goddard (2009: 32) claimed that the strategies did not meet the needs of 'an aspirationally democratic society of extraordinary cultural diversity and fragmentariness', were not sufficiently flexible, were too authoritarian and as such alienated teachers and students alike, concluding that they were 'not fit for purpose'.

EAL: meeting diverse needs

How might you respond to the needs of EAL students in your school when planning to teach texts from the literary heritage, texts from different cultures and traditions, or any other aspect of the curriculum? You might wish to consider the place of texts in translation, the role of visual learning, and strategies for encouraging speaking and listening activities that are multi-lingual.

Alexander (2006: 6) argues that the new emphasis on literacy was not motivated 'by altruistic concerns for young people' but rather 'functional' demands of a global economy: the reformulation of English to focus on literacy has 'exerted huge pressure on pedagogy, which has responded to the demand for an instrumental approach, skills, systemisation and prescription'. The strategy also received criticism from those outside educational practice and research. The author Philip Pullman (2002: 12) described an audit he had carried out of what children were to be doing when reading text, according to the strategy. He records that the word 'enjoy' was not present.

While the strategy has received much criticism from teachers and researchers alike, there are some elements that *have* been creatively adopted and modified. For example, while there was a tendency to focus on extracts rather than full texts, the focus on shared text work has been regarded positively (Ofsted 2009). As Dickinson (2010: 26–7) stresses:

> The literacy strategy has had its day and yet its legacy will take time to be forgotten. Reflective teachers will hold on to its 'lessons' such as the importance of modelling expectations, sharing the meta-cognitive processes of writing with their students and sideline the negative experiences of bite-size approaches to literature to cover the multitude of objectives in the Framework for Teaching English: Years 7, 8 and 9.

Professional reflection: creativity and curriculum

Consider your reactions to the quotations below.

> Uniformity might seem to have much to recommend it. It would certainly be a way for central government to control what is taught in schools, but it would only work if those who go into teaching were different sorts of people. At the moment the great majority of people who decide to go into teaching do so because they like their subject and want to pursue it, they have interests and values which they want to share with young people and they enjoy the creative process of thinking up lessons, trying them out, discussing them, and rethinking them. This process may produce problems as well as successes but at least its alive, and always 'on the move'.
>
> (Barnes *et al.* 2003: 18–19)

> The National Strategies have recently revised the frameworks and guidance that teachers use for planning. There have been changes to the National Curriculum in Key Stage 3, including an end to national tests at 14, and GCSE courses are being rewritten to include a new element of functional skills. New A-level courses began in 2008. At the same time, schools are being encouraged to personalise the curriculum, in order to meet students' needs more effectively. The best schools visited during the last year of the survey were revising their programmes in the light of national recommendations and this was leading to positive developments. Where the curriculum was least effective, the teachers had found it difficult to respond creatively to the new opportunities. They were implementing national policy changes unthinkingly, often because they had no deeply held views about the nature of English as a subject and how it might be taught.
>
> (Ofsted 2009: para 31)

[T]here is a danger that the creative nature of the subject may be undermined.

(Allen 2002: 9)

When creativity is lost, English as a subject will lose its point.

(Barnes *et al.* 2003: 19)

How do you respond to fears that the years of NLS teaching have potentially led to a generation of students who lack creativity? What does this imply for the future of English teaching?

The revised National Curriculum 2007

The revised programmes of study for the National Curriculum have a shared format across the subjects. Each contains: an 'importance statement' describing why the subject matters; key concepts underpinning the subject; key processes; an outline of the range and content of the subject; and curriculum opportunities which identify opportunities to enhance and enrich learning, including making links to the wider curriculum. This offers more flexibility than has been enjoyed by teachers of English in recent years.

ICT: literacy and ICT

Goodwyn and Findlay (2003) question what is meant by literacy within schooling. They argue that the definition of 'school-centric' literacy that resonates from official documentation is too narrow and reductive; they suggest that the type of literacy skills needed to succeed at school, therefore those which are deemed necessary, are 'vocationalised with an economic imperative' and linked to 'our economic survival and competitiveness' (2003: 24). They also make the point that to be successfully literate within school means to be able to succeed within a 'traditionally/elite academic curriculum' (2003: 28).

Do you agree with this? Does the National Curriculum for English (2007) promote different types of literacy (print, visual, media, computer, multi-modal, critical ...)? How might a broader understanding of notions of literacy acknowledge what children can bring to school and consequently empower those who exist on the border of the traditional elite?

How does ICT fit in with this?

Do you agree with Goodwyn and Findlay that ICT 'remains outside the English school-centric' notions of literacy? What kinds of 'newer' literacies are children in and out of schools used to working with? How can newer technologies of literacy be utilised to improve student learning within English?

Key reading
- Goodwyn, A. and Findlay, K. (2003) 'Shaping literacy in the secondary school: policy, practice and agency in the age of the National Literacy Strategy', *British Journal of Educational Studies* 51:1: 20–35.

Within English, the revised programme of study has been built around the four key concepts (the four Cs) of competence, creativity, cultural understanding and critical understanding (concepts which developed from a QCA 'discussion' with the English education community, *Taking English Forward*: QCA 2005).

Into practice: creativity in the revised National Curriculum

How can you shape a KS3 English scheme of work that goes beyond the reductive notions of 'literacy'? Look at the descriptions of creativity in the key concepts and the accompanying explanatory notes on page 62 (Key Stage 3) of the revised Programme of Study for English. How might you plan to ensure that your students are provided with opportunities to understand this concept?

Research some of the projects described in the Creative Partnerships website in order to explore ways in which we can think beyond narrative and poetry. What is the place of drama in this? Are there ways in which there could be cross-curricular links with other creative subjects such as dance, art and design, and music? What about media and digital texts? Can we move beyond notions of creativity as being an elitist concept housed in galleries, theatres and museums? Read the Hall and Thomson (2010) article to help you to consider whether there are ways in which students can be encouraged to look to their local community to find examples of creativity that they could utilise in their work in school.

Key reading
- Jones, K. (2010) 'The twentieth century is not yet over: resources for the remaking of educational practice', *Changing English* 17:1: 13–26.
- Marshall, B. (2006b) 'What do we know in English? Facts and fiction in an arts-based English curriculum', *English in Education* 40:3: 7–20.
- Hall, C. and Thomson, P. (2010) 'Grounded literacies: the power of listening to, telling and performing community stories', *Literacy* 44:2: 69–75.
- Creative Partnerships website: www.creative-partnerships.com.

Lesson planning

The activity of planning is complex, and takes place at a number of different levels: scheme of work planning, medium-term planning, lesson planning. Below is some guidance as to what should be included at each level of planning (see Table 4.1). It also involves the interaction of a wide range of issues (see Figure 4.1). This model illustrates the many different components that go into planning. It demonstrates the way that planning works, bringing together two component parts – content and pedagogy.

The figure is divided into differently shaded sections, as follows:

- Content component, or what to teach. The different cells outline various documents or initiatives that provide guidance or requirements regarding the content of English lesson planning.

Table 4.1 Levels of planning

Scheme of work planning	Medium-term planning	Lesson planning
• Topic/title	• Sequence of objectives (usually over a week) to show progression	• Links to previous learning
• Overall aims		• Detailed lesson objectives
• Broad links with National Curriculum	• More specific resource requirements	• Detailed links to National Curriculum
• Major resources	• Major lesson objectives	• Detailed activity breakdown
• Major student tasks	• Main lesson activities	
• Major assessment	• Main interim assessment opportunities	• Detailed assessment
• Outline plan (introduction of topic, number of lessons, possible sequence of lessons, main objectives)		• Clear timings
		• Specific resources

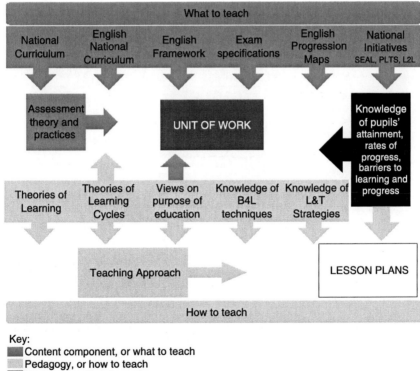

Figure 4.1 A conceptual model of planning

- Pedagogy, or how to teach. Some of these are theories or policies, but others relate to personal views on the purpose and means of English education.
- Student-specific information: this feeds into thinking about planning for individuals and classes.
- The unit of work, a document which outlines the coverage of a particular unit for teaching, particularly concentrating on its content.
- The individual lesson plan, which outlines practically how the content of a particular lesson will be explored, focusing on matters of teaching and learning as they relate to the content for the lesson.

Individual lesson planning

It is probable that your ITE provider and/or school will have their own lesson planning pro forma for you to use. However, there is a suggested template in Figure 4.2 that you may use, with an explanation of what goes in each section.

LESSON PLAN		Date:		Time:	
Unit of work: Title of unit	Group:	Room:		Boys/Girls:	
Work covered in previous lesson(s): Include here key information that helps locate the lesson you are going to teach (e.g. names of poems covered, types of writing addressed, major topics dealt with).		**Resources:** Include here all resources required (e.g. pens and sugar paper, DVDs, texts, stimulus materials, etc.).			
Intended Learning Objectives: By the end of this lesson students will understand These are a succinct statement of the learning you want to take place, so steer clear of anything activity-based (e.g. write a poem is not a learning objective). Using words such as 'understand' or 'conceptualise' will help you focus on learning. Do not have too many objectives for one lesson (usually 2 or 3 is plenty). Try to make these as specific as possible (e.g. 'Understand the poem' is a very broad and unhelpful objective, whereas 'Understand how the poet uses water imagery' is much more specific and helpful).		NC Demonstrate how your objectives relate to the National Curriculum.		Key Words Identify any words you find particularly important in this lesson.	
Lesson Outline: This section is the 'narrative' of the lesson. It will provide an outline of the content, activities and outcomes of the lesson. Write this in enough detail that it serves as a good aide memoire for you and a suitable guide for anybody else who may be observing the lesson.	ILO Use this column to map where your objectives are covered.	Time Indicative timings for sections of the lesson.		Differentiation Indicate here where specific provision has been made for individuals or groups within the class.	
Homework Details of any homework task set.		Extension Explain here additional work prepared in case students finish quickly or you mistimed the lesson.			

Figure 4.2 Exemplar lesson planning pro forma

Common mistakes in planning

It is also worth noting common mistakes made in planning (see Table 4.2).

Table 4.2 Common mistakes in planning

Learning objectives	The objective(s) of the lesson does not specify what the student will actually learn that can be observed. Remember, an objective is a description of what students are intended to learn. Poorly written objectives lead to faulty inferences.
Lesson assessment	The lesson assessment is disconnected from the behaviour indicated in the objective. An assessment in a lesson plan is simply a description of how the teacher will determine whether the objective has been accomplished. It must be based on the same behaviour that is incorporated in the objective. Anything else is flawed.
Prerequisites	The prerequisites are not specified or are inconsistent with what is actually required to succeed with the lesson. Prerequisites mean just that – a statement of what a student needs to know or be able to do to succeed and accomplish the lesson objective. It is not easy to determine what is required, but it is necessary. Successful learning obviously depends on students having the appropriate prerequisites.
Materials	The materials specified in the lesson are extraneous to the actual described learning activities. This means keep the list of materials in line with what you actually plan to do. Overkilling with materials is not a good idea.
Instruction	The instruction in which the teacher will engage is not efficient for the level of intended student learning.
Lesson activity	The learning activities described in the lesson plan do not contribute in a direct and effective way to the lesson objective(s). Don't have your students engaged in activities just to keep them busy. Whatever you have your students do should contribute in a direct way to their accomplishing the lesson objective.

In summary

- The curriculum for English is a social and political project.
- Wider societal issues play a key role in shaping content and pedagogy.
- Professional identity is something that evolves over time.
- There is a wide variety of 'models' of English.
- Planning is a complex and multi-faceted process.
- Teachers need to consider their individual response to teaching the National Curriculum for English.

Recommended reading

- Andrews, R. (2001) *Teaching and Learning English: A Guide to Recent Research and its Applications.* London: Continuum.
- Berry, J. (2009) 'Can there be an alternative to the centralised curriculum in England?', *Improving Schools* 12:1: 33–41.
- Ellis, V. (2007) *Subject Knowledge and Teacher Education: The Development of Beginning Teachers' Thinking.* London: Continuum.
- The English Association, www.le.ac.uk/engassoc/index.html.
- Goddard, R. (2009) 'Not fit for purpose: the national strategies for literacy considered as an endeavour of government', *Power and Education* 1:1: 30–41.
- Jones, K. (2006). 'Part of the main: a project for English', *English in Education* 40:1: 80–91.
- Marshall, B. (2000) *English Teachers: The Unofficial Guide.* London: Routledge.
- National Association for the Teaching of English, www.nate.org.uk.
- United Kingdom Literacy Association, www.ukla.org.

Acknowledgements

The earlier sections of this chapter have evolved from ideas and discussions with the English team in the School of Education, University of Nottingham.

Figure 4.1 was developed initially by Marie Hamner.

References

Alexander, J. (2006) 'The uncreating word or some ways not to teach', *Why English? Conference,* University of Oxford, 26–28 October, 2006.

Alexander, R. (2004) 'Still no pedagogy? Principle, pragmatism and compliance in primary education', *Cambridge Journal of Education* 34:1: 7–33.

Allen, N. (2002) 'Too much, too young? An analysis of the Key Stage 3 National Literacy Strategy in practice', *English in Education* 36:1: 5–15.

Barnes, A., Venkatakrishnan, H. and Brown, M. (2003) *Strategy or Strait-jacket? Teachers' Views on the English and Mathematics Strands of the Key Stage 3 National Strategy.* Final report. London: Association of Teachers and Lecturers.

Clark, U. (1994) 'Bringing English to order: a personal account of the NCC English Evaluation Project', *English in Education* 28:1: 33–9.

Dearing, R. (1993) *The National Curriculum and its Assessment: An Interim Report.* London: HMSO.

DES (1987) *English for Ages 5–16: A Consultation Report.* London: HMSO.

DES (1988) *A Report of the Committee of Inquiry into the Teaching of English (Kingman Report).* London: HMSO.

DES (1989) *English for Ages 5–16 (Cox Report).* London: HMSO.

DES (1990) *English in the National Curriculum.* London: HMSO.

Dickinson, D. (2010) 'Developments in English', in S. Clarke, P. Dickinson and J. Westbrook (eds), *The Complete Guide to Becoming an English Teacher.* London: Sage.

Dixon, J. (2003) 'The battle for English', in J. Davison and J. Dowson (eds), *Learning to Teach English in the Secondary School*. London: RoutledgeFalmer.

Eagleton, T. (1983) *Literary Theory*. Oxford: Blackwell.

Goddard, R. (2009) 'Not fit for purpose: the national strategies for literacy considered as an endeavour of government', *Power and Education* 1:1: 30–41.

Goodwyn, A. and Findlay, K. (2003) 'Shaping literacy in the secondary school: policy, practice and agency in the age of the National Literacy Strategy', *British Journal of Educational Studies* 51:1: 20–35.

Hall, C. and Thomson, P. (2010) 'Grounded literacies: the power of listening to, telling and performing community stories', *Literacy* 44:2: 69–75.

Harvard Education Review (1998) *The Changing Curriculum* (summer). Available online at www.hepg.org/her/booknote/176 (accessed 12 September 2010).

Jones, K. (2003) *Education in Britain: 1944 to the Present*. Cambridge: Polity.

Jones, K. (2006) 'Part of the main: a project for English', *English in Education* 40:1: 80–92.

Jones, K. (2010) 'The twentieth century is not yet over: resources for the remaking of educational practice', *Changing English* 17:1: 13–26.

Marshall, B. (2000) *English Teachers: The Unofficial Guide*. London: Routledge.

Marshall, B. (2006a) 'The future of English', *FORUM* 40:1: 69–79.

Marshall, B. (2006b) 'What do we know in English: facts and fiction in an arts-based English curriculum', *English in Education* 40:3: 7–20.

Ofsted (2009) *English at the Crossroads*. London: HMSO.

Protherough, R. and King, P. (1995) *The Challenge of English in the National Curriculum*. London: Routledge.

Pullman, P. (2002) *Perverse, All Monstrous, All Prodigious Things*. Sheffield: NATE.

QCA (2005) *Taking English Forward*. London: QCA.

Torrance, H. (2002) 'Can testing really raise educational standards?', *Professorial Lecture Delivered at the University of Sussex*, 11 June 2002. Available online at www.enquirylearning.net/ELU/Issues/Education/HTassess.html (accessed 24 September 2010).

UK Parliament (1988) *The Education Reform Act*. London: HMSO.

Wrigley, T. (2009) 'Rethinking education in the era of globalisation', in D. Hill (ed.), *Contesting Neoliberal Education*. London: Routledge.

5

DEBRA MYHILL AND ANNABEL WATSON
Teaching writing

In this chapter you will consider

- the principal theoretical perspectives on writing;
- how writing is re-framed by digital technologies;
- process approaches to writing;
- how metacognition supports writing development;
- how to teach writing reflectively, supporting writers in thinking about their own writing process and becoming designers of text.

Introduction

Writing is a mirror of the self, the soul and the world. Through writing, we can give voice to our most intimate thoughts and give free rein to our imagination; through writing, we can shape and articulate new knowledge, new ideas, and new philosophies; through writing, we can reflect on the past and imagine the future. Yet the sad truth is that, for many students in secondary English classrooms, writing is a chore, something which has to be done and which many would avoid if they could. English teachers often choose teaching English as a career so that they can open up the world of reading to young minds, but we need to be just as aspirational and as inspirational in the way we think about teaching writing. Enabling young writers to be confident communicators of the written word, both on paper and in digital formats, gives them access to power. Writing remains the dominant mode for accessing educational success (most examinations are still written examinations) but, more than this, writing gives students the power to voice themselves and to challenge and change the world in which they live.

Professional reflection: your views of writing
· How do you approach the writing process?   · How can you support students who approach it in different ways?   · What values do you bring to your teaching of writing?   · What can you do to draw links between your students' writing in and out of school?

Theorising writing

Research into writing can be grouped into three main disciplinary approaches, cognitive psychology, linguistics and socio-cultural theory. Recently, there has been an increase in interdisciplinary methodologies which provide more holistic understandings of writing, and we would argue that an appropriate pedagogy for teaching writing adopts an inclusive approach. Students as writers do have to manage the complex mental processes involved in writing; they do have to manage language effectively to shape and create text; and they always write within a social context which influences how they see and value the writing they produce. Below we present a brief overview of the three disciplinary approaches but encourage you to draw on all three in your own professional thinking about teaching writing.

Cognitive approaches

Cognitive or psychological research conceptualises writing chiefly as a problem-solving activity, attempting to describe the internal mental processes that occur. The first influential model of the writing process was developed by Hayes and Flower in 1980. They defined separate stages of planning (goal-setting, generation of content, organisation of ideas), translating (turning thoughts into words and sentences, graphic transcription) and reviewing (evaluating and editing what has been written). These stages are contextualised by the 'task environment', which incorporates the nature of the assignment and the text produced so far – a prompt for further ideas as well as an object to be analysed and edited. Finally, the model includes the long-term memory from which writers draw their knowledge of topic, audience and generic structure. The monitor switches the writer's attention between planning, translating and revising during the writing process.

Figure 5.1 depicts the writing process as a flowchart, but it is not intended to suggest that writing is a linear process; indeed, in expert writers the stages are recursive and some elements become automatic. The operation of the process is also highly individual; for example, some writers may prefer to create detailed plans and minimise their reviewing process, while others may plan 'online' as they write, then edit extensively afterwards (Sharples 1999: 112).

The model in Figure 5.1 provided the starting point for a number of more sophisticated models (e.g. Hayes 1996; Kellogg 1996), many of which expand on our understanding of the different stages of the process, as well as considering aspects absent from the initial model such as the roles of motivation, affect and working memory. Other models, such as Bereiter and Scardamalia's models of 'Knowledge-telling' and

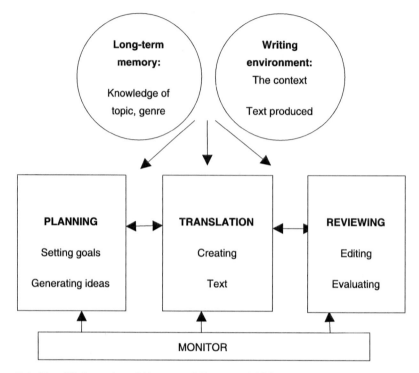

Figure 5.1 Simplified version of Hayes and Flower's (1980) model of the writing process

'Knowledge-transforming' (1987) have explored differences in the processes of novice and expert writers.

While such models are necessarily reductive, they can provide useful ways for teachers and students to think about writing. One important insight is that different children find different stages of the process difficult to manage. Beginner writers often find planning particularly difficult and tend to focus on content generation rather than organisation of ideas or the needs of the audience. They will also struggle more with the act of graphic transcription, something that becomes almost entirely automatic for more experienced writers, and find the reviewing process difficult (Negro and Chanquoy 2005), tending to correct surface features rather than considering deeper changes to the structure or organisation of ideas. By paying attention to these stages when planning lessons on writing, teachers can ensure that they support all of the different aspects of the writing process.

Socio-cultural approaches

Criticisms that cognitive research has been decontextualised, tending to be carried out in laboratory settings often using 'expert' writers, have been countered by socio-cultural approaches. These aim to study the writer in context, acknowledging that writing is a social act, using socially constructed tools (languages, genres, technologies of writing) for social purposes. Rather than formulating universal models, this research centres on differences of experience, often studying minority or disadvantaged groups. It also often has an historical element which is sensitive to changing understandings of literacy and the values attributed to different forms of writing (Cook-Gumperz 2006).

Socio-cultural researchers are concerned with the diverse experiences that children have with literacy and how they construct identities as 'writers'. They argue that differences in social experience often far outweigh differences in the cognitive abilities of students, citing factors such as motivation, self-confidence and perceptions of the value of assignments as significant influences on writing development (Ball 2008). The influence of class, gender and ethnicity have been widely explored, with a movement away from simplistic classification towards a sensitivity to the influence of expectations: for example, it has been suggested that teachers' perception that boys are less able writers may actually contribute to their under-achievement (Jones and Myhill 2007: 458).

EAL: EAL students as writers

- Always establish the EAL student's level of achievement in writing, rather than judging by oral competence. Depending on their language history, some orally fluent EAL writers will struggle to achieve similar levels of competence in writing; alternatively, some EAL students will be better at writing, than orally.
- Support the different stages of the writing process in specific ways. Moving from thoughts into words may be challenging, as they may not have the linguistic resources in English to match their thoughts in their first language. Encourage diagrammatic or pictorial ways of representing ideas, or capturing ideas in first language before moving to writing in English. Give them word banks to support vocabulary building.
- Actively help the process of revising text by teaching them strategies for revision (reading aloud, checklists, separating attention to spelling from punctuation and from the communicative message).
- Encourage collaborative work with first-language speakers but set this up carefully so that it is a learning experience, not simply a more expert writer doing the work.

Dominant and subordinate literacies, the ideologies inherent in the types of writing that are valued in school, and the 'role that writing plays in challenging or perpetuating social positions and injustices' (Englert *et al.* 2008: 217) are also key focuses of socio-cultural research. Experiences of speaking, reading and writing in families and communities can complement or conflict with school literacies (Heath 1983); for example, students from middle-class backgrounds whose spoken dialect more closely reflects the rules of written language have an advantage over those whose home dialect is further from Standard English. To combat this, teachers are urged to 'build bridges' between home and school to 'strengthen students' academic writing' (Ball 2008: 297).

Socio-cultural research also studies relationships and power in the classroom, questioning the image of a lone writer translating thought into words, seeing writing as an intersubjective process. Prior (2008: 58) suggests that 'teachers in schools are always co-authors (often dominant ones) in students' writing', taking the role of task-setting, deadline-monitoring, specifying style and topic, structuring the writing process, and evaluating writing. Within genre theory, researchers have also investigated how writers learn to operate within and challenge social codes and conventions (Czerniewska 1992: 149), as well as the ways in which genres are used to construct and maintain identities.

Linguistic approaches

Linguistic approaches to writing research conceptualise writing as a form of linguistic mastery. One strand of linguistic focus has been genre theory, particularly the Sydney School in Australia, which advocated explicit teaching of the linguistic features of genres to young writers. Drawing on the work of Halliday, Australian theorists such as Martin and Rothery (1980), Derewianka (1996) and Rose (2009) developed teaching materials which illustrated the grammatical and textual characteristics of genres such as explanation, instruction and recount. This has been heavily influential in our own National Curriculum and particularly in the NLS. In the USA, the genre movement has been more influenced by socio-cultural theory than linguistics, and focuses on demonstrating how genres are socially and culturally determined (Swales 1990).

Linguistic approaches to writing also include studies of vocabulary acquisition and development, the development of grammatical structures in students' writing, differences between speech and writing, and descriptive grammars such as systemic functional linguistics (Halliday and Matthiessen 2004).

A number of studies have explored the developing maturity of young writers by analysing samples of writing. Loban (1963), Harpin (1976) and Perera (1984) all suggested that it is possible to trace key stages of development in linguistic mastery, looking particularly at the ability to handle complex structures at clause and sentence level, and highlighting the use of complex sentences and subordinating connectives as one indicator of maturity. However, the focus of linguistic research has shifted away from trying to define a simple linear model of development that equates syntactical complexity with linguistic ability, instead suggesting that linguistic maturity evolves as a writer develops a repertoire of structures and choices (Beard 2000: 71). Linguistic mastery is thus defined as an ability to craft text, selecting and deploying a range of words and (text and sentence level) structures for effect (Myhill *et al.* 2008). Research has also moved away from a deficit model focused on the prevention or correction of errors in writing, towards recognition that mistakes can be a sign of ambition, a necessary part of developing linguistic control. Indeed, students can seem to regress in their writing as they try out more complex structures and apply them incorrectly at first (Perera 1984, 158: Myhill 2001: 35).

M level: a variety of tasks

- Plan a writing lesson and write a critical rationale for your pedagogical decisions, drawing on your reading about research in writing.
- Find three journal articles which reflect different theoretical perspectives on writing. You could try *Learning and Instruction* for cognitive perspectives, *Written Communication* for socio-cultural perspectives, and *Language and Education* or *Applied Linguistics* for linguistic perspectives. Be warned, however: the latter journals in particular may have articles which represent other perspectives. Read your selected three articles carefully and write a critical commentary on each one, analysing its strengths and weaknesses in supporting classroom practice in writing.
- Observe one or two students writing, and interview them about their writing processes; you could use the methodology outlined in Myhill (2009). How does what they do and say link with what research tells us about writing? The role of explicit grammar teaching in improving students' writing is a highly contentious aspect of linguistic research. Studies have repeatedly reported that decontextualised grammar teaching does not benefit students as they fail to make links between their knowledge of grammar and the decisions they make as writers (Wyse 2001). Research in this area has been limited, with sentence-combining the only strategy that has shown any transferable benefit with some degree of consistency (Andrews *et al.* 2006). However, there have also been suggestions that teaching grammar in context, drawing attention to structures and patterns of language in real texts and encouraging students to explore the effects of structures in their own writing may benefit students, making them more aware of the choices they have as writers (Carter 1990; Myhill *et al.* 2008). Our own 'Grammar for Writing?' project, funded by the ESRC, has investigated the potential of contextualised grammar teaching on a larger scale than previous studies, and the statistical data indicate that it can have a significant benefit for some students.

Writing as design

A more recent attempt to understand writing draws on all three of the above: the concept of writing as design. This idea has been elaborated by Sharples (1999), who conceptualises writing as a problem-solving activity, with authors approaching a design solution through a number of different strategies. The notion of a writer as a 'designer' emphasises the writer's active role in crafting their work, making choices which to draw from a repertoire of rhetorical resources. Comparing writers to architects and graphic designers (who often work in teams), the concept suggests a way of understanding collaborative writing, and Sharples also integrates psychological theories of creativity into an understanding of the 'design' process. In pedagogical terms, the concept urges teachers to move away from an emphasis on error correction, rules or formulaic approaches, towards discussion and exploration of the links between the communication of meaning and rhetorical impact of the writer's linguistic choices (Myhill 2010).

Into practice: writing as design

- Approach a writing task like a design task: with discussions about audience and purpose, design briefs as plans, drafts as prototypes and market testing through evaluation.
- Give students opportunities to reflect on their own writing processes and compare with others, including through invited professional writers in the classroom.
- Teach writing explicitly: not just through modelling and analysis of texts, but also teaching students about the writing process and strategic ways to manage it.
- Build connections between writing and reading, and writing and oracy, and encourage reading aloud of written text to help students hear the voice of their own writing.

Writing futures: new technologies and multi-modal texts

Developing technologies have influenced how we read, compose and disseminate texts to the extent that the very meaning of the word 'writing' has been called into question (Sorapure 2006). Fundamental changes have been identified by Kress (2005: 6), who outlines the increasing predominance of image and the movement away from a linear structure, arguing that 'the semiotic changes are vast enough to warrant the term "revolution"', and highlighting a shift in the dominant mode from writing to image, and in the dominant medium from book to screen. New technologies have created a growing convergence of modes and processes: text, image and sound are increasingly interlinked, as are the activities of reading, listening and composing text. One example of this is the convergence of speech, text and image in instant messaging exchanges, where emoticons are used to convey information that would be carried by tone of voice or facial expression in face-to-face conversation. Arguably, multi-modality has become the norm. Media convergence is also collapsing traditional oppositions such as producer/consumer, expert/amateur, with collaborative platforms raising questions of authorship and ownership. Wikipedia, for example, is a site 'not just of converging media, but also converging notions of authorship, research, and knowledge production' (Alexander 2008: 4).

This poses considerable challenges for teachers, not least in the need to recognise the varied ways in which students are engaged in literacy beyond the classroom and to make links between practices in and out of school. In many cases students are ahead of their teachers in their ability to use technologies, but teachers have an important role in developing students' critical understanding of multi-modal texts.

ICT

- Even though, regrettably, at present all examination of writing is handwritten or very basic word-processed text, develop students' ability to compose on screen, and to use all the affordance of word-processing to develop as writers. Beyond school, most workplace writing is electronic.

- Exploit the potential of blogging, wikis and online publication to encourage writing within and beyond classroom boundaries and use shared writing tools, such as Google Docs, to actively support and teach the collaborative production of text.
- Analyse the differences between electronic genres such as email, Twitter, SMS and other conventional written genres.
- Give students opportunities to write multi-modal texts, both print versions, such as leaflets, and onscreen versions, such as web pages. When teaching these, treat the whole enterprise as a writing design activity, in which fonts, colours, layout, hypertext and so on are all an important part of the composing process. Research has also investigated the use of technology to support writing in the classroom. There is some evidence that word-processing programmes can help students to break away from a linear approach and move towards a more 'mature cycle of composing, reflecting and revising' (Sharples 1999: 190), although without careful instruction they have tended to produce superficial error correction rather than deep revisions (MacArthur 2008). A growing area of inquiry is the potential of wiki technologies to promote collaborative writing (Wheeler *et al.* 2008), and the use of other platforms, such as podcasts, to promote writing have also been explored (Walsh 2008).

In this context, the model of 'writing as design' may provide a helpful way to approach the study of multi-modal texts. The concept of 'design' can apply across all modes and media, giving equal weight to both visual and linguistic elements, and a design approach can also focus students on the need to combine images, sounds, language and interactive features to produce an effective whole.

Process approaches to writing

The term *writing process* is subject to multiple interpretations, often due to the particular field of research in which the term is used. Cognitive psychologists, as we explained earlier, see the writing process as made up of the sub-processes of planning, translating and revising, but their use of the word *process* is very much concerned with mental processes. However, the dominant understanding of the notion of writing as process derives from educational research and practice in the 1970s and 1980s, which argued that the teaching of writing should pay far more attention to the process of writing than the product. In England, in the 1950s and 1960s, writing tended to be regarded as simply a product which needed to be marked or assessed, and little teaching time was given to helping students draft or revise. They just wrote! The seminal work of Britton *et al.* (1975) highlighted the limited range of writing students were asked to undertake, something which Emig (1971), in the USA, had also found. Emig was arguably the first educationalist to frame writing as a composing process and to suggest that the teaching of writing needed to acknowledge this. Graves (1983) and Murray (1982) advocated creating writing classrooms where drafting and discussed work-in-progress were central to the teaching of writing: teachers were encouraged to hold writing conferences with students in the classroom, giving students one-to-one time to discuss their emerging texts. The Gravesian approach highly valued personal voice and the narration of personal experience, and discouraged interventionist actions from the teacher which might silence the emerging voice. The influence of process approaches to writing has been evident in the National Curriculum from its first iteration in 1989, which for the first time formally included planning, drafting, revising and editing as part of the writing curriculum. The most recent version of the National Curriculum for English (QCA 2007: 67) mandates that students should be able to 'use planning, drafting, editing, proofreading and self-evaluation to shape and craft their writing for maximum effect'.

There are many valid and robust critiques of process approaches to writing which deserve attention here. Some have critiqued the quality of the research which under-pins the ideas. Emig's study, for example, is based on a case study of eight students and detailed analysis of just one. Smagorinsky (1987: 339) condemned Graves's work as reportage, rather than research, and argues that he has 'a distinct bias for certain writing styles and processes that the researchers praise in certain children, and note critically the absence of in others'. Others have critiqued the approach as privileging the already privileged: just as Heath (1983) had drawn attention to the disadvantage of those whose home literacies were different from school literacies, so critics of proc-ess writing argued that it privileged those who come to school already accessing the socially valued ways of writing,. Because it eschews explicit or interventionist teaching strategies, and values personal, self-expressive forms of writing over others, it is both culturally and socially biased: as Martin (1985: 61) puts it:

> With its stress on ownership and voice, its preoccupations with children selecting their own topics, its reluctance to intervene positively and constructively during conferencing, and its complete mystification of what has to be learned for children to reproduce effective written products, it is currently promoting a situation in which only the brightest middle-class children can possibly learn what is needed.

In essence, Martin was highlighting that the process approach as espoused in the 1980s valued one genre, personal writing, over other genres, and ignored the social context in which the writing was produced. Both the genre movement (Martin and Rothery 1980; Derewianka 1996) and the writing as social practice movement (McComiskey 2000; Prior 2006) grew out of this.

Creativity

- Create opportunities for writing beyond the classroom, particularly for specific and authentic purposes. Rather than just 'creative writing' clubs, think more creatively and, for example, produce a poetry anthology for publication on one occasion, and an invitation prospectus for the new Year 7 to go to all feeder schools on another occasion.
- Foster independence and autonomy by using student leadership to run specific tasks, like a school newspaper, and by encouraging digital writing activities and collaborations (which could go beyond school or national boundaries).

- In the writing lesson, foster creativity by showing students repertoires of possibility, the multiple ways in which meaning can be conveyed, rather than giving formulaic guidance on writing.
- Teaching writing as design is an intrinsically creative approach! However, we do believe that there is an important place for process approaches within a reflective pedagogy of writing because attention to the composing process and how we write supports the development of the writer. Like Martin, we agree that over-emphasising the personal expressive genre at the expense of helping students develop confidence in a range of genres is inadvisable, and, unlike Graves, we do think that teachers do need to be explicit in showing writers how a text is shaped. Our definition of a process approach to writing, fit for the twenty-first century, is less about personal writing and more about writer awareness and strategic management of the way they write. A process approach to writing acknowledges that the composing process is an important part of the writing produced and that teaching should help writers to analyse and reflect on their own composing process, and to become more confident as planners, drafters and revisers of their own texts. We need to remember that we are helping students to become writers in the real world, not just for classrooms or examination purposes. And, of course, we do know, from the testimonies of professional authors, that writers do not all compose in the same way. Some writers, J.B. Priestley for example, plan their work meticulously in advance of beginning writing; others, such as David Almond, write to find out what they want to say. Neither educational research nor the accounts of professional writers yet provides a consistent interpretation of the writing process, and we owe it to our student writers to open up the mysteries of the writing process to them.

Writers as thinkers

If we accept the principle that teaching writing needs to involve students actively in thinking about their composing processes, then we can hope to develop writers who are reflective thinkers, writers who understand themselves as creators of text. Our own research reveals just how thoughtful and reflective students can be when given appropriate opportunities. It also indicates that young writers have different ways of composing, or different *composing profiles*, as we have called them (Myhill 2009). We observed students from Year 8 and Year 10 undertaking a piece of writing in an English lesson, and then interviewed them afterwards to discuss their reflections on their writing process and the decisions they made. We also timed their writing and pausing patterns and created profiles of the different types of writers in the sample. What is very evident is that students, like professional writers, have different writing profiles. Hayes and Flower (1980) found that writers could be characterised as Mozartians, who undertook extensive planning, or Beethovians, who generated a first draft quickly, then revised intensively. Sharples (1999) called these two kinds of writers planners and discoverers, and our students very much fitted these profiles. In particular, students do not all approach the starting period of writing in the same way: some writers

Table 5.1 Students' reflections on their composing processes

Planner writers	Discovery writers
· I think about it in my head first. I think before I write.	· I just really get on with it and things start coming into your head.
· I'll probably just think about it in my head, how I'm going to set it out, and then do it after I've thought about it.	· Well, I didn't know what I was going to write about and then I just decided that, start and see if I got any ideas when I started writing.
· I think about what we have to do and how we've got to do it.	· It just flows really; I just start writing … as I write it just comes to me and new words, new sentences, just different things, different ideas…
· I think about how I'm going to start the story and how I'm going to continue it.	· As I'm writing it just kind of comes from there; it just flows and I just get more and more ideas.

like to spend time thinking about the writing, mentally planning or creating written plans, whereas others write to find out what they want to say (see Table 5.1).

The teenagers we worked with demonstrated that, with the right kind of prompting and encouragement, they were capable of high-level reflection on themselves as writers, not simply at the level of describing whether they were planners or discoverers, but in much more sophisticated accounts of their writing process. One girl explained that 'when I pause, I'm not thinking about what I'm going to write next, I'm thinking about what's going to happen in two or three paragraphs' time', while other writers described re-reading their work during writing, thinking about how to 'change it to make it better' or about how to 'shape the sentence'. One boy knew that, even while he was writing at one point in the text, his reader's eye could be elsewhere, as he explained:

> There was one time that you might have thought was a bit strange where I got to about three-quarters of the way down and then just went straight back up to the top and I changed something … because that just actually caught my eye … just something looked out of place and I happened to see it.

Inclusion: working with SEN and gifted students
· Use the principles of personalised learning to make sure that you meet the needs of all learners in the class: this requires focused and purposeful assessment of writing and writing progress.   · Think carefully about differentiation in writing and do not repeatedly rely on differentiation by outcome; for example, how can the writing task be varied appropriate to need, or the expectations of the task varied?

- For students with specific learning difficulties in literacy, ensure that you know the nature of their learning needs and any recommended strategies for support. Use teaching assistants wisely to address need: this might mean that you work with a child with Special Needs while the teaching assistant is working with the class.
- For very able writers, ensure that the writing task demand is appropriate, and give opportunities for extended writing tasks. Make sure that formative feedback gives high-level information on what could be improved and on what has been successful. Remember, though, that the most able writers may need *more* time to do justice to a piece of writing than less able writers as they are more sophisticated about their goals and revision processes.

These writers are showing metacognitive awareness of writing. Right from the earliest investigations on the cognitive processes involved in writing, research (Hayes and Flower 1980; Martlew 1983; Kellogg 1994; Butterfield *et al.* 1996) has shown the importance of metacognition, or thinking about writing, in successful writers. Bereiter and Scardamalia (1982: 57) maintained that this relationship between effective writing and effective thinking about writing is because metacognition makes 'normally covert processes overt', thus making 'tacit knowledge more accessible'. In other words, teaching students how to think about themselves as writers brings thoughts and activities which are normally hidden to the surface of consciousness for visible scrutiny and reflection. This allows students to be more strategic about their writing – for example, knowing what to do when they reach a writing block, or knowing they need to remind themselves to re-read their emerging text periodically during writing, or that they need to spend more time working on the overall structure of their text. A recent large-scale US review of research (Graham and Perin 2007) found that the most successful teaching strategy for developing effective writers was explicitly teaching them writing strategies to help them manage the composing process. Indeed, Kellogg (1994: 213) argued that successful teachers 'must teach the student how to think as well as write'. Successful writers are also successful thinkers about writing.

In summary

- Writing needs aspirational and inspirational teachers just as reading does.
- Writing has been theorised from different perspectives, principally through cognitive psychology, socio-cultural theory and linguistics. An appropriate pedagogy for writing needs to draw on all three.
- Writing in the twenty-first century is not just about handwritten text; it includes all the affordances and possibilities of digital and multi-modal texts.
- Writing is an act of design: writers make linguistic, creative, visual and social choices in creating their texts. Teaching needs to help writers develop creative repertoires for writing in a range of modes and formats.
- Writing is a process and teaching should support writers in thinking about and reflecting on their composing processes and the design choices they make in creating texts.

Further reading

- Christie, F. and Derewianka, B. (2008) *School Discourse*. London: Continuum.
- Cope, B. and Kalantzis, M. (2000) *Multiliteracies: Literacy Learning and the Design of Social Futures*. London: Routledge.
- Graham, S. and Perin, D. (2007) *Writing Next: Effective Strategies to Improve Writing of Adolescents in Middle and High Schools – A Report to Carnegie Corporation of New York*. Washington, DC: Alliance for Excellent Education.
- Hillocks, G. (2006) 'Research in writing, secondary school 1984–2003', *L1 – Educational Studies in Languages and Literature* 6:2: 27–51.
- MacArthur, C.A., Graham, S. and Fitzgerald, J. (eds) (2008) *Handbook of Writing Research*. New York: The Guilford Press
- Myhill, D.A. (2009) 'Children's patterns of composition and their reflections on their composing processes', *British Educational Research Journal* 35:1: 47–64.
- Myhill, D.A. and Jones, S. (2007) 'More than just error correction: children's reflections on their revision processes', *Written Communication* 24:4: 323–43.
- Sharples, M. (1999) *How We Write: Writing as Creative Design*. London: Routledge.
- *English Teaching: Practice and Critique* (New Zealand journal)
- *Written Communication* (US)
- *Journal of Writing Research* (European journal)

References

Alexander, J. (2008) 'Media convergence: creating content, questioning relationships', *Computers and Composition* 25:1: 1–8.

Andrews, R., Torgerson, C., Beverton, S., Freeman, A., Locke, T., Low, G., Robinson, A. and Zhu, D. (2006) 'The effect of grammar teaching on writing development', *British Educational Research Journal* 32:1: 39–55.

Ball, A. (2008) 'Teaching writing in culturally diverse classrooms', in C.A. MacArthur, S. Graham and J. Fitzgerald (eds), *Handbook of Writing Research*. New York: The Guilford Press: 293–310.

Beard, R. (2000) *Developing Writing 3–13*. London: Hodder and Stoughton.

Bereiter, C. and Scardamalia, M. (1982) 'From conversation to composition: the role of instruction in a developmental process', in R. Glaser (ed.), *Advances in Instructional Psychology*, vol. 2. Hillsdale, NJ: Lawrence Erlbaum Associates: 1–64.

Bereiter, C. and Scardamalia, M. (1987) *The Psychology of Written Composition*. Hillsdale, NJ: Lawrence Erlbaum Associates.

Britton, J., Burgess, T., Martin, N., McLeod, A. and Rosen, H. (1975) *The Development of Writing Abilities (11–18)*. London: Macmillan Education.

Butterfield, E.C., Hacker, D.J. and Albertson, L.R. (1996) 'Environmental, cognitive and metacognitive influences on text revision', *Educational Psychology Review* 8:3: 239–97.

Carter, R. (ed.) (1990) *Knowledge about Language and the Curriculum*. London: Hodder and Stoughton.

Cook-Gumperz, J. (ed.) (2006) *The Social Construction of Literacy*, 2nd ed. Cambridge: Cambridge University Press.

Czerniewska, P. (1992) *Learning about Writing: The Early Years*. Oxford: Blackwell.

Derewianka, B. (1996) *Exploring the Writing of Genres.* London: UKRA.

Emig, J. (1971) *The Composing Processes of Twelfth Graders.* Urbana, IL: NCTE.

Englert, C.S., Mariage, T.V. and Dunsmore, K. (2008) 'Tenets of sociocultural theory in writing instruction research', in C.A. MacArthur, S. Graham and J. Fitzgerald (eds), *Handbook of Writing Research.* New York: The Guilford Press: 208–21.

Graham, S. and Perin, D. (2007) *Writing Next: Effective Strategies to Improve Writing of Adolescents in Middle and High Schools – A report to Carnegie Corporation of New York.* Washington, DC: Alliance for Excellent Education.

Graves, D. (1983) *Writing.* Exeter, NH: Heinemann.

Halliday, M. and Matthiessen, C. (2004) *An Introduction to Functional Grammar.* London: Hodder Education.

Harpin, W. (1976) *The Second 'R': Writing Development in the Junior School.* London: Allen & Unwin.

Hayes, J.R. (1996) 'A new framework for understanding cognition and affect in writing', in C.M. Levy and S. Ransdell (eds), *The Science of Writing: Theories, Methods, Individual Differences and Applications.* Mahwah, NJ: Lawrence Erlbaum Associates: 1–27.

Hayes, J.R. and Flower, L.S. (1980) 'Identifying the organisation of writing processes', in L.W. Gregg and E.R. Steinberg (eds), *Cognitive Processes in Writing: An Interdisciplinary Approach.* Hillsdale, NJ: Lawrence Erlbaum Associates: 3–30.

Heath, S.B. (1983) *Ways with Words: Language, Life and Work in Communities and Classrooms.* Cambridge: Cambridge University Press.

Jones, S.A. and Myhill, D.A. (2007) 'Discourses of difference? Examining gender difference in linguistic characteristics of writing', *Canadian Journal of Education* 30:2: 456–82.

Kellogg, R.T. (1994) *The Psychology of Writing.* Oxford: Oxford University Press.

Kellogg, R.T. (1996) 'A model of working memory in writing', in C.M. Levy and S. Ransdell (eds), *The Science of Writing: Theories, Methods, Individual Differences and Applications.* Mahwah, NJ: Lawrence Erlbaum Associates: 57–72.

Kress, G. (2005) 'Gains and losses: new forms of texts, knowledge, and learning', *Computers and Composition* 22: 5–22.

Loban, W. (1963) *The Language of Elementary School Children: A Study of the Use and Control of Language and the Relations among Speaking, Reading, Writing, and Listening*, NCTE research reports. Champaign, IL: National Council of Teachers of English.

Martin, J. (1985) *Factual Writing.* Geelong, Victoria: Deakin University Press.

Martin, J. and Rothery, J. (1980) *Writing Project Report No. l.* Sydney: University of Sydney, Department of Linguistics.

Martlew, M. (1983) *The Psychology of Written Language: Developmental and Educational Perspectives.* Chichester: John Wiley and Sons.

MacArthur, C.A. (2008) 'The effects of new technologies on writing and writing processes', in C.A MacArthur, S. Graham and J. Fitzgerald (eds), *Handbook of Writing Research.* New York: The Guilford Press: 248–62.

McComiskey, B. (2000) *Teaching Composition as a Social Process.* Logan, UT: Utah State University Press.

Murray, D. (1982) *Learning by Teaching.* Montclair, NJ: Boynton-Cook.

Myhill, D.A. (2001) *Better Writers: Applying New Findings about Grammar and Technical Accuracy.* Bury St Edmunds: Courseware.

Myhill, D.A. (2009) 'Children's patterns of composition and their reflections on their composing processes', *British Educational Research Journal* 35:1: 47–64.

Myhill, D.A. (2010) 'Changing classroom pedagogies', in A. Denham and K. Lobeck (eds), *Linguistics at School: Language Awareness in Primary and Secondary Education.* Cambridge: Cambridge University Press: 92–106.

Myhill, D.A., Fisher, R., Jones, S., Lines, H. and Hicks, A. (2008) *Effective Ways of Teaching Complex Expression in Writing*, report number DCFS-RR032. London: DCFS.

Negro, I. and Chanquoy, L. (2005) 'The effect of psycholinguistic research on the teaching of writing', *L1 – Educational Studies in Language and Literature* 5:2: 105–11.

Perera, K. (1984) *Children's Writing and Reading: Analysing Classroom Language*. Oxford: Blackwell.

Prior, P. (2006) 'A sociocultural theory of writing', in C.A. MacArthur, S. Graham and J. Fitzgerald (eds), *Handbook of Writing Research*. New York: The Guilford Press: 54–66.

QCA (2007) *English in the National Curriculum*. London: QCA.

Rose, D. (2009) 'Writing as linguistic mastery: the development of genre-based literacy pedagogy', in R. Beard, D. Myhill, J. Riley and M. Nystrand, *The Sage Handbook of Writing Development*. London: Sage: 151–66.

Sharples, M. (1999) *How We Write: Writing as Creative Design*. London: Routledge.

Smagorinsky, P. (1987) 'Graves revisited: a look at the methods and conclusions of the New Hampshire study', *Written Communication* 14:4: 331–42.

Sorapure, M. (2006) 'Text, image, code, comment: writing in Flash', *Computers and Composition* 23:4: 412–29.

Swales, J. (1990) *Genre Analysis*. Cambridge: Cambridge University Press.

Walsh, M. (2008) 'Worlds have collided and modes have merged: classroom evidence of changed literacy practices', *Literacy* 42:2: 101–8.

Wheeler, S., Yeomans, P. and Wheeler, D. (2008) 'The good, the bad and the wiki: evaluating student-generated content for collaborative learning', *Journal of Educational Technology* 39:6: 987–95.

Wyse, D. (2001) 'Grammar. For writing? A critical review of empirical evidence', *British Journal of Educational Studies* 49:4: 411–27.

6

ANGELLA COOZE
Teaching reading

In this chapter you will consider

- some of the key debates regarding the ways in which children become readers;
- the potential impact and implications of these debates;
- how policy and guidance link with theoretical debate regarding reading;
- the complexity of the reading process and what it is to be a reader;
- some of the skills, knowledge and experience that may inform a student's understanding of text.

Introduction

As you are a beginning teacher of English, reading is, presumably, something that you can do well and, hopefully, enjoy. It is, after all, one of the things that led you to be holding this book in your hands. The kinds of reading skills that you will have developed over time are, no doubt, sophisticated and enable you to engage with many different types of texts in many different ways and at different levels. To skilled readers such as you, an understanding of subtext and structure, of 'how' a piece of text works and what impact it has on you and/or 'the reader', probably seems second nature. The 'process' of reading seems spontaneous and traceless to higher-level readers. The complex relationship between symbol and meaning – both surface and more profound – is negotiated at a deep and quite hidden level. The complex and multiple processes that somehow enable us to draw 'meaning' from text are not, however, quite so straightforwardly negotiated by many. 'The reader', so casually and frequently called upon in examination questions, is not such a straightforward figure, nor is there a definitive 'response' or series of reading practices that can be relied upon by every reader.

It wulod be a pttery sfae bet taht you can mganae to raed this wtoiuht too much toulrbe. Yuo have no dubot seen smeohtnig like tihs bferoe. In Elgnhis at lsaet, it semes taht our brains make snese of the ltteres and cearte mneaing. How we do this is a much researched and debated topic.

Reading as a topic of study covers a vast number of related, though quite distinct disciplines and debates. For reasons of expediency, this chapter will focus on the issues surrounding reading acquisition and development that have informed the notion of reading underpinning statutory and guidance documents. In many secondary school classrooms, the actual processes of reading are as much, if not more, of a focus than response to literature.

The UK context

The position of reading in the English classroom is at once central and obscure – something highlighted by the Rose Report (DfES 2006), which placed reading at the centre of learning, while recognising that it is complex and hard to define. The ongoing, heated debates about the right approach to early reading (see, among many others, SEED 2002; Smith 2004; DfES 2006; Ellis 2007) demonstrate the importance of reading to learning. The 2010 end of Key Stage assessments in England (DfE 2010) saw a fifth of students fail to reach expected standards in English at the end of Key Stage 3. This issue continues into adulthood. Recent figures (Basic Skills Agency 2004; National Literacy Trust 2010) suggest that as many as one in four adults have a reading and writing age of eleven or below. The results of the most recent PISA reading assessment (2009) raised similar concerns about students' reading skills. In an assessment of around 500,000 students aged fifteen in 65 countries, students in the UK were placed 25th (Bradshaw *et al.* 2010a, 2010b, 2010c). Similarly, in the PIRLS (Progress in International Reading Literacy Study) survey of 2006, both England and Scotland had fallen down the table in reading – England by some twenty points (IEA 2007). More worryingly, England and Scotland were in the 'top' three in terms of the reading gap between the lowest and highest achievers.

Of course, figures such as these should not be taken at face value. The PISA tests and scores are often debated in terms of reliability and methodology, and the average results for the rest of the UK were negatively impacted by falling results from Wales. Similarly, despite the decline, both Scotland and England were above average on the PIRL scale. Nonetheless, the importance of good reading skills cannot be overstated. The ability to read well, both functionally and critically, has ramifications well beyond the classroom (Cox 1998). In terms of economic opportunity, adults with poor literacy skills are far less likely to be in full-time employment by the age of thirty than their more literate peers (National Literacy Trust 2010). In terms of personal growth and development, independence, social and creative opportunities, and cultural engagement, the advantages of good reading skills are immeasurable.

Still, reading as such is not taught in most secondary schools. Students are expected to read a variety of texts from social networking sites to Metaphysical poetry both in and out of the classroom, but they will come to secondary school at very different stages of reading development and will have multifarious attitudes towards and expectations of reading. Yet it remains the case that the actual skills and knowledge called upon in the process of engaging with texts are seldom explicitly approached by teachers.

What is 'reading'?

Following from Chomsky's notions of innatism, Goodman (1967) influentially advanced the notion that reading was developed through textual or language 'experiences' rather than through the formal teaching of discrete features. This model posits the idea that reading develops in much the same way as speaking – through use, rather than through decontextualised, structured tuition in specific hierarchical skills. The teaching of reading through distinct rules, skills and stages was criticised by Goodman and others as not reflecting the experiential nature of language development.

Goodman claimed that there were three inter-related areas of knowledge or 'cueing systems' that played a part in the reading process:

- the graphophonic system (our understanding of sound–letter correspondence);
- the syntactic system (our understanding of the structural aspects of language); and
- the semantic system (our understanding of context).

These ideas were taken up by others, such as Clay (1985) in a move towards a holistic, context-embedded model of reading. In this view of reading, often referred to as the 'whole language' approach, readers draw upon these three systems concurrently so as to secure meaning. The cues that Goodman (1967, 1995) outlined suggest that students draw understanding from a number of sources rather than simply from their understanding of the relationship between, and ability to decode, graphemes and phonemes. The graphophonic cueing system – that is, an understanding about the relationship between sounds and letters – is still important to this view of reading as it enables students to 'hear' words and then make sense of them. It is, however, seen as just a part of the reading process. Importantly, whole-language reading approaches do not situate reading as a set of discrete skills. Rather, text is approached as a whole and meaning-making is explored contextually. Meaning is seen as being produced and understood through the interplay of the cueing systems in reading experiences. In this model, readers draw variously on their knowledge, skills and experience to make sense of texts.

Into practice: try it out

Fill in the gaps in the sentences below.

1. The sun rises in the East and sets in the _____.
2. This animal is a klinger. This is another klinger. There are two _____.
3. The flag is red, black and y_____.

(from Gibbons 2002: 78)

Think carefully about the types of clues you picked up on when deciding which word to use.

In example 1, your knowledge of the world predicts that the missing word is *West*. In the second example, your knowledge of how English works allows you to predict *klingers* using other plural words as an analogy. Example 3 is different again: here graphophonic knowledge is important. The letter 'y' allows you to predict yellow. Without this cue, you would have guessed the missing word was a colour, but not which one.

While the example shows each cueing system used separately, adherents of this view of reading claim that readers draw upon these knowledges simultaneously and that each reader may draw upon different aspects of their knowledge and understanding when reading a piece of text. Meaning-making is more than a simple decoding process. The reader participates in the production of meaning, drawing upon various resources, skills and experiences.

Goodman's ideas are not, however, without flaws. While they are undoubtedly related, reading and speaking are not the same. Critics of the 'whole-language' approach, such as Allington (2002) and Shaywitz (1996), maintain that reading, unlike speaking, does not 'occur' without some form of instruction – it is a learned skill. Those favouring phonics-based approaches would argue that reading primarily occurs through recognition of sound cues, and that context simply affirms meaning gained through decoding, rather than forming part of its creation. Research by the United States National Reading Panel (2000) concluded that students who had had no explicit instruction in phonics performed less well in tests that required them to read words in isolation. It was argued that for a child to be able to begin to engage with syntax or semantics, a certain level of phonetic competence must be in place. However, the kinds of engagement with text that we ask of students in secondary schools require reading for meaning on a whole-text level.

Professional reflection

Speak to a selection of primary and secondary school teachers about the use of phonics as a means of teaching reading. What do they see as its advantages and disadvantages? Do they use it as a sole method or as part of a wider battery of approaches?

Reading in the National Curriculum and the National Strategy

The whole-language theory of reading as an integrated process that draws simultaneously on different types of knowledge during textual 'experiences' has had considerable influence on the teaching of reading in secondary schools. Independent reading practices, for example – a familiar part of the English classroom – can be seen as giving students opportunities for textual 'experiences'. Even at the inception of the curriculum, The Cox Report (DfES 1989) highlighted the importance of wider reading and exposure to literature to the development of pupils' language skills. Schools have moved away from rules- and skills-based reading instruction, and the NLS in general and the 'Searchlights' model of reading in particular draw on Goodman's ideas, while also recognising (Adams 1994) that reading requires more than experience. The idea that reading can be developed through greater experience with a wider range of texts can be seen in the range of reading experiences offered to students in secondary classrooms. The notion, too, that readers come to reading from different places, using different skills, can also be evidenced in the documentation relating to the National Strategy and the National Curriculum Orders for English.

Influential here was the 'Four Resources' model of reading (Freebody 1992; Luke and Freebody 1999). Rather than positing whole language or decoding processes as the organising principle of a reading model, Luke and Freebody propose a balanced view of reading, where each aspect develops different literacies. This model identifies four key areas of reading or 'resources' that readers need to draw upon in order to fully engage with text (see Table 6.1). These aspects of reading are not to be taught sequentially and are not hierarchically ordered. The model echoes the kinds of reading practices found in the National Curriculum. It was used by Wray (2001) in his analysis of effective literacy practices in secondary schools and recognised by the Nuffield Review of English in 2005 (Ellis 2006) as offering an 'enriched' view of reading as language that was compatible with the range of reading activities and skills in which students participate.

The NLS 'searchlights' (DfEE 1998) that students use to enable them to read a text are:

- phonics;
- word recognition and graphic knowledge;
- grammatical knowledge; and
- knowledge of content.

The clear connections to aspects of whole-language systems and also to the balanced model of reading offered by Luke and Freebody (1999) are apparent. Reading is

Table 6.1 Four key resources

Reader as code breaker	Engagement with the mechanics of reading text such as sound–symbol relationship, directionality and phonemic understanding
Reader as text participant	Drawing upon knowledge of the world, of how texts and types work so as to infer meaning from text, including understanding of social and cultural mores
Reader as text user	The ability to use and understand reading skills in social and other contexts
Reader as text analyst	Critical analysis of texts in order to understand how they produce effects, including understanding of the social and cultural context of texts and their intention

figured as an holistic process, drawing upon four equally important aspects of language in the process of meaning-making. In the Four Resources model, too, the aspects are seen as distinct but interlinked. Reading includes, but is not confined to, an understanding of decoding processes, and meaning can be drawn from many places.

Interestingly, the Rose review recommended that 'Searchlights' should be revised so as to include discrete daily phonics work for beginning readers. This was due to the 'necessary' and central role of phonetic knowledge in the reading process. The report acknowledged that reading was more than phonics, but maintained that 'learning to read progresses to reading, effortlessly, to learn' (DfES 2006: 36).

There is some clear recognition to be found in the review of the other 'searchlights' or cueing systems, although these are seen as part of a more sophisticated reading repertoire. It is considered vital that readers are competent decoders before they use the 'full range of strategies' available to them to gain deeper understanding. Rather than drawing meaning from a number of places, readers need to have the skills of decoding in place and then work out meaning from there.

Another development was the simple view of reading, influenced by the work of Gough and Tunmer (1982) (see Figure 6.1). Reading, in this model, has two basic elements: decoding , 'the ability to recognise words presented singly out of context', and comprehension, 'the process by which, given lexical (i.e. word) information, sentences and discourse are interpreted' (DfES 2006: 41).

Students can figure anywhere in the quadrant. Their position indicates the progress made in each aspect of reading and the areas that would benefit from further

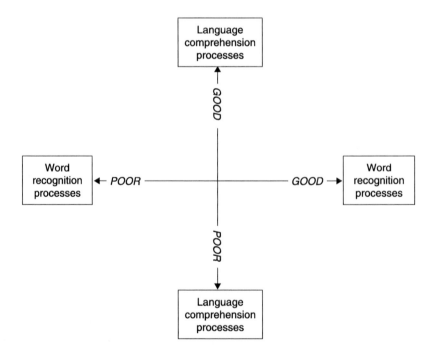

Figure 6.1 The simple view of reading

instruction. Implicit in this model is the premise that decoding is necessary for comprehension, but comprehension is not necessary for decoding. Both are seen as central to the development of effective reading skills, although this importance will shift significantly in balance as the child develops his or her reading skills.

M level

Read through the En2 reading section of the National Curriculum. Consider the range of reading it requires of students at Key Stages 3 and 4. Think carefully about the views of teaching reading you have read about in this chapter. How do you relate the theory to practice?

Comprehension is, perhaps, simplified in this model to the same process as that of spoken language. Once a word has been decoded, it 'becomes' spoken language and is understood in the same way. The reading of texts seems more complicated than this and relies on a wider system of knowledge and understanding. The other 'reading' systems seem to come into play as readers develop their understanding, rather than of ways of 'decoding' in themselves. The key word here is 'comprehension'. As noted by Smith (2004), comprehension is a word generally associated with reading rather than spoken language (where 'understanding' is more commonly used) and which involves engagement with text at several levels. The balanced reading view offered by Luke and Freebody (1999) seems to suggest that, while decoding skills are central to the reading process, other aspects of reading have similar importance, and not only as the reader develops in skill.

The concepts outlined in Goodman or Luke and Freebody can, broadly, be broken down or linked to word-, sentence- and text-level knowledge or skills. Graphophonemic cues are primarily used in word-level decoding processes, syntactic knowledge is generally employed at sentence level, and semantic knowledge at the level of the whole text. This is, of course, a simplistic division of these processes, and meaning does not necessarily build in a sequential way. Think about the times when you have read on in a sentence to understand a single word or the instances when you have obtained a general impression from a text rather than a specific word-level understanding.

Other processes in reading

There seems to be some agreement that readers bring to the text key skills and experiences – linguistic and other – that are engaged in the process of reading and understanding. Since James Britton's observation in the early 1970s that 'reading and writing float on a sea of talk' (Pradl 1982: 11), there has been a considerable focus on the close links between reading, and speaking and listening. Spoken and written languages are not the same. Neither, however, are they discrete, easily compartmentalised aspects of language. Much research (for example, DfES 2006; ESTYN 2008) has stressed the importance of recognising and strengthening students' skills in speaking and listening as a key part of developing their skills in reading and writing. There is considerable agreement that reading, writing, speaking and listening are closely interwoven parts of a complex and shifting language capacity. The importance of developing students' oracy, not simply as an important end in itself but also as a fundamental means of developing their language skills per se, cannot be overstated.

Into practice

In the light of what you have read so far, spend some time developing responses to the questions in Table 6.2.

What does 'reading' mean in secondary school?

Much of the focus on reading at Key Stage 3 and beyond builds upon skills that teachers assume are already in place. That is, teachers of English do not teach children how to read per se, but how to be more sophisticated readers of a wider range of texts. In other words, by and large, students are assumed to be operating at text level and to have acquired word- and sentence-level skills prior to arriving at Key Stage 3. This can be seen quite clearly in the sort of skills and texts found in the National Curriculum.

Table 6.2 Models of reading

Reflection	Implementation
• Why should the mechanics of reading acquisition be of concern to the secondary school teacher?	• Which aspects of reading do you feel are most explored in your classroom? Why?
• Which model of reading most closely fits with your experience of the classroom – as a student and as a teacher?	• Do your students engage with text on a critical or cultural level when their word- or code-level skills are not strong?
• Is reading a series of skills that can be taught sequentially? Can students 'get something' from a text without a secure word level of skills?	• Do the different cultural and linguistic backgrounds of students need to be taken into account when teaching reading? Why? What does this suggest about reading practices?
• What are the possible limitations and potentials of these models?	• How much explicit reading instruction occurs in your classroom? Why is this?
• Are they equally suitable for every student?	• In what ways are speaking and listening tasks used in your classroom? Are they supported? Purposeful?
• How can spoken language be supported and developed in such a way as to improve students' reading skills?	

Four key concepts underpin the curriculum for English: competence, creativity, cultural understanding and critical understanding (see Chapter 4). Again, links can be made to both the Four Resources model and to some aspects of Goodman's work. Crucially, reading is situated as a set of cultural and critical practices, without neglecting the process-based aspects of reading proficiency.

The debates surrounding the teaching of the process of reading such as those concerning approaches based on whole language (top-down) and phonics (bottom-up), and then of the merits of analytic or synthetic phonics-based reading strategies do not seem, perhaps, of that much concern to teachers in secondary school. After all, by the time students reach this stage in their education, 'reading' becomes something quite different from the actual mechanical process of decoding and processing meaning from text. Instead, 'reading', as it is figured in curriculum orders and examination requirements, seems to be concerned more with engaging with different types of texts and exploring how they work. However, these debates do matter. Underlying the various debates about models of reading are fundamental assumptions about what reading is, how reading skills develop and what approaches work best in the classroom. The underlying concept of reading – as linear, with a foundation in teachable skills or as the interweaving of several systems of understanding which operate in a more holistic way – informs how students learn, and for a considerable number of students reading is a constant struggle and needs further support.

In secondary school English lessons, reading is 'not a specific quantifiable act, or collection of such acts, but an amalgam of a whole set of cultural practices' (Dean 2000: 3), covering a huge range of skills, knowledge and understanding (QCA 2007). In the 'Reading for Meaning' section of the curriculum alone (QCA 2007), students should be able to, among other things, 'extract and interpret information, events, main points and ideas from texts' – that is, exercise the functional skills of skimming and scanning and the more critical skills of interpretation and selection – and understand 'how meaning is constructed within sentences and across texts as a whole' – something that requires sophisticated critical and analytical skills. The 'Author's Craft' section of the curriculum makes reference to similarly sophisticated reading skills. Students should be able to comment on how text is constructed – evaluating the use of grammar, literary devices, layout and structure and the impact these have on the reader – as well as demonstrate their understanding of the relationship between texts and their 'social, historical and cultural' contexts. The reading skills outlined in the programme of study call upon students' graphophonic, semantic and syntactic knowledge. Students are expected to demonstrate their ability to read a considerable range of texts in a number of different ways, responding to a huge variety of cues and using an array of skills. Reading, then, is both functional process, and skills and engagement with text in a deeper sense.

Professional reflection

Using the questions in Table 6.3 as a basis, consider the personal, professional and pedagogic demands placed upon teachers in relation to reading.

Table 6.3 Working with readers in secondary school

Some things to consider	Implementation

• In what ways do the Attainment Targets of the National Curriculum and the reading skills outlined in the National Strategy demonstrate a progressive reading structure?
 	
• What models of reading can be seen as underpinning 'reading' in the English curriculum and guidance?
 	
• Are reading skills taught in a systematic way, building upon each other?
 	
• Should reading in secondary school be primarily concerned with the development of skills or with exposing students to different types of text?
 	
• How confident do you feel in your understanding of reading skills and how best to teach them?
	• In your experience, what reading practices or roles take place in the classroom?
	
	• Do any particular aspects of reading dominate your lessons? Why?
	
	• What explicit reading skills are taught in your classroom? How?
	
	• How are reading texts explored? As a whole class? In groups?
	
	• Do your tasks call upon and develop students' skills as:
	  • Code breakers?
	  • Text participants?
	  • Text users?
	  • Text analysts?
	
	• In what ways are students skills developed:
	  • Graphophonic?
	  • Syntactic?
	  • Semantic?

Reading and multi-modal texts

Text itself is also broadened to include multi-modal media, image and ICT (DfES 2004; DCELLS 2008). Many students engage with a wide variety of electronic media in their everyday lives, using fluid and sophisticated reading practices to decode and comprehend. Students who may well struggle with analysing character in a set text may be able to demonstrate those skills quite confidently when discussing film, games or media personalities. There is a case for exploring the kinds of reading skills students use when they engage with these types of text and examining the reading practices that are being developed, as well as how we can best make use of them in the classroom. It is important to help students develop genuinely transferable skills as readers.

ICT: ICT and media text

Students are engaged in reading a vast array of text both in and out of school. Much of this is ICT or media text. Use the questions that follow to help you reflect on issues surrounding this type of reading and its relation to the classroom.

- Which type of text do you think is most important? Why?
- What could be lost if the others were abandoned? Are they easily separable?
- Are some types of texts privileged over others in the curriculum? Why?
- Do students demonstrate more sophisticated reading skills when engaging with electronic or media texts?
- What conventional texts do your students engage in outside of the classroom? Is this important?
- What sorts of electronic and media texts do your students read?
- Do they use social networking sites? Watch films? Are they gamers?
- What reading skills do they employ when engaged in these activities?
- How can these skills be used in the classroom?

Subject knowledge for teaching reading

The subject knowledge demanded of English teachers has expanded rapidly since the beginning of the twenty-first century to cover a broad spectrum of language, media and non-fiction as well as the conventional literary knowledge – much of which may not feature in English degree courses. The comprehensive models of reading offered in statutory and guidance documentation bring with them concomitant bodies of knowledge and skills concerned with various print media and multi-modal texts. Reading, as figured in the curriculum, involves personal growth, literary heritage, functional skills and cultural understanding, as well as semantic, syntactic, phonetic and critical skills.

Into practice: pedagogy

The National Strategies document (DfCSF 2008) outlines some key pedagogical approaches to reading (see Figure 6.2), which reference the need to teach active reading strategies and give students the opportunity to explore and develop these strategies for themselves. Do they link to any of the models and ideas about reading already discussed? Make a copy of Figure 6.2 and fill in the links that you can find.

Gifted readers

While for a significant number of students reading is an area of difficulty, others have reading skills that are already sophisticated and well developed. These students may well be voracious readers who need to be challenged through genuinely extended reading experiences, and whose advanced abilities need to be developed further. There are a number of ways in which the reading models already discussed can be used to facilitate this.

National Strategies – Secondary: Teaching for Progression: Reading (DfSCF 2008)	
Pedagogical approaches	**Links to models or theories of reading**
The explicit teaching of active reading strategies.	
Shared reading – where the teacher, for example, displays an enlarged text and models good reading practices which are then used by students.	
Guided group reading – where students who share a similar learning need are given opportunities to practise active reading skills and strategies with a clear learning outcome.	
Paired reading – again with a focus on students developing active reading strategies.	
Interactive starter and plenary activities which enable students to sort, categorise, explore and respond to texts at word, sentence and whole-text level.	
The development and extension of PEE (Point Evidence Explanation) strategies so as to develop personal and critical response (PEERP), closer analysis of language (PEE+) and links to other texts (PEEL).	
Peer- and self-assessment opportunities which enable students to identify features of successful responses to text and identify meaning targets.	
Use of structured speaking and listening activities with clear outcomes in terms of reading objectives.	

Figure 6.2 National strategies: suggested pedagogic approaches

---

Professional reflection: working with gifted readers

Refresh your memory of the Four Resources model, then consider how each 'resource' could be used to extend able readers (see Figure 6.3). Take a copy of Figure 6.3 and use it to record your thoughts.

For many able students, differentiation is often by quantity – they simply do more of the same. By considering the multiple ways in which students engage with text and the resources they draw upon when making sense of text, we should be able to provide opportunities for them to develop qualitatively, not simply quantitatively. Too often, higher-order reading skills are facilitated by way of the tick-list approach. Students are often encouraged to identify and label features of text, as if this in itself is a sign of sophistication. With more able students, it may be useful to consider ways of exploring a wide range of texts and different ways of reading texts – perhaps using appropriate theoretical approaches. It is patronising, for instance, to assume that able students cannot deal with the basic tenets of feminism, Marxism and structuralism as ways of reading text. This provides a richer view of reading.

Resource	How could this reading role be used so as to challenge and extend students' reading skills?
Reader as Code Breaker	
Reader as Text Participant	
Reader as Text User	
Reader as Text Analyst	

Figure 6.3 Working with gifted readers

Despite the rich complexity of the reading process and of the readers in our classrooms, it is, perhaps, an unfortunate consequence of a results-driven classroom that reading often becomes reduced to a narrow set of identifiable 'ingredients'. The study of fiction texts often becomes an extraction of character, plot, atmosphere and theme, while the study of non-fiction texts and poetry is frequently dominated by the 'list of features'. In both cases, the actual complexities of students' engagement with and understanding of text seem to be sidelined. This seems to be a little like putting the cart before the horse and is likely to lead to able readers quickly becoming disaffected. Text is not, after all, simply a collection of identifiable features, nor is every reader's response to those features likely to be the same. Having the 'ingredients' is not the same as having the cake.

There are, of course, strong arguments for reading responses being structured through 'features' lists. We need to give our students the metalanguage with which to discuss texts. However, it is fair to say that, for many students, being able to identify an instance of 'tripling' (the ubiquitous 'rule of three') in a persuasive piece is neither really necessary nor sufficient to their developing meaningful response to the text.

Into practice: planning for teaching reading

Select a short text that you might use with a class. Using a copy of the grid at Figure 6.4, plan some reading activities you could do with a class to address each aspect of reading. What kinds of supporting resources might you need? How might these learning activities need to be differentiated?

Aspect of reading	Possible learning activities
Graphophonic: understanding of sound–sign correspondence	
Syntax: understanding of the structural aspects of language	
Semantic: understanding of context and how it informs/creates meaning	

Figure 6.4 Planning for reading

The difficult part comes in identifying the necessary reading challenge. Does it mean simply selecting a text by a more 'adult' or serious writer? One that deals with more challenging ideas? One that is written in a more complex way? Can students engage with undemanding text in a complex way? How? How can we, as educators, facilitate meaningful opportunities for this?

Inclusion

Use the questions in Table 6.4 to help you think about how you might use the simple view of reading (Figure 6.1) to help you support the reading needs of a variety of students.

Table 6.4 Reading and inclusion

Providing support	*Implementation*
How could you use the quadrant in Figure 6.1 to target reading support for your students?	What evidence would be needed so as to position a student's reading skills within the quadrant? How would you collect this? Why would it be useful?
In what ways could you gather evidence about a student's comprehension skills that didn't depend upon their decoding skills?	Consider ways in which a student's reading for meaning skills can be assessed if their decoding skills are not strong.
Would you expect a student to be in the same position within the quadrant for all/most reading tasks? Why?	What could be done about this? How could various reading systems help support reading skills?
What sorts of tasks could you set for a student who had: • Strong decoding skills but weak comprehension skills? • Weak decoding skills but strong comprehension skills?	What sorts of reading support programmes or approaches are you familiar with? Do they address decoding skills? Comprehension skills? Both?

EAL readers

Where a student who was in the process of acquiring English would appear on the 'simple view' of reading is, perhaps, less clear cut. It is also uncertain that the 'simple view' quadrant would capture the difficulties a student may have with different types of text. Also, the 'comprehension' skills of a student are figured as potentially distinct from decoding, even though decoding is placed as central to meaning. As useful as this tool may be for providing a snapshot of a student's reading profile, perhaps a richer view of reading suggested by the models discussed in this chapter would be more useful, along with an awareness that students draw meaning using a number of skills, and that applying different knowledge areas is a useful teaching tool. Certainly, when you are teaching students who are EAL learners, the awareness that reading has a cultural dimension and that cultural experiences and knowledge form part of the meaning-making process can help identify reading needs and point the way to specific support.

EAL: working with previous reading experience

Consider the questions below:

1. What skills and experiences might an EAL learner bring to the reading process? How could this be discovered? How could this be used to inform teaching and learning?
2. Do you think that reading practices and development are 'universal'? Why? How would this impact upon English language reading provision?
3. Can you think of ways in which EAL students' graphophonic, syntactic or semantic knowledge or skills could be confused during their reading of English language texts? Can reading experiences or progress be managed so as to avoid this? How? What knowledge or understanding would a teacher need so as to plan effectively for this?
4. How could a student's reading skills in a language other than English be built upon? What information would be needed by the class teacher? How could this be planned effectively?

Conclusions

The reading needs of students in secondary schools are many and various. Some students, for a variety of reasons, will require input at the most basic level. Others will be gifted readers who will require stimulation and extension in higher-order reading skills. There will also be every shade in between on the reading spectrum. It is essential to realise that as teachers we need to approach reading as both practice *and* process. This is challenging and complex, but opens up possibilities and approaches that should expand students' reading horizons rather than limiting them.

In summary

- Reading as a process has been understood in many ways.
- Teachers at secondary level need to understand a range of theories regarding the teaching of reading.
- The English curriculum now incorporates an ever-widening range of text types.
- Notions of what constitutes the act of reading are constantly changing as technology advances.
- Teachers need to provide rich and stimulating reading environments.

References

Adams, M. (1994) *Beginning to Read*. Boston, MA: The MIT Press.

Allington, R. (2002) *Big Brother and the National Reading Curriculum: How Ideology Trumped Evidence*. Portsmouth, NH: Heinemann.

Basic Skills Agency (2004) *National Survey of Adult Basic Skills in Wales*. London: BSA.

Bradshaw, J., Ager, R., Burge, B. and Wheater, R. (2010a) *PISA 2009: Achievement of 15-Year-Olds in England*. Slough: NFER.

Bradshaw, J., Ager, R., Burge, B. and Wheater, R. (2010b) *PISA 2009: Achievement of 15-Year-Olds in Northern Ireland*. Slough: NFER.

Bradshaw, J., Ager, R., Burge, B. and Wheater, R. (2010c) *PISA 2009: Achievement of 15-Year-Olds in Wales*. Slough: NFER.

Cox, B. (ed.) (1998) *Literacy Is not Enough: Essays on the Importance of Reading*. Manchester: Manchester University Press.

Clay, M. (1985) *The Early Detection of Reading Difficulties*, 3rd ed. Tadworth: Heinemann.

DCELLS (2008) *English in the National Curriculum for Wales*. Cardiff: Welsh Assembly Government.

Dean, G. (2000) *Teaching Reading in the Secondary School*. London: Fulton.

DfCSF (2008) *National Strategies – Secondary: Teaching for Progression: Reading*. London: DfCSF.

DfE (2010) *National Curriculum Tests and Teacher Assessments at Key Stages 2 and 3 (PROVISIONAL)*. London: DfE.

DfEE (1998) *The National Literacy Strategy Framework for Teaching*. London: DfEE.

DfES (1989) *English for Ages 5–16*. London: DfES.

DfES (2004) *ICT Across the Curriculum: English*. London: DfES.

DfES (2006) *Independent Review of the Teaching of Early Reading*. London: DfES.

Ellis, V. (2006) 'Rethinking English in English schools: asking questions of a "sack of snakes"', *English in Aotearoa* 58: 5–10.

Ellis, S. (2007) 'Policy and research: lessons from the Clackmannanshire synthetic phonics initiative', *Journal of Early Childhood Literacy* 7:3: 281–97.

ESTYN (2008) *Best Practice in the Reading and Writing of Students aged 7 to 14 Years*. Cardiff: ESTYN.

Freebody, P. (1992) 'A socio-cultural approach: resourcing four roles as a literacy learner', in A. Watson and A. Badenhop (eds), *Prevention of Reading Failure*. Sydney: Ashton-Scholastic: 48–60.

Gibbons, P. (2002) *Scaffolding Language, Scaffolding Learning*. Portsmouth, NH: Heinemann.

Goodman, K. (1967) 'Reading: a psycholinguistic guessing game', *Literacy Research and Instruction* 6:4: 126–35.

Goodman, K. (1995) *On Reading*. Portsmouth, NH: Heinemann.

Gough, P.B. and Tunmer, W.E. (1986) 'Decoding, reading, and reading disability', *Remedial and Special Education* 7: 6–10.

IEA (International Association for the Evaluation of Educational Achievement) (2007) *PIRLS 2006 International Report*. Boston, MA: TIMMS and PIRLS International Study Centre.

Luke, A. and Freebody, P. (1999) *Further Notes on the Four Resources Model*. Available online at: www.readingonline.org/research/lukefreebody.html (accessed 24 February 2011).

National Literacy Trust (2010) *Literacy: State of the Nation*. London: NLS.

National Reading Panel (2000) *Report of the National Reading Panel. Teaching Children to Read: An Evidence-based Assessment of the Scientific Research Literature on Reading and its Implications for Reading Instruction: Reports of the Subgroups*. Washington, DC: Government Printing Office. Available online at www.nationalreadingpanel.org/publications/subgroups. htm (accessed 24 February 2011).

Pradl, G.M. (ed.) (1982) *Prospect and Retrospect: Selected Essays of James Britton*. London: Heinemann.

QCA (2007) *Programme of Study for Key Stage 3 and Attainment Targets*. London: QCA.

SEED (2002) *A Seven Year Study of the Effects of Synthetic Phonics Teaching on Reading and Spelling Attainment*. Edinburgh: SEED.

Shaywitz, S. (1996) 'Dyslexia', *Scientific American* 275:5: 98–104.

Smith, F. (2004) *Understanding Reading*. London: Routledge.

Wray, D. (2001) 'Literacy in the secondary curriculum', *Reading* 35:1: 12.

7

ROBERT FISHER
Dialogic teaching

In this chapter you will consider

- dialogic methods in teaching for thinking and deep learning and the theory and research underpinning them;
- how teachers can use classroom dialogue to engage learners in talk for thinking;
- collaborative learning;
- creating a community of enquiry;
- making thinking more 'visible' through dialogue;
- facilitating deep learning in classrooms;
- dialogic routines that effective teachers use to facilitate deep learning in the classroom.

Introduction

> When we get to talk about it I understand it more. Some teachers get us to do this. Others are not interested.
>
> (Gary, aged 14)

The quality of talk in the classroom has the power to enhance or inhibit students' thinking and learning. The kinds of talk that facilitate learning and stimulate thinking can be described as 'dialogic'. Dialogic teaching, in this chapter, refers to the kinds of verbal interaction that stimulates thinking, facilitates learning and expands awareness of self, task and environment.

The concept of 'dialogic teaching' builds upon a long tradition of theoretical and empirical research into the role of talk in learning and teaching. This research has included the work of cognitive and cultural psychologists (Vygotsky 1978; Bruner 1987), discourse analysts (Coulthard 1992), psycholinguists (Halliday 1993; Wells 1999), socio-cultural linguists (Barnes 1995) and philosophers (Bakhtin 1981;

Habermas 1991; Lipman 2003), as well as many classroom researchers (Alexander 2000; Littleton and Howe 2009) who have provided influential perspectives on the role of dialogue in learning.

What is dialogism?

In recent years there has been a growing emphasis on the central importance of dialogue in stimulating thinking and learning (Fisher 2008; Mercer 2008). Most teacher talk has traditionally not been dialogic but monologic – talk in which the teacher informs the student of certain prescribed forms of knowledge. This is sometimes called learning by rote, recitation or instruction. These forms of traditional teacher talk are characterised by the superiority of the *first* voice (the teacher) over the *second* voice (the student). The theorist Bakhtin describes this form of dialogue as 'official monologism'. It depends upon an asymmetry of power between two voices within a dialogue. This asymmetry arises from a *third voice* implicit in the dialogue (Bakhtin 1986).

This 'third person', or 'third voice', stands outside the dialogue and acts as a point of reference or authority for the teacher. It may be a set of rules, a sacred text, a received view, a school curriculum or some other source of authority. This authority can constrain the openness or creativity of the discussion. It sets the educational goal and directs the discussion. The questions Bakhtin poses for any dialogue are – where is the reference point of authority? Who decides what should be open for discussion? Who, in effect, asks the questions?

Traditional teacher talk is useful for teaching through instruction or demonstration, but it does not facilitate self-expression, thinking or dialogue. In traditional classrooms it is the teacher's voice that is authoritative and persuasive. Wertsch (1991) describes the process of appropriating the voices of others (such as the teacher) by children as a process he calls 'ventriloquation'. There are dialogic strategies that put equal communicative rights and the personal voice of the student at the heart of the learning process, strategies such as collaborative reasoning and community of inquiry, discussed below.

Researchers argue that teachers in secondary schools do not always fully exploit the learning potential of talk for learning in the classroom. This, to summarise Alexander (2006), is because they often:

- view talk only as a *means* for learning and not an *aim* of learning;
- fail to use talk to challenge children cognitively;
- focus on the social and affective functions of talk rather than the cognitive;
- do not plan for sustained and effective group dialogue;
- do not teach the ground rules for effective dialogue;
- rely on written and ignore oral learning tasks and modes of assessment;
- use feedback to praise and support rather than diagnose and inform;
- employ teacher questions but not questions from students;

- use closed questions inviting recall, rather than challenging questions inviting speculation; and
- do not allow children enough time for of thinking, reasoning and enquiry.

Students do not naturally engage in sustained intellectual enquiry. Talking together does not necessarily lead to learning or to 'communicative rationality' (Habermas 1991) or to cognitive challenge (Mercer 2000; Fisher 2008). Getting students, individually or in groups, to speak and listen together is not enough. Teachers need to ensure through appropriate, non-monologic interventions that students engage in effective dialogue and other kinds of talk if speaking and listening is to promote learning in the classroom.

Kinds of talk

Talk in classrooms can take many forms. These include:

- *instruction* – telling the student what to do, and/or imparting information
- *recitation* – teaching through questions designed to test or stimulate recall
- *monologue* – one person speaking, without engagement with others
- *conversation* – talk with others characterised by uncritical sharing, lacking depth and challenge, speaking and listening at a low level of cognitive demand
- *argument* – where individuals' views compete and monologic viewpoints are aired
- *discussion* – exchanging ideas with others, to share information or solve problems
- *dialogue* – exploratory talk with others, co-operative enquiry, with dialogic space to agree or disagree, challenge, question and appeal to reason, allowing possible self-correction.

All these kinds of talk serve useful purposes and have their place in learning conversations. What we need to ensure is that there is the right balance of talk and that every lesson or learning experience includes opportunities for cognitively challenging dialogue.

Professional reflection: assessing kinds of talk

Observe a lesson, either a live lesson in the classroom or one that has been filmed.
  Use the above categories listed on p. 92, or others you devise, to identify examples of the kinds of teacher talk or student talk being used in the classroom. Discuss your findings with a colleague. Consider the questions:

- What are the prevailing kinds of talk?
- What kinds of talk could be further developed?

Many interactions between teachers and learners in secondary classrooms are characterised by the traditional routines of instruction and recitation. Most teachers

Table 7.1 Traditional vs dialogic teaching

Traditional teacher–student interaction	Dialogic teaching
Teacher's questions	Children's questions
Teacher's agenda	Shared agenda
Informative	Imaginative
Limited focus	Exploratory
One directing view	Variation of viewpoint
Calculative	Reflective
'I–it' relationship	'I–thou' relationship
Authoritative	Persuasive
Right answers	Possible answers
Competitive answer-giving	Co-operative enquiry
Content-focused learning	Personalised learning
Related to functional outcomes	Related to inner purposes

and parents, though by no means all, extend this repertoire through discussion and dialogue. But to engage effectively in dialogue students need to be trained in its skills. This means learning to be able to:

- listen to and be receptive to alternative viewpoints;
- ask effective questions;
- think critically and creatively about the issues under review; and
- exercise good judgement in what they think and do.

Table 7.1 sums up some of the differences that might distinguish traditional teacher–student interaction from dialogic teaching. Traditional teacher–student interaction is a necessary feature of learning, but it is not sufficient or necessarily the best means for maximising learning. It tends to place limits on learning, whereas dialogic teaching opens up students' thinking and challenges their capacity to frame ideas in words.

Discussion between students may incorporate many types of talk, from random conversation to the disputational, where participants simply want to assert their own point of view. Sometimes dialogue will be cumulative, where participants add information and build on each others' contributions, and at other times it will be exploratory, encouraging participants to explore ideas and work things out together (Mercer 2000). Another aspect of any dialogue is its level of creativity. Creative dialogue is characterised by flights of fancy and imagination, by story-telling and narration, by hypothesis and experimentation with ideas (Fisher 2009). To summarise, any discussion may include:

- conversational talk: the cumulative sharing of thoughts usually without critical challenge
- disputational talk: centred on disputed ideas and competitive argument
- exploratory talk: the process of shared inquiry, co-operative reasoning and research
- creative dialogue: the inclusion of imaginative and playful ideas.

By age nine or ten, children should have developed all the language strategies they need to engage actively in exploratory and creative dialogue. It is the job of the secondary teacher to build and develop these skills through practice and the planning of a range of dialogic tasks.

Exploratory talk – which interrogates the quality of claims, tests hypotheses and proposals, and enables groups of individuals to reach consensual agreement – is the type of talk most valued in higher levels of society, such as in the fields of politics, law and the professions (Mercer 1995). Teaching students these skills could therefore help them in later life to participate in educated discourse and in the persuasive dialogue that will help them realise their life goals. Exploratory talk also has a significant role to play in enabling learners to assimilate new knowledge, evaluating it in the light of old knowledge and appropriately negotiating new meaning (Barnes 1976). Such exploratory talk is recognised through extended utterances, including the use of 'um' and long pauses, often evidence of students thinking aloud – talking their way through a problem and reshaping it to find an answer. Barnes (1976) identifies that such talk is frequently punctuated by hesitations, and that speakers often rephrase ideas and change direction as they shape new understanding.

Exploratory talk shares many of the characteristics of dialogic talk, which Alexander (2006) characterises as being:

- collective (learning together)
- reciprocal (listening to each other)
- supportive (each is able to express ideas freely)
- cumulative (each builds on their own and each others' ideas)
- purposeful (keeping educational goals in sight).

Alexander argues that dialogic teaching has the greatest potential for developing cognition, when classroom talk is explicitly used to probe and extend thinking. But dialogue, when effective, is not just a cognitive process; it also depends on empathy, the social and emotional intelligence that enables dialogic partners to relate and respond to each other. It is not just about curriculum objectives but should also be about personal, everyday knowledge. If curriculum objectives are seen as a set of answers to be grasped they may be inimical to dialogue which thrives on epistemological openness, uncertainty and personal concerns (Lefstein 2009). We should try to engage students with the curriculum by weaving curricular with everyday knowledge.

Into practice: responding to poetry

The teaching of poetry in schools is often about working to a closed set of issues for examination purposes rather than about genuine inquiry. Choose a poem to discuss with students and ask them in what ways the poem relates to or is different from their own lives and experience. Use this discussion as a way into what genuinely motivates and excites the students in relation to the poem and its concerns. This will provide a ready springboard for further discussion of the language of the poem and its effects. It also foregrounds the importance of personal experience in how we respond to and make meaning from texts.

In all English lessons dialogue should encourage students to consider and reflect upon their own, and others', thoughts and beliefs (everyday knowledge) as well as to deepen their understanding of the taught topic (curricular knowledge). Dialogue, when it weaves curricular with everyday knowledge, embodies four processes (see Table 7.2)

Information processing

Student: I know what kind of play *Hamlet* is. It's a tragedy.
Teacher: But what is a tragedy?

All dialogue involves information processing about some kind of knowledge stimulus. Information processing is not only about 'facts' but also about 'know-how'; that is, knowing what rules and strategies to use to find things out or solve problems. For knowledge to be fully understood it must be expressed in words or concepts. Concepts are the words or organising ideas we use to communicate and understand what we think, know and believe. In every field of study there are key ideas or concepts that students may or may not fully understand. Students need to be challenged to interpret the meanings of key words so that they learn not only at the literal level of thinking, but also at strategic and conceptual levels of understanding.

Table 7.2 Dialogic processes and questions to ask

Dialogic processes	Questions to ask
Information processing	Does it relate to what we believe and know?
Critical thinking	Does it challenge claims and call for reasons?
Creative thinking	Does it generate and extend new ideas?
Caring thinking	Does it embody care and respect for others?

Table 7.3 Information processing and dialogic questions

Information processing	Dialogic questions
at the literal level: 'knowing that'	What do you know about …?
at the strategic level: 'knowing how'	What strategy do you use to …?
at the conceptual level: 'interpreting meaning'	What does (the concept) mean?

Information processing is facilitated by dialogic questions at different levels (see Table 7.3). Students become able to interpret information in their own words through processes of critical and creative thinking.

Critical thinking

There are reasons for everything, if only you can find them.

(Child aged 11)

Critical thinking helps young people develop insight into the problematical nature of learning, and the need to subject what they read, see and hear to critical inquiry. Critical dialogue is about challenging them to perform a number of tasks (see Table 7.4). Critical dialogue is about giving reasons, probing evidence and making reasoned judgements – or as Danny, aged 15, said, 'It's about trying to be logical in an illogical world'.

Creative thinking

Unless you think of new ideas you are always going to be stuck with old ideas.

(Gareth, aged 14)

Dialogue is creative if it involves students in generating and extending ideas, suggesting hypotheses, applying imagination, or expressing new or innovative ideas. What

Table 7.4 Critical thinking and dialogic questions

Critical thinking	Dialogic questions
make reasoned evaluations	What reasons are there for …?
make choices informed by evidence	What kinds of evidence support …?
ask critical questions	What questions could be asked?
argue a case	How would you justify thinking …?

Table 7.5 Creative thinking and dialogic questions

Creative thinking	Dialogic questions
apply imagination	What might be ...?
generate hypotheses, ideas and outcomes	What is a possible (idea/way/solution)?
develop creative skills or techniques	What methods could you use for ...?
assess own or others' creative work	How well did you/they succeed in ...?

promotes creativity is a questioning classroom, where teachers and students value diversity, ask unusual questions, make new connections, represent ideas in different ways (visually, physically and verbally), try fresh approaches and solutions to problems, and critically evaluate new ideas and actions. Try to include opportunities for creative dialogue in the lessons you teach. Prompt creative thinking through asking dialogic questions (see Table 7.5). Creative dialogue cannot be left to chance, it must be valued, encouraged and expected, and seen as essential to good teaching and learning (Fisher 2009).

Creativity

Creativity involves using imagination to expand on existing knowledge. This is done through building on existing ideas or thinking of new ideas and possibilities. Teachers need to ask students to build on what is given in the way of stimulus or concept; to expand an idea to make it more complex. This may involve both visual and verbal thinking, working by themselves or with others.

Choose a text you might use with a class. Read the text, but stop half way through. Ask students to speculate on what might happen from that point, then ask them to try to complete the text for themselves. For example:

'After the war, Earth was dead; nothing grew, nothing lived. The last man sat alone in a room. There was a knock on the door...'. Can you continue and complete the story?

Dialogic questioning can be used to encourage creative thinking *before* the task, *during* a task or *after* any task is completed. At the end of a task this can often come in the review, plenary or de-briefing stage. Dialogue at this stage depends on:

- the tasks being worth serious thought;
- the thinking and reasoning of students being valued; and
- adequate time being given for discussion and review.

Caring thinking – the expression of empathy

Empathy, which can defined as 'caring thinking', is not just the by-product of our brain's evolutionary expansion, but is the very ground of the growth of human consciousness. Likewise, empathy should not just be a by-product of learning but the very ground of English teaching. Empathy does not develop simply through reasoning or through exposure to the narratives of life. Observing or reading about the experience of others will not necessarily enhance students' capacity to care. They need not just to know that others have different desires, intentions and points of view, but to feel care and respect for others and their views. Buber (2004 [1923]) distinguishes between empathetic and non-empathetic thinking. The empathetic ('I–thou') type of relationship is characterised by mutual responsiveness; the non-empathetic ('I–it') relationship is typified by an active subject confronting and dominating a passive object. A similar distinction is found in the work of the Russian thinker Mikhail Bakhtin, who contrasts the 'authoritative' voice that demands that we either accept or reject it, with the 'persuasive' voice that enters into us and invites our own response. Such persuasive dialogue Bakhtin (1981) calls 'inter-animation' or 'inter-illumination'.

M level: read and apply

Try reading either or both of Bakhtin's seminal works: *The Dialogic Imagination* (1981) and *Rabelais and His World (1984)*.

Bakhtin's idea of 'carnival' can be interpreted as sanctioning a role for playfulness in lesson planning. As George Bernard Shaw once said 'You see things and say "Why?" But I dream things and say "Why not?"' What if animals could speak? What if we could live forever? What if the earth stopped revolving and the sun did not rise? 'What if' questions are playful but also offer a provocation to thinking by adding some impossible feature or picking out some feature of an item and imagining it was missing. This kind of playful imagination is a kind of conceptual exploration or thought experiment. By examining what can or cannot be imagined or conceived, students are exploring the possibilities and limits of their thinking. For example: What 'essential' features of the following could you imagine leaving out of a house, school, bicycle, library, birthday? (e.g. 'What if your house had no …?'). What features could you imagine adding to school, parents, clothes, sleep, sports (e.g. 'Wouldn't it be nice if …'). Can you or your students create a 'What if …' question about the text or topic in hand?

A dialogic teacher also tries to create the conditions where 'I–thou' interactions can take place; where students can relate and connect with each other, creating not just what the German philosopher Habermas (1991) calls the 'ideal speech situation' embodying equal rights but a 'community of enquiry' which is critical, creative and caring.

The capacity to engage in dialogue is inextricably connected to emotions and dispositions, including 'emotional' and 'social' intelligence, the ability to understand our own emotions and the emotions of others (Goleman 1995, 2006; Dweck 2005).

Caring dialogue should be governed by ground rules that have been mutually agreed, by relationships of 'reasonableness' and by a care for the rights of others.

Care is also shown by carefully listening to what is said and by building in 'thinking time'. Teachers, perhaps embarrassed or even intimidated by silence in response to a question or proposition, frequently leave very little space for students to reflect and respond. Increasing thinking or 'wait time' to 3–5 seconds can result in significant changes in dialogue, such as students giving longer answers, more students offering to answer, students being willing to ask more questions and students' responses becoming more thoughtful and creative. Allowing silence is a deliberate act by the teacher to encourage a more thoughtful response. Some teachers provide their students with a learning log, journal or 'think book' to provide another space to show their thinking and help reflection through writing.

Questioning

A number of questioning skills have been identified in research. These include:

- sequencing a set of questions – moving from literal to higher-order conceptual questions
- pitching appropriately – putting the questions clearly, for example by re-phrasing
- distributing questions around the class – to the shy as well as the dialogic 'stars'
- prompting and probing – giving clues where necessary, asking 'follow-ups'
- listening and responding in a positive way – inviting student questions
- challenging right as well as wrong answers – playing 'devil's advocate'
- using written questions effectively – using key questions for further thinking.

Formative interaction, however, involves more than having good questions. Questions should open up a dialogue, with students being given time to discuss their learning with the teacher and with one another, and being provided with meaningful opportunities to share their ideas with others. Students need more than questions to facilitate dialogue.

Dialogic alternatives to questions

There is a danger, however, even with skilful questioning, of teachers following a pre-set agenda, and not encouraging student initiative. In adopting a 'teacherly role' we can dominate the talk by asking too many questions and imposing our own meaning. Teachers who ask too many questions tend to discourage students from giving elaborate or thoughtful answers. Overusing a pattern of repetitive fixed questions – who? what? where? when? why? – will create students who ask fewer questions themselves, who give undeveloped responses, who rarely discuss ideas with their peers, who volunteer few thoughts of their own and who show confusion. What then is to be done?

In dialogic talk more extended answers are sought and the teacher takes on a more challenging role, disagreeing or putting an opposing argument and not rewarding

Table 7.6 Alternatives to questions

Withhold judgement	Respond in a non-evaluative fashion; ask others to respond
Invite students to elaborate	'Say more about ...'
Cue alternative responses	'There is no one right answer.' 'What are the alternatives?' 'Who's got a different point of view?'
Challenge students to provide reasons	'Give reasons why ...'
Make a challenging statement	'Supposing someone said ...'
Contribute your own thoughts or experience	'I think that ...' or 'I remember when ...'
Use 'think–pair–share'	Allow thinking time, then instruct students to discuss the issue with their partner, then with the whole group
Allow 'rehearsal' of response	'Try out the answer in your head and then to your partner'
Invite student questions	'Anyone like to ask Pat a question about that?'
Use 'think alouds'	Model rhetorical questions. 'I don't quite understand'
Child to invite response	'Ali, will you ask someone else what they think?'
Don't ask for a show of hands	Expect everyone to respond

students simply for making a response. Often the 'puzzled listener' role will be effective, if it reflects genuine interest and attention to the learner's answer. To stimulate more effective and thoughtful discussion, therefore, alternative strategies may be more productive than questioning. Table 7.6 outlines some effective options.

The task of promoting learning through dialogue is difficult. It is a delicate balance between letting discussion wander at random, and dominating it so students do not feel free to say what they think. The crucial indicators of good dialogue are the ways:

- thinking is challenged by teachers ('What do you mean by ...?'); and
- students' responses show extended reasoned thinking ('Give me three good reasons why ...').

Students must be encouraged to express arguments in fully formed sentences using such words as 'think' and 'because', not merely give short one-word or one-phrase answers. For many students school may be the only place where they experience and develop habits of reasoned talk (Alexander 2006).

Into practice: beyond questioning to dialogue: observing a lesson

Observe or film a lesson and note your observations of the type of questions being used.

Use your observations as a basis for professional dialogue, either with colleagues in school or with other students on your course. Discuss alternative ways of responding to children that do not involve the use of questions. Give an example for each of the alternatives to show how it might be used in practice. Share and discuss your ideas. Compare them to the suggestions in Table 7.6 and add any further examples. Create an agreed guide to 'developing dialogue' that could be shared with staff and parents.

Discourse and metacognitive knowledge

Dialogue helps students to develop 'discourse knowledge' through:

- constructing and reconstructing ideas through talk;
- learning the implicit rules of dialogue; and
- monitoring, self-regulating and learning to internalise dialogue.

The process of acquiring strategic dialogic knowledge allows students to determine what it is legitimate to say in any given domain or discipline and what 'breaks the rules'. They can then begin to monitor their thinking and dialogic responses. As they become more expert in doing this, they are able to conduct these conversations in their own heads, or with others without the support of a teacher or mentor. Initially they may need a teacher or peer to take responsibility for the ground rules of dialogue. When they are then able to 'self-regulate' their dialogue with others they have become 'metacognitively wise'. Metacognition, or knowledge of one's own thinking processes, is thus an essential part of dialogic understanding.

The term *metacognition* was introduced by Flavell (1979) and refers to learners' awareness of the strategies they use to engage with new learning or problems, and the extent to which they are explicitly able to reflect upon these. Flavell argues that if we can bring the process of learning to a conscious level, we can help children to be more aware of their own thought processes and thus enable them to gain control or mastery over the organisation of their learning (Flavell *et al.* 1995). Vygotsky (1986) argued that such *conscious* reflective control was an essential factor in human learning. Effective dialogue involves gaining discourse knowledge but also the ability to reflect on and exercise conscious control over knowledge acquisition.

Students who are trained in metacognitive self-checking routines improve their learning skills and become more successful learners. One of the best ways to engage them in metacognitive dialogue is through formative feedback (see also Chapter 8).

Dialogic formative assessment

The key feature of formative assessment is interaction through dialogic feedback. Interaction is through dialogue – that is, talk about teaching and learning between student and teacher or between students. Dialogic assessment helps learners to assess themselves and to modify and improve their learning behaviour. Dialogic feedback from teachers is helpful if it does not just say what was right or wrong, but helps students understand why it was right or wrong. Improvement in learning is about change in the student's self-awareness about learning behaviour. No change in self-awareness and learning behaviour usually means no improvement in outcomes.

Effective interaction in formative assessment is about 'thinking together' through questioning and dialogue, leading to peer and self-assessment. Through such interaction we can create the conditions for metacognitive discussion to take place, which is crucial to the ultimate aim of students taking greater responsibility for their own learning and becoming independent, self-directed learners.

Opportunities for formative assessment often occur in a plenary review. Like any good dialogue, a good plenary review will include:

- a high proportion of open or Socratic questions
- lengthy student responses, encouraged by the teacher
- reference to the 'big' ideas or concepts being taught
- connections made to other areas of learning and life.

Dialogic tasks and research projects

Involving students in research topics, 'rich tasks' and challenging contexts can help to engage learners in practising the skills of research and dialogue. This may involve teachers in looking differently at the content of learning, working in teams with colleagues from across subjects and across sectors, and presenting challenges to students which are engaging, extending the scope of their research and trying to embed their understanding of key concepts and processes through dialogue with others, for example through semi-structured interviews.

Inclusion: generating questions

Thinking and questioning in lessons are often the sole preserve of the teacher. Rigid adherence to teacher-generated learning objectives often encourages this. In order genuinely to engage students in their learning, it is essential that they are given the opportunity to generate and discuss their own questions in relation to any given topic or text.

1. Ask students to generate questions on a chosen topic in twos or threes.
2. Instruct them to share and analyse the questions together. How many different questions were created?
3. Discuss the kinds of questions that were asked with the group.
4. What were the most interesting questions? What made them interesting?

The questions students ask can be divided into different types. A useful distinction can be drawn between 'closed' questions that require one answer and 'open' questions that have many possible answers. These can also be called 'factual' (closed) or 'enquiry' (open) questions. When applied to a text a closed question is a comprehension question where the answer is in the text. An open question may require use of the imagination to read 'beyond the lines' and to make an inference, speculation or hypothesis. Once the students' questions have been identified, they can then be analysed using the question quadrant in Figure 7.1. Could they turn any of the closed questions into more interesting open enquiry questions?

Several research studies have now demonstrated that teaching students how to talk together effectively improves their thinking and learning (Mercer 2000). These studies show that good talk does not always just happen – it needs to be planned and practised. One strategy for doing this is called collaborative reasoning.

Collaborative reasoning

Research has shown that the kind of teacher-led talk with students called collaborative reasoning (CR) leads to improvements in reading comprehension and the quality of written argument for older (secondary/high school) students (Anderson *et al.* 1998; Rheznitskaya *et al.* 2001). The assumption underpinning this research is that reasoning is fundamentally dialogic, and is best nurtured in supportive dialogic settings such as group discussion. 'Empirical studies show that the quality of children's reasoning is high during CR discussions ... and they display higher levels of thinking than in conventional classroom discussion' (Kim *et al.* 2007: 342).

Research has shown that conceptual understanding is enhanced by students' discussion of ideas during group work. Some features of dialogue are particularly associated with solving complex problems, such as the requirement that the partners should try to achieve consensus in their discussion (Howe and Tolmie 2003). The most productive interactions seem to involve students proposing ideas, giving reasons and explaining their reasoning to each other (Mercer 2008).

TEXTUAL QUESTIONS

Reading Comprehension The answer is in the text	*Literary Speculation* Using your imagination
CLOSED QUESTIONS	**OPEN QUESTIONS**
Factual knowledge One right answer	*Enquiry questions* Many possible answers

INTELLECTUAL QUESTIONS

Figure 7.1 Question quadrant
Source: adapted from Cam 2006: 34.

Another strategy for achieving these aims is by creating a community of inquiry in the classroom.

Community of inquiry

Community of inquiry is a simple and powerful technique for developing dialogic skills that has been used effectively from pre-school through to adult contexts. It provides the opportunity for learners to practise the skills of shared inquiry by engaging in discussion about philosophical or conceptual questions of their own choosing as well as issues of personal concern. The community of inquiry pedagogy has been developed through research undertaken in many countries into ways of facilitating philosophical dialogue in the classroom – also called philosophy for children (Lipman 2003; Fisher 2008).

Through engaging in a community of inquiry students learn how to set their own learning agenda by asking questions; how to explore ideas, views and theories; how to explain and argue their point of view with others; how to listen to the views and ideas of others; and how to build on ideas and engage in discussion, recognising and respecting differences of opinion. A community of inquiry can help develop skills as critical readers, as well as initiate students into public discussion about philosophical issues and existential questions about personal identity, change, truth and time.

The following summarises the elements of a community of inquiry in the classroom (Fisher 2003):

- community setting: sit so all can see and hear each other, teacher as part of the group
- agreed rules: for example, 'Only one speaks at a time', 'Everyone listens to the speaker'
- shared stimulus: for example a chosen text, experience or problem
- thinking time: time is given to think about the shared stimulus or problem
- questioning: a forum is provided for raising questions, problems and ideas
- discussing: each with a right and opportunity to express his or her own views and feelings
- extending thinking: through further activities that apply and extend leading ideas.

Collaborative philosophical inquiry with children has been shown to produce gains along a range of educational measures, including verbal reasoning (Trickey and Topping 2004, 2008). Such communities can often extend beyond the activity of the classroom, and this can be effectively supported by the use of developing ICTs.

ICT: online dialogue

ICT can also play a role in extending dialogue beyond the classroom. Look at a range of virtual learning environments (VLEs) in schools, in your university and elsewhere.

How do these VLEs provide the conditions for and encourage effective online dialogue? What kinds of stimulus or other input do you see teachers providing in these forums? What are the advantages and potential pitfalls of online discussion forums? What is the role of the teacher in these forums? How might student learning be extended by the possibilities of online dialogue?

What a community of inquiry needs is a stimulus for thinking. The following are some questions raised by a group of able 13–14-year-olds about Franz Kafka's story *Metamorphosis*, about a man who wakes one morning to find he has turned into a giant insect. After the students spent some time thinking about the story and discussing possible questions in pairs, the teacher listed the chosen question of each pair to create a research and discussion agenda. The students then chose what they thought was the most interesting question to begin the discussion, which was 'What's the point of the story?' The following is an excerpt from their discussion:

Child 1: I don't think the point of the story is to ask questions about the story but to ask questions about yourself. How can you relate to this? Does he really turn into a bug? Or does he feel mostly that he's ugly or something?

Child 2: Maybe he's like worried or something. Maybe he is feeling like everything is difficult, like his voice is changing., and he's just feeling really scary, about growing up and all that lot …

Child 3: Suddenly you just feel that your legs are so long, and your arms so much longer than you thought they'd be. And these are things you wouldn't normally think about so maybe its just how he feels. He's just realised it and that's it.

Child 4: Maybe he's just buried up so he thinks he's a bug.

Child 2: Or it could represent something else.

Child 1: Yes, but if you are buried you don't think you are a bug!

Child 3: It might have represented a change in your life or something, like he's changed into a bug and that represents a change in his life.

Child 4: But what does a bug represent?

Child 1: I don't know. It's just a comparison. Maybe he just chose that because that happened in a dream. Just that.

Child 3: Yes, but you can't choose your dreams can you?

Child 2: How do you know it was a dream? How do we know we are not dreaming now?

Child 4: Maybe it's just the writer's way of telling us how the boy is feeling.

Child 3: Maybe there's no point to the story. Perhaps it's just the writer's way to keep people confused. [Laughter from the group]

Child 1: Well I think he succeeded.

Child 2: I think the more questions you ask the more confused you get.

Child 1: Yes, maybe … or do I mean definitely?

(from Fisher 2010: 53–4)

Here students can be seen playing with ideas and possibilities in a creative way, interrogating the meaning behind the story and starting to use their own experience as a reference point. Later the dialogue focused on the differences between dreams and reality and led to more philosophical discussion.

Professional reflection task

After a lesson in which dialogic learning takes place, reflect on the dialogic learning that has taken place in relation to the learning objectives. To help in this process you could use a positive, negative, informative (PNI) formula, as follows:

- Positive: identify the strengths of the lesson in terms of evidence of learning and positive features of the dialogic strategies used.
- Negative: identify the weaknesses, negative or problematical features of the teaching and learning strategies.
- Informative: identify the strengths, the interesting outcomes of the teaching and learning experience and the ways it will inform your future planning and practice

Ask students to reflect on the value of the dialogue and to assess the value of the learning that has taken place, possibly using the PNI formula above.

Identify how you would use this information to plan future interventions and opportunities for dialogic learning with the students who took part in the above dialogue.

Developing dialogic teaching

The following are characteristics of dialogic teachers, identified by research into teachers in schools whose students achieve better learning outcomes (Alexander 2006; Mercer 2008). Such teachers regularly:

- used question sequences to guide the development of understanding, asking 'why' questions to get students to reason and reflect about what they were doing;

- explained the meaning and purpose of classroom activities – not just 'subject content', but also problem-solving strategies and characteristics of good language users and learners;

- planned and organised opportunities for teacher–student and student–student dialogue, encouraging students to take an active, vocal role in their education;

- modelled the habits of good dialogue, including giving thinking time, and being comfortable in not knowing;

- challenged students' thinking through open-ended questions, provoking argument and debate on contestable issues;

- let learners ask and answer the questions, fostering the concept of students as researchers in setting their own agenda and identifying criteria for success; and

- provided opportunities for collaborative and co-operative working, with opportunities for self-, peer and group assessment.

M level: discuss dialogic teaching and learning

Discuss with colleagues the characteristics listed on pp. 106–7 and suggest ways in which teachers can (or should) exhibit these in everyday classroom practice.

The following are questions to aid reflection and discussion about the principles and practice of 'dialogic learning', which is the way we apply the principles and practices of formative assessment to develop successful and independent teachers and learners.

- In what ways do we use dialogue to support formative assessment?
- What strategies do we use to develop dialogue between teacher and students and between students?
- What is our policy and practice on giving feedback on learning?
- In what ways do we use questioning?
- How do we support co-operative learning (e.g. through activities such as paired learning, group work or community of inquiry)?
- What opportunities do we give for peer assessment?
- What opportunities do we give for self-assessment?
- How do we create communities of inquiry in our classrooms?
- What evidence is there that we are training our students in dialogic research skills?
- How might we pursue our own dialogic research into teaching and learning?

Conclusions

Dialogue makes thinking more 'visible' and facilitates deep learning. It is essential that teachers think in detail about how they will provide contexts for genuine dialogue where the questions that matter are the questions that the students themselves raise, and where the voices that matter are the students' voices. Without this, teaching and learning are in danger of serving the needs of the teacher rather than the needs of the learner. Creating classroom conditions where such genuine dialogue is possible can be a long process, but it is central to the development of powerful teaching and learning communities. As Tom, aged 13, put it: 'The best teachers make you think together'.

In summary

- Dialogue between teacher and student and between students is crucial in facilitating deep learning in classrooms.
- Opportunities should be planned for in each lesson or learning experience.
- Plan for dialogue in every lesson.
- Engage learners in dialogue about learning.
- Develop explicit awareness of the habits of good dialogue.
- Involve learners in leading and assessing the quality of dialogue.
- Engage learners in their own dialogic research.

Recommended reading

- Fisher, R. (2005) *Teaching Children to Learn*, 2nd ed. Cheltenham: Nelson Thornes.
- Fisher, R. (2007) 'Dancing minds: the use of Socratic and Menippean dialogue in philosophical inquiry', *Gifted Education International* 22:2–3: 148–59.
- Fisher, R. (2008) 'Philosophical intelligence: why philosophical intelligence is important in educating the mind', in M. Hand and C. Winstanley (eds), *Philosophy in Schools*. London: Continuum: 96–104.
- Fisher, R. (2008) *Teaching Thinking: Philosophical Inquiry in the Classroom*, 3rd ed. London: Continuum.
- Fisher, R. (2009) *Creative Dialogue: Talk for Thinking in the Classroom*. London: Routledge.
- Fisher, R. (2010) 'Thinking skills', in J. Arthur and T. Cremin (eds), *Learning to Teach in the Primary School*. Abingdon: Routledge: 374–87.
- www.robinalexander.org.uk: Robin Alexander's website on dialogic teaching
- www.sapere.org.uk: the UK's philosophy for children website
- www.teachingthinking.net: Robert Fisher's website

References

Alexander, R. (2000) *Culture and Pedagogy*. Oxford: Blackwell.

Alexander, R.J. (2006) *Towards Dialogic Teaching: Rethinking Classroom Talk*, 3rd ed. Cambridge: Cambridge University Faculty of Education: Dialogos.

Anderson, R.C., Chinn, C., Waggoner, M. and Nguyen, K. (1998) 'Intellectually stimulating story discussions', in J. Osborn and F. Lehr (eds), *Literacy for All: Issues in Teaching and Learning*. New York: Guilford Press: 170–86.

Bakhtin, M. (1981) *The Dialogic Imagination*. Austin, TX: University of Texas Press.

Bakhtin, M. (1984) *Rabelais and His World* (translated by Hélène Iswolsky). Bloomington, IN: Indiana University Press.

Bakhtin, M. (1986) *Speech Genres and Other Late Essays*. Austin, TX: University of Texas Press.

Barnes, D. (1976) *From Communication to Curriculum*. Harmondsworth: Penguin.

Barnes, D. (1995) *Communication and Learning Revisited*. London: Heinemann.

Bruner, J. (1987) *Actual Minds Possible Worlds*. Cambridge, MA: Harvard University Press.

Bruner, J. (1996) *The Culture of Education*. Cambridge, MA: Harvard University Press.

Buber, M. (2004) *I and Thou*. London: Continuum [1923].

Cam, P. (2006) *20 Thinking Tools*. Melbourne: ACER Press.

Coulthard, M. (1992) *Advances in Spoken Discourse Analysis*. London: Routledge.

Fisher, R. (2005) *Teaching Children to Think*, 2nd ed. Cheltenham: Nelson Thornes.

Fisher, R. (2005) *Teaching Children to Learn*, 2nd ed. Cheltenham: Nelson Thornes.

Fisher, R. (2008) *Teaching Thinking: Philosophical Inquiry in the Classroom*, 3rd ed. London: Continuum.

Fisher, R. (2009) *Creative Dialogue: Talk for Thinking in the Classroom*. London: Routledge.

Flavell, J. (1979) 'Metacognition and cognitive monitoring: a new area of cognitive-developmental enquiry', *American Psychologist* 34: 906–11.

Goleman, D. (1995) *Emotional Intelligence: Why It Can Matter More Than IQ*. New York: Bantam.

Goleman, D. (2006) *Social Intelligence*. London: Hutchinson.

Habermas, J. (1991) *The Theory of Communicative Action*, vol. 1. Cambridge: Polity Press.

Halliday, M.A.K. (1993) 'Towards a language-based theory of learning', *Linguistics in Education* 5.

Howe, C.J. and Tolmie, A. (2003) 'Group work in primary school science: discussion, consensus and guidance from experts', *International Journal of Educational Research* 39:1–2: 51–72.

Lefstein, A. (2009) 'More helpful as a problem than solution', in K. Littleton and C. Howe (eds), *Educational Dialogues: Understanding and Promoting Productive Interaction.* London: Taylor and Francis.

Lipman, M. (2003) *Thinking in Education.* Cambridge: Cambridge University Press.

Littleton, K. and Howe, C. (eds) (2009) *Educational Dialogues: Understanding and Promoting Productive Interaction.* London: Taylor and Francis.

Mercer, N. (1995) *The Guided Construction of Knowledge: Talk among Teachers and Learners.* Clevedon: Multilingual Matters.

Mercer, N. (2000) *Words and Minds: How we use Language to Think Together.* London: Routledge.

Mercer, N. (2008) 'Talk and the development of reasoning and understanding', *Human Development* 51:1: 90–100.

Mercer, N. (2008) 'Classroom dialogue and the teacher's professional role', *Education Review* 21:1: 60–5.

Rheznitskaya, A., Anderson, R., McNurlen, B., Nguyen-Jahiel, K., Archodidou, A. and Kim, S. (2001) 'Influence of oral discussion on written argument', *Discourse Processes* 32: 155–75.

Trickey, S. and Topping, K.J. (2004) 'Philosophy for children: a systematic review', *Research Papers in Education* 19:3: 365–80.

Topping, K. and Trickey, S. (2007) 'Collaborative philosophical enquiry for school children: cognitive effects at 10–12 years', *British Journal of Educational Psychology* 77:2: 271–88.

Vygotsky, L.S. (1986) *Thought and Language.* Cambridge, MA: The MIT Press.

Vygotsky, L.S. (1978) *Mind in Society: The Development of Higher Order Processes.* Cambridge, MA: Harvard University Press.

Wells, G. (1999) *Dialogic Enquiry: Towards a Socio-cultural Practice and Theory of Education.* Cambridge: Cambridge University Press.

Wertsch, J.V. (1991) *Voices of the Mind.* New York: Harvester.

8

BETHAN MARSHALL
Assessing English

In this chapter you will consider

- what is meant by summative and formative assessment;
- some of the issues surrounding summative and formative methods of assessment;
- some historical dimensions of assessment in English;
- Assessment for Learning;
- self- and peer-assessment; and
- practical issues of assessment.

Introduction

When the word assessment is used people tend to think of examinations, and those sweaty afternoons in May or June – what are known as terminal exams. But English has maintained a somewhat different stance on exams, arguing for at least part of the examination to be done through coursework, thus avoiding the last-minute panic of summer. This chapter will look at the changing nature of these exams, the coursework involved and the importance of Assessment for Learning (AFL).

Summative assessment

Coursework vs terminal exams

London Association for the Teaching of English

In the period following the Second World War English teachers began to be restive about the examination system that confronted them. At first this was about O levels, which examined the top 20 per cent or so of students in the country. This was because only about 20 per cent went to grammar schools and were seen fit for examination. Some did enter the exam at secondary modern but these were few and far between. Very early on, English teachers in London began to question whether or not the O level tested what children did best. The London Association for the Teaching of English (LATE) was founded in 1947, just two years after the war, and by 1951 they were already holding meetings looking at the O levels in language and literature.

It is important to note that these teachers were not looking to rid students of the O level, rather they were wanting to make it more appropriate to the kind of teaching that they did and the experiences they felt these children had. In 1950, a year before they started looking at the exams, Britton, with a number of London teachers, began looking at how they marked what were then called compositions. This was significant because Britton was trying to see if teachers could agree on the marking of them if they did so holistically. He was concerned that English teachers do not agree philosophically about what they are looking at when assessing, something that has been the case ever since. Some may mark technical errors while others look, for example, at the imagination displayed, and this could make them mark a piece of work differently unless there are very clear or 'analytic' guidelines. He called the project *The Meaning and Marking of Imaginative Composition* (Britton 1950).

What is interesting is that he included the word 'meaning' in the title. In this respect he was perhaps indicating that meaning is not considered enough in analytic mark schemes. Analytic marking tends to move away from what the text is actually saying and just looks for specific things to mark out such as technical considerations. If it does look at meaning, such as whether or not a student has understood a passage, it tends to outline appropriate responses but does not look at whether or not a child has actually understood what is being said. The flaws of such a system were particularly exposed in the Key Stage 3 comprehension tests, where a student might have fully grasped what was being said but failed to use terminology from the text, which in turn meant that it did not register in the analytic mark scheme.

In selecting the word 'meaning' Britton might have been stressing the importance of examining what the student was actually trying to say. In this respect he was also moving away from teaching to the test. In English, in particular, as we shall see, teaching to the test, even in apparently creative writing, was a major concern. The temptation was to teach to what was in the mark scheme. If a tight analytic mark scheme did not exist then teachers would be freer to encourage students to write more freely, to write what they meant to say.

He was still equally committed to a more holistic way of marking over a decade later. In 1964, in work done for the Schools Examination Council, he again looked at how teachers marked compositions in exams in *The Multiple Marking of Compositions* (Britton 1964). This time he compared what he now called multiple-impression marking with the exam boards' analytic mark schemes. Writing about the experiment twenty-five years later, along with Nancy Martin, he said: 'The upshot of the experiment was to indicate that parcelling out scripts to examiners is a considerably less reliable process than parcelling them out to teams of three rapid impression markers' (Britton and Martin 1989: 2). They also found it more accurate than the traditional 'very careful analytic marking system' (1989: 2–3).

Throughout his career, then, Britton was interested in making exams meet the needs of the students rather than the other way around. In 1955, he wrote:

It seems to me that, in principle, there ought not to be any better way of preparing a student for examination than good teaching: and that the examining authorities ought to recognise the principle and make themselves responsible for providing an examination which as nearly as possible satisfies it. … One effect of the English language paper is to encourage training in certain restricted techniques at the expense of more broadly based language teaching.

(Britton 1955, cited in Gibbons 2009: 22)

Joint Matriculation Board

In expressing this opinion he was echoing a broader feeling among English teachers that all was not well with the examination system. The Joint Matriculation Board (JMB) had also been interested in considering the system for assessing O level and had even in the 1950s looked at what was going on in London. In 1964 they set up a group, which was somewhat different from Britton's, but which also had the apparent wrongs of the O level as the basis for trying to alter the system. In their first interim report they wrote:

The GCE O-level examination in English language is under bitter criticism as conducive to dull and cramped teaching and to crabbed rote learning and practice. The lively interest which should be aroused by learning to read and write English is killed, so it is asserted, by the need to prepare for writing stereotyped answers.

(Wilson 1965: 1)

Although the procedures that they went through changed somewhat over the course of time, the method that they used, which became known as trial marking, involved a combination of the class teachers and a panel of experts looking at the files students produced. The so-called experts were those who were the most consistent in the marks they gave during this procedure, and in the end these people became what was known as the Review Panel. Unlike Britton they did not mind that English teachers often disagreed in their philosophy of English. They believed that as long as people were 'adaptable' (Wilson 1965: 12) this would not prove a problem; it might even be an asset. What was important was that people met regularly to discuss students' work. In the last report they wrote, 'Experience has shown that it is essential for groups to meet together to discuss the results of trial marking and procedures for assessment' (Rooke and Hewitt 1970: 14). They went on to recommend that, on the extension of the scheme, 'Provision must therefore be made for groups to meet for discussion' (1970: 14). And this is what they did.

The JMB and later the Northern Examination Association Board (NEAB) sent out trial marking bi-annually. This consisted of the work of the previous year's candidates. The folders always contained a selection of candidates' work, including some that were difficult to assess (e.g. work falling on the C/D borderline). All teachers marked these folders blind then met with the rest of the department in order that a school grade could be decided. The individual scores and the school's agreed grades were sent back to the board. A standardisation meeting was then held by the board, in which the grades, agreed by a Review Panel, were given out. The Review Panel was made up of practising teachers, who, as with the original experiment, had been chosen for the accuracy of their assessments, through the trial marking.

Professional reflection

It is always important to gauge whether or not our view of a student's work coincides with the rest of the department. Although you might do some kind of departmental moderation for GCSE it is important to do it at Key Stage 3 as well.

In a departmental meeting it may be worth discussing three students' pieces of work to see if you are assessing them in a similar way.

The system by which the actual work of students was assessed was similarly rigorous. To ensure the reliability of these judgements checks and double checks were introduced. All candidates were marked both by their own teacher and another member of department. Where there was any disagreement, or when the candidate was on the borderline between two grades, their folder was submitted for scrutiny by the whole department.

The whole school entry was then moderated to ensure that the candidates' work was placed in the correct rank order, from grade A to U, before sending the papers to the exam board. Here the work was moderated by a member of the Review Panel. All Review Panel members worked with partners; when one panel member moderated a school's entry, the other checked their judgement. The Review Panel members had the power to alter a school's grades, either up or down, if they felt that they had placed more than 50 per cent of the candidates on the wrong grade. A 'C' could become a 'D' or a 'B' an 'A'. (The rank order of individual candidates could be changed only when the Review Panel members felt that an individual candidate had been wrongly graded by at least two complete grades.) The work of the vast majority of candidates was, therefore, read by at least five different English teachers before a final grade was awarded. One final check was built into the system. A sample of the cohort was sent to an Inter School Assessor. This teacher marked the entries blind and then sent their grades to the Review Panel. Again, if there were any serious discrepancy between the Assessors' grades and the school's, the panel members would moderate the school's entry.

The exam boards returned all coursework to the schools, after they had been externally moderated, with comments on any adjustments that had been made as well as on the quality of the work. In this way the whole process of exam boards' decisions and moderations was entirely made by ordinary teachers whose own students were being examined. Moreover, a national network began to develop where the teachers were firmly in charge, but learning constantly from the dialogues that were created by the process.

The era of 100 per cent coursework reached its zenith around the time the GCSE was introduced in 1998. Schools could either opt for 100 per cent or 50 per cent coursework, and many schools that did not already do coursework opted for it at this point. This only lasted for four years. In 1992 the Conservative government abandoned the practice, and by 1994 no school was allowed to do more than 20 per cent written coursework in the English language exam and 30 per cent in their literature despite vigorous campaigns by people such as Mike Lloyd, a Birmingham teacher, who launched the Save English Coursework Campaign. It has not resurfaced since.

ICT: ICT and malpractice

One of the major concerns surrounding the use and validity of coursework assessment in English and other subjects has been the issue of malpractice facilitated by ICT.

Discuss this with a range of colleagues and others on your course. What are the major areas of malpractice students might engage in, both wittingly and unwittingly? Is the answer to this problem to withdraw the possibility for coursework assessment, as has been done with the current system of controlled assessments, or could other approaches be adopted? How should teachers work with their students to ensure they are responsible and ethical users of ICT?

Assessment for Learning

Guild knowledge

What both these examples of examination demonstrate is that English teachers have often sought a different more holistic means of assessment. What neither of them does, however, is say how, if at all, the approach worked. This is where the work of the Australian Royce Sadler comes in. In 1989 he wrote a seminal paper in which he put forward the concept of 'guild knowledge' (Sadler 1989). In essence, he said that teachers, in this case English teachers, carried around with them an idea of what it meant to be good at a subject, as people who were in a guild would have. In this respect his notion of guild knowledge was not unlike Britton's idea of an impression.

The notion of guild knowledge is important for both summative assessment and for AFL. Sadler suggests that the way in which teachers cope with the multiplicity of variables confronting them, when marking an essay, for example, is by making what he calls 'qualitative judgements' about students' work. A teacher of English, therefore, has a guild knowledge of what makes a good essay and this is why it is important summatively.

Yet it is also important formatively, for what is important in teaching is that in some way the teacher imparts this knowledge to the student. But, he admits, 'How to draw the concept of excellence out of the heads of teachers, give it some external formulation, and make it available to the learner, is a non trivial problem' (Sadler 1989: 127). This becomes very important in AFL, particularly in peer-assessment, but also in sharing criteria with the learner, as Black and Wiliam (1998a) suggest when they discuss formative assessment.

M level: guided reading task

Compare the two following publications:

- Black, P.J., Harrison, C., Lee, C., Marshall, B. and Wiliam, D. (2003) *Working Inside the Black Box*. London: NFER.
- Marshall, B. (2005) *English Inside the Black Box*. London: NFER Nelson.

Consider some of the ways in which the general principles of AFL are interpreted in English. But to pursue the notion of guild knowledge just a little further first – essentially, Sadler argues that criteria are unhelpful in improving performance. 'For complex phenomena, use of a fixed set of criteria (and therefore the analytic approach) is potentially limiting' (Sadler 1989: 132). Instead he argues for what he calls 'configurational assessment' which he explains 'do[es] not require the specification of all the criteria in advance, neither do[es] they assume operational independence among the criteria' (1989: 132).

Into practice: AFL in practice

The Teacher Training Resources Bank identifies that AFL should:

- be part of a teacher's effective planning
- focus on how students learn
- be a central feature of classroom practice
- be seen as a key professional skill for all teachers
- be viewed as a sensitive and constructive process
- never underestimate the importance of student motivation
- encourage a shared understanding of the criteria by which learning goals are assessed
- ensure learners receive constructive guidance on how to improve their learning
- develop the learners' capacity for self-assessment
- recognise the full range of educational achievement.

Read the general assessment policy in your school and the policy of the English Department. How do these policies relate to the ten principles above? Discuss with colleagues in school and/or other students on your course the practicalities of working with AFL.

One reason Sadler appears to give for the inter-relatedness of criteria – and therefore the difficulty, not to say impossibility, of separating them out – is because

> The greater the divergence in outcomes which can be regarded as acceptable, the more likely it is that a variety of ways can be devised to alter the gap between actual and reference levels, and therefore the less likely it is that information about the gap will in itself suggest a remedial action.
>
> (Sadler 1989: 139)

In other words, if a child writes a descriptive piece there are any number of ways it could be improved. Identifying, for example, the increased use of complex sentences among higher-achieving students, and so teaching that element explicitly, is insufficient. Only with surface features such as spelling and punctuation is such a simple procedure possible. Moreover, he goes on to argue that with extended writing

> Any attempt to mechanise such educational activities and creative efforts [as for example with … software packages] is unlikely to be successful because of the large number of variables involved, the intense relationship existing among them, and their essential fuzziness.
>
> (1989: 140)

What Sadler calls 'their essential fuzziness' and perhaps James Britton calls an impression, for others is 'judgement'. Protherough *et al.* (1989: 31), when talking about assessment, write, 'In the end, grade descriptions for English have to be matters of judgement and not of objective fact, and developing this judgement is one of the skills that young English teachers have to acquire'. In other words, the guild knowledge of which Sadler writes is acquired over time. And this applies to students too. One of the main ways in which teachers can encourage students into an understanding of what it is to be good at the subject without using strict criteria is to peer assess each other's work.

Peer-assessment

If we look at a piece of work that was peer assessed in some detail the point becomes clearer. The peer assessment is on the first draft of a piece of Year 10 coursework on Tybalt and Mercutio's deaths in *Romeo and Juliet*. This is in itself interesting for a number of reasons. To begin with, it shows that there can be a link between the formative and summative. The coursework is used ultimately as a piece of summative assessment for GCSE. So this essay is being looked at formatively, through peer assessment, where the student can, as a result, improve on their work, and summatively for an examination. This is one of the reasons that many English teachers are worried about the new GCSE. Although there is a course-based element, all the work done has to be done in controlled conditions which can be, in effect, mini exams. This means, for example, that students cannot take any work done previously in class, including a peer-assessed essay, into the exam and make improvements on what had previously been written.

To return to the essay on *Romeo and Juliet*, here the intention is that the student will read the comments made on their piece of work and rewrite it. Table 8.1 includes peer comments offered on one essay. For the purposes of this activity, the essay was photocopied onto a piece of A3 paper and the comments were written down both sides of the essay. Here again there is a difference between what this student has written and what might be found in many peer-assessed documents. It reads as an account of what the marker, as student peer assessor, thought of the piece as they were reading it. There is no grid by which the comments are to be assessed, no Assessing Pupils' Progress (APP) remarks or similar, although many of the points do relate to APP focuses in some respects.

Table 8.1 Example of Year 10 peer assessment (points not numbered in original)

Written in left margin	Written in right margin
1. Lots of points blended together. It gets confusing without any	7. Too brief 'Mercutio wants to fight' … 'then they were fighting'. You need more info and emotions in between what causes them to fight do they threaten each other first.
2. This sentence doesn't work well. You can't use two becauses in a sentence	8. Good explanations and emotions
3. Too many ands	9. Good thoughts and opinions from Romeo on the situation
4. A bit vague. Mercutio doesn't just die, he suffered. Maybe add some quotes from Mercutio	10. I like this bit when he says 'it was over' you could maybe add finally into to describe how glad he is for it to be over.
5. Good choise [sic] of words. They are good to describe Romeo's feelings	11. Lots of good points. Everything is included. Try to space out all of the events instead of blending them all together. This makes it a bit confusing to read. Second half a lot better than the first half
6. More descriptive bits for Tybalt's death not just he fell over dead	

What is most impressive about this piece of peer assessment is the range and type of comments. In some respects this is suggestive of the kind of assessment that is done on students' work in general. Students learn to peer assess through constant modelling as well as practice. In order for them to peer assess well, the teacher must also assess in detail for them to see what good assessment is like. But more fundamentally, through their assessment and their teaching, this teacher appears to have begun to share their 'guild knowledge' of the subject. What you have here, therefore, possibly unarticulated, is the beginnings of the students' understanding of what that guild knowledge of the subject looks like in practice.

SEN: supporting AFL

Engaging in AFL is beneficial for learners of all abilities, but students with SEN may well require more support in order to undertake this kind of classroom activity. Considering the above AFL activity in relation to *Romeo and Juliet*, explore some of the ways in which this activity could be differentiated to enable students with SEN beneficially to participate.

The English teacher must make a variety of remarks that shows a holistic view of English and the assessment process in particular. The peer markers' comments then pick up on this. They make technical comments but also talk about the overall shape of the essay. In fact the first and last points they make are about clarity. Their first comment is, 'Lots of points blended together. It gets confusing' and this is echoed in the last point, too: 'Lots of good points. Everything is included. Try to space out all of the events instead of blending them all together. This makes it a bit confusing to read. Second half a lot better than the first half'.

This is not quite teacher speak but very close. One knows what the peer marker is trying to say when they comment on points being 'blended'. It is quite an interesting turn of phrase. They do not say overlap, which is a comment that might be made by a teacher, but blended. The image of a blender mixing in all the points would indeed be 'confusing'. It would blur things to the point of a disparate mush. What they ask is for the student 'to space out all of the events'. In other words they are to separate them, giving clarity.

Indeed, they go on to say what you might add in 'spac[ing] out all the events'. On three separate occasions they talk about how the author might add to what they have written. Comments three, five and six are concerned with a more detailed look at how characters feel about events, what motivates them. This, in a tentative way, shows the peer marker's view of the importance of subject knowledge, and it is twofold. They argue that you can tell what a character is thinking or feeling and that it is what they say that gives you this information. And once more, to add such information would prevent the point from being 'a bit vague' and give it clarity. Clarity, then, works at the level of subject knowledge as well as overall structure.

So, for example, 'Mercutio doesn't just die, he suffered'. In order to demonstrate that this is true the author should, 'Maybe add some quotes from Mercutio'. The word 'suffered' is also telling. It shows that the peer assessor recognises a degree of anguish on the character's part that is derived from the text, hence 'add some quotes'. Or, again, the description of the fight between Mercutio and Tybalt is 'Too brief'. The peer assessor tells the author to add 'more info and emotions' and in so doing requires them to examine the text further, to see 'what causes them to fight do they threaten each other first'.

This sense of engagement with the characters, but a realisation that such knowledge must be found in the text, demonstrates the way in which the teacher must have imparted guild knowledge through the way she both taught and assessed. It is even true of the technical comments that the peer assessor gives, for they do not stop at the technical. In point two they write that there are 'too many ands' and 'becauses'. To begin with they appear to be making a point about repetition, though the word is not used. But this is elaborated on 'It doesn't make the sentence work well'. Here the peer assessor is possibly developing an ear for language, for what does work well as well as what does not. It may be confusing to the reader but also it does not sound right and this is, perhaps, what is important.

Ironically, it is the way criteria in English all 'blend together' that, on the one hand, make it so hard to assess and, on the other, can make peer assessment so effective. Significantly, the teacher has not singled out any particular criterion for the peer assessor to look at but has just asked them to comment on what they read. Confronted with this the author of the piece will have a good commentary on their essay, including positive comments like 'Good choise [sic] of words. They are good to describe Romeo's feelings'. These will give the author a better idea of what to build on when the peer assessor makes suggestions as to what might be improved.

Although it is not possible to know what effect this had on the peer assessor themselves, one can tentatively presume that they may have learned something about how an essay is presented as well, that they will have seen the importance of putting in quotes and description and that they have begun to learn why: that they are gaining in guild knowledge.

Dialogue and AFL

Perhaps the predominant way in which both guild knowledge and what makes up the 'stuff' of English is made known, however, is through the dialogue in English lessons between the teacher and student and between the students themselves. In their original article on AFL Black and Wiliam (1998a: 16) write, 'All such work involves some degree of feedback between those taught and the teacher, and this is entailed in the quality of the interaction which is at the heart of pedagogy'. In other words 'feedback' becomes the type of remark that you give in response to what someone has said.

Typically, in classroom terms, this can be somewhat limited. The teacher asks a question to which they know the answer and the student tries to guess what is in the teacher's head. This kind of closed questioning led Black and Wiliam to look at the whole issue of questioning in the booklet they produced on formative assessment (Black and Wiliam 1998b). In particular they focused on 'big' questions that a teacher might ask to avoid the usual closed questions. In the later booklet *Working Inside the Black Box* (Black *et al.* 2003) they extended this further. So, for example, in English they asked essay-type questions, such as 'Is Macbeth a villain or a hero?'

Creativity: creative responses to text

Think about the assessment of either *Romeo and Juliet*, or this title in relation to *Macbeth*. The predominant method of formal assessment in English remains the analytical essay, but there are strong cases for assessing students through creative responses to literary (and other kinds) of text. Develop a range of creative responses you might use with students studying either *Romeo and Juliet* or *Macbeth* (or indeed any other text). Spend some time thinking about:

· the kinds of support students will need to undertake such tasks – how does this differ from the support required for conventional analytical responses; and
· the particular types of learning students will engage in doing creative tasks of this sort – how does this differ from discursive responses?

While there is no doubt that English teachers asked such questions this did not get to the heart of what Black and Wiliam (1998a: 16) originally meant when they talked about 'the interaction which is at the heart of pedagogy'. In fact, the English teachers who were involved in the research carried out by King's (Black and Wiliam n.d.) into formative assessment never mentioned questioning at all.

This, in many respects, is the kind of dialogic classroom that Alexander (2006a) discusses and wishes to encourage in his booklet *Towards Dialogic Teaching: Rethinking Classroom Talk*. Ultimately Alexander (2006b: 5) observes that the dialogic classroom '[r]equires willingness and skill to engage with minds, ideas and ways of thinking other than our own; it involves the ability to question, listen, reflect, reason, explain, speculate and explore ideas'. If we look at an extract of dialogue from the classroom the significance of this, and the way it relates to guild knowledge, becomes clearer.

In this lesson the teacher, Angela, wanted the students to peer assess a group performance of a pre-twentieth-century poem. She began the lesson by asking the students to draw up a list of criteria for performing a poem, which is in itself important because she is making them decide what criteria to use rather than imposing a checklist on them. Through the interaction that followed she also developed the students' critical vocabulary, as the students' contributions were negotiated with the teacher who, through exchange, refined them.

> Student: You could speed it up and slow it down.
> Teacher: Yes – pace, that's very important in reading [teacher then writes the word 'pace' on the board].

Substituting the word 'pace' is important, for in so doing she introduces them to technical vocabulary. It might have been even better if she had told them what she was doing, but it is, nevertheless, significant. Interestingly, the Japanese have a useful term for describing such a process – *neriage* – which literally means polishing. In Japan recapitulating the contributions made by students is an important part of teachers' classroom practice. It provides an opportunity for teachers to synthesise the contributions made by different students, to interject specific vocabulary, and also to refine or re-contextualise ideas.

In another series of exchanges between the students and Angela, it is again the students' ideas that are being sought. They are discussing a reading by the learning support assistant (LSA), which was accompanied by a freeze frame by the teacher. Students were invited to comment on both the reading and the freeze frame and in so doing drew not just on the criteria but also on their interpretation of the poem. In this way the dual nature of the lesson – developing their understanding of the literature and of speaking and listening – was also served. As with the previous dialogue, it is the teacher who tries to understand what the students are saying.

> Student: It [the performance] was boring.
> Teacher: What do you mean boring?
> Student: There wasn't enough expression in your face when the poem was being read or in the reading.
> Teacher: So what could I have done to make it better?
> Student: You could have looked and sounded more alarmed.
> Teacher: Like this? [strikes a pose]
> Student: Not quite.
> Teacher: More like this? [strikes another pose]
> Student: Yeah.

Although this is only a brief extract we can see that the teacher is attempting to do all those things which Robin Alexander requires. She listens to the student's ideas. She questions the student's response and reflects upon it. She looks for explanation and speculates, albeit a little, on the answer. But, as important, the dialogue in which she engages is formative because in asking the student to clarify what they mean by 'boring' she is feeding back the notion that the student needs to be more specific. Their response is one that shows that formative feedback works as each answer improves on the one that went before. In this way she is also communicating guild knowledge.

But the lesson is also an example of the spirit of formative assessment as opposed to the letter (Marshall and Drummond 2006) in that the activities help the students become independent learners. This included encouraging the students to create their own criteria, which in turn helped them to think for themselves about what might be needed to capture the meaning of the poem in performance. But it was also the way each activity built on the one that preceded it.

Inclusion: setting criteria for assessment

Speaking about or writing out what kind of criteria students might use is vital in getting students to engage in their own learning because it helps them think about what quality means. Discuss with colleagues in school or other students on your course a range of ways in which you might actively involve students at a range of levels and of a range of abilities in this process.

If we look at each activity in the lesson we can see this:

- The class draw up a list of criteria guided by the teacher.
- The teacher and the LSA perform the poem.
- Students are asked to critique the performance.
- Students rehearse a performance.
- Students peer assess poems based on the criteria.
- Students perform poems based on the criteria.

Each of the activities had an open, fluid feel which corresponded with the notion of promoting student independence; it reinforced a sense of holistic and limitless progress whereby assessment is always seen as a tool for future rather than past performance. And this is important too. Rather than dwelling on what they had done, as so much summative assessment in the UK does, they were concentrating on how they could perform the poem better next time. Finally the lesson created tasks designed to enable children to enter the subject community 'guild' (Sadler 1989).

In summary

- Assessment in English will continue to be controversial.
- Since the end of the Second World War teachers have battled to assess their subject in a way that they think is compatible with a holistic view of what English is meant to be about.
- In doing so they have developed a kind of guild knowledge that is invaluable when they apply it to their everyday teaching.
- Through meaningful peer assessment and through supportive dialogue, teachers assess students formatively and so improve the performance of those they teach.

References

Alexander, R. (2006a) *Towards Dialogic Teaching: Rethinking Classroom Talk.* Cambridge: Dialogos.

Alexander, R. (2006b) *Education as Dialogue: Moral and Pedagogical Choices for a Runaway World.* Cambridge: Dialogos.

Black, P. and Wiliam, D. (1998a) 'Assessment and classroom learning', *Assessment in Education: Principles, Policy and Practice* 5:1: 7–73.

Black, P. and Wiliam, D. (1998b) *Inside the Black Box.* London: NFER Nelson.

Black, P. and Wiliam, D. (n.d.) *Changing Teaching through Formative Assessment: Research and Practice. The King's Medway Oxfordshire Formative Assessment Project,* available online at www.oecd.org/dataoecd/53/30/34260938.pdf (accessed on 9 March 2011).

Black, P.J., Harrison, C., Lee, C., Marshall, B. and Wiliam, D. (2003) *Assessment for Learning: Putting It into Practice.* Buckingham: Open University Press.

Britton, J. (1950) *The Meaning and Marking of Imaginative Compositions.* London: LATE.

Britton, J. (1955) 'The paper in English Language at Ordinary Level', *Use of English* 6:3: 178–84.

Britton, J. (1964) *The Multiple Marking of Compositions.* London: Her Majesty's Stationery Office.

Britton, J. and Martin, N. (1989) 'English teaching: is it a profession?', *English and Education* 23:2: 1–8.

Gibbons, S. (2009) 'Back to the future: a case study', *English in Education* 43:1: 19–31.

Marshall, B. and Drummond, M.-J. (2006) 'How teachers engage with assessment for learning: lessons from the classroom', *Research Papers in Education* 21:2: 133–49.

Protherough, R., Atkinson, J. and Fawcett, J. (1989) *The Effective Teaching of English.* London: Longman.

Rooke, H.M. and Hewitt, E.A. (1970) *An Experimental Scheme of School Assessment in Ordinary Level English Language: Third Report.* Manchester: Joint Matriculation Board.

Sadler, R. (1989) 'Formative assessment and the design of instructional systems', *Instructional Science* 18:2: 119–44.

Wilson, J.G. (1965) 'Preface', in E.A. Hewitt and D.I. Gordon, *English Language: An Experiment in School Assessing (First Interim Report).* Manchester: Joint Matriculation Board.

9

MAGGIE PITFIELD
Drama in English

In this chapter you will consider

- how the relationship between drama and English has developed over time;
- the ongoing debate around the role of drama in the secondary curriculum;
- the position of drama in English as set out in the National Curriculum (DCSF/QCA 2007a);
- drama teaching practices within English; and
- some key debates and theoretical positions which underpin the role of drama as a learning medium in English.

Introduction

In many secondary schools drama exists as a subject in its own right and yet it also has a place within the curriculum for English. This raises some interesting questions about the specific role of drama in English, how English teachers can utilise drama-based approaches to enrich teaching and learning, and what kinds of collaboration between drama and English specialists might be expected.

Professional reflection: drama in the curriculum

Look closely at the National Curriculum. All three sections identify content and processes that relate closely to drama. Identify what these are, and then consider how you understand the relation between drama and English at Key Stage 3 and at Key Stage 4.

Background

Since the introduction of the National Curriculum (1989) and in all subsequent revisions (1993, 1995, 2000, 2007), drama has appeared as a requirement of the National Curriculum Order for English. The original version, known as *The Cox Report* (DES 1989), placed drama within the programme of study for speaking and listening (S&L). The link with S&L has remained to this day. It is important, however, to consider what had gone before. In the days before the National Curriculum a combination of factors influenced the progression of drama as a school subject, not least the enthusiasm and 'grassroots' practice of some inspired English practitioners who promoted drama as a tool for exploring texts and language in the classroom. Theirs was an interpretation of drama that moved beyond the ever-popular school play and into the curriculum. Such teacher-led developments were taken up by subject-specific professional bodies and supported in emerging centres of educational innovation, such as the former Inner London Education Authority.

Also playing its part was the introduction of the comprehensive system of state education and the subsequent abandonment in many (if not all) areas of the country of selection at age eleven via a common examination. Increasingly, the curriculum in the non-selective setting of the comprehensive school had to be responsive to the needs and interests of the full range of learners. Over time the re-thinking of education that took place as a result of such changes saw a focus on particular theories of learning, and this too had a positive impact on the profile of drama in education. The work of Piaget, which emphasised the importance of child play, child-centred learning and the social purpose of role play, was particularly influential at primary school level. Of similar importance was the social constructivist approach, based on the writings of Vygotsky, in which it is interaction with others and 'cooperation that lies at the basis of learning' (DfES 2004: 21). More specifically in English, language studies that focused on classroom discourse and 'the language resources students bring to the school' (Dixon 2009: 249) brought about the kinds of developments in classroom practice that would see drama-based learning thrive and grow.

However, in 1989 the decision to include drama as part of the Order for English meant that it was not recognised as a separate subject within the National Curriculum structure. This was considered by some practitioners to be a stumbling block to the development and wider acceptance of drama as a valid and valued school subject.

Professional reflection: drama and English

The statutory association between drama and English has been debated extensively over time.

- Drama and English are so closely linked as subjects that it is appropriate to recognise this connection in the National Curriculum for English.
- A place for drama in the secondary curriculum has been secured by its inclusion as a statutory part of the National Curriculum for English.

- There is always a danger that drama as a discrete discipline might be marginalised in schools, perhaps even excluded, because it is not a National Curriculum subject and is therefore 'officially invisible' (Neelands 2000: 55).
- Drama is rightly considered to be part of the core curriculum precisely because of its statutory association with English (one of the subjects designated as 'core').

Place the above statements in rank order starting with the one that most closely reflects your view. Justify your ranking. Whether it is an adjunct to, or (as claimed by Arts Council England 2003; DfES 2003; Bunyan and Moore 2005; NATE 2006) at the very heart of the secondary curriculum because of its formal association with English, drama as a discreet subject has remained free from the constraints of the high-stakes national testing regime (known as SATs) at Key Stage 3. By contrast these tests, prior to being abandoned in 2008, have had a significant impact on the English curriculum (Coles 2009; Yandell 2010).

Key reports and policy documents

The Cox Report (DES 1989) identified five models of, or approaches to, English (remind yourself of the details in Chapter 4). These models accommodated a wide range of views about the subject, and envisaged a place for drama within all the models. The report seemed, therefore, to propose a wider definition of the contribution of drama than its positioning within S&L might imply.

M level: Cox and drama

Look at each of the five models proposed by Cox (personal growth view; cross-curricular view; adult needs view; cultural heritage view; cultural analysis view).
    How does the role of drama seem to vary in each?

In 1997, the New Labour Government's National Strategy for Education at Key Stage 3 implemented an objectives-led, skills-based model of literacy and English teaching, the underlying philosophy of which has generated much debate. In this model, as exemplified in the *Key Stage 3 National Strategy Framework for Teaching English: Years 7, 8 and 9* (DfEE 2001), the direct link between drama and S&L was upheld, and the drama objectives were situated within the lists of S&L objectives for each of the three years.

The attainment targets and level descriptors designed to measure students' performance in meeting these objectives did not give detailed guidance on how English teachers might assess students' achievements in S&L through drama. The publication of the *Key Stage 3 National Strategy Drama Objectives Bank* (DfES 2003) was an attempt to remedy this situation. It provided English teachers with a 'making, performing, responding' model of learning in drama which drew on an approach identified in *Drama in Schools* (Arts Council England 2003). It also gave a set of performance indicators for assessment purposes.

Into practice: making, performing, responding

The *Drama Objectives Bank* (DfES 2003: 2–3) defines these processes:

- 'Making (or creating) in drama involves working alone or with others to shape ideas into actions and exploring the conventions, resources and techniques of drama with increasing confidence ... Creativity in drama is imaginative, linguistic and physical.'
- 'Performing refers to the work of a class, group or individual exploring, preparing and sharing ideas through enactment.'
- 'Responding to drama involves students in reflecting on their own experience of drama. They also need to express their understanding of what the drama is saying and how it is saying it through dramatic conventions and techniques. Responses can be emotional or intellectual, individual or shared, spoken or written.'

What types of activity does each of these processes require? One problem with a number of the drama objectives was that they offered too broad a focus to serve as particular lesson objectives and were better suited to planning across a sequence of lessons. Nevertheless, the *Drama Objectives Bank* did make a good attempt to show that drama contributes to learning across all aspects of English and that it should not be confined to S&L.

A similar approach is taken in a more recent publication entitled *The National Strategies Secondary. Developing Drama in English: A Handbook for English Subject Leaders and Teachers* (DfE 2010). The 'Assessment in Practice' section shows how the new assessment system known as Assessing Pupils' Progress (APP), instituted following the abolition of national tests at Key Stage 3, relates to assessment of drama in English. Here suggestions are given for using drama activity to contribute to the assessment not only of S&L but of reading and writing too.

Ofsted inspection reports can be useful in shedding some light on what is happening in English classrooms in response to policy initiatives. In the 2005 review, drawing on evidence from inspections of English in schools over a five-year period, concern is expressed about the lack of attention and time given to S&L in comparison with reading and writing. Although it comments favourably on the fact that there are often separate drama departments in secondary schools, as 'This makes sensible use of specialist teachers to develop skills and understanding in drama, as well as contributing to students' speaking and listening skills' (Ofsted 2005: 19–20), the report also claims that assessment in drama 'remains an area for improvement' (2005: 20). *English at the Crossroads* (Ofsted 2009), based on inspection evidence between April 2005 and March 2008, criticises the lack of focus on S&L and drama (among other aspects of the curriculum) in 'less effective schools' (2009: 22), but suggests that overall the situation has improved since the 2005 report.

While it is the purpose of inspections to make judgements on the effectiveness of schools and teaching, they do not probe the wider context in which teaching takes place and in that sense offer a limited view. It is worth remembering, for example, that the national tests at Key Stage 3, which until their abolition contributed to the construction of school league tables, were only based on the results of the reading and writing papers, and did not include S&L. In this respect policy has actually contributed to the 'poor relation' status of S&L.

The *English 21* consultation does offer a wider perspective, however, as it involved a range of stakeholders in the field of English education and was instrumental in shaping the revised National Curriculum for English (DCSF/QCA 2007a). The report's findings, published as *English 21 Playback: A National Conversation on the Future of the Subject English*, highlight English teachers' concerns about the effects of the testing regime on the curriculum and suggest 'a widely-held belief that the tests drive, rather than support, the English curriculum' (QCA 2005: 40).

Professional reflection

The following excerpts from a focus group interview involve two early career English teachers. They are discussing why they wish to introduce more drama-based learning into their English lessons, and reflect on some of the perceived barriers.

> Teacher 1: The pressure, I'm already feeling it with Year 10, I can't waste a lesson. They need to know these poems well and they need to be able to write about them. So if you come in and spend a lesson doing drama, and then in the end you're having to squeeze in two poems, because it's not integrated, you kind of feel the pressures of 'what *are* they going to be tested on?' I know that every teacher knows that you shouldn't just base it on...
>
> Teacher 2: ... teaching to the test ...
>
> Teacher 1: ... but especially if you're an NQT, you don't want your whole class not to fulfil their potential.
>
> Teacher 2: Sometimes the kids themselves, because of their preconceptions of the subject, and obviously what's expected of them ...
>
> Teacher 1: ... say 'What's the point of this?'
>
> Teacher 2: Yeah, sometimes you have to convince them. They say, 'Are you sure we've got time? I'm not going to be assessed on it, I'm not going to get a grade or a level, why should I do it?'

Think about your own attitudes towards and/or experience of drama in English in the light of the above conversation. Apart from test and examination pressures, what other factors might contribute to:

1. students' concerns; and
2. teachers' concerns regarding drama in English?

How might you, as an English teacher, justify and explain the importance of using curriculum time to explore texts through drama?

Creativity

In *Playback*, English teachers are reported as wanting 'to give more time and space to the creative and arts aspects of English' (QCA 2005: 6), and 'argue drama has a key role to play in engaging students and deepening their responses, combining emotional engagement with a text or an issue with the ability to think and reflect on it' (2005: 9). Such views find resonance in an important report from the National Advisory Committee on Creative and Cultural Education (NACCCE) (1999), *All Our Futures*. This report argued in favour of a 'national strategy for creative and cultural education' (1999: 6), as the Key Stage 3 National Strategy (which at the beginning focused on literacy and numeracy) did not really concern itself with these aspects of education. Relevant to drama is the definition of creativity given in *All Our Futures:* 'Imaginative activity fashioned as to produce outcomes that are both original and of value' (1999: 29). Significantly for the drama–English association, the report also cited drama as 'a powerful way of promoting skills in reading, writing and in speech' (1999: 36).

Creativity

In the 2007 National Curriculum for English, creativity is identified as one of the four 'key concepts' underpinning the whole curriculum across S&L, reading, writing, and language study, and this has the potential to open up extensive opportunities for drama in English. Creativity is defined in the following ways:

a.   Making fresh connections between ideas, experiences, texts and words, drawing on a rich experience of language and literature.
b.   Using inventive approaches to making meaning, taking risks, playing with language and using it to create new effects.
c.   Using imagination to convey themes, ideas and arguments, solve problems, and create settings, moods and characters.
d.   Using creative approaches to answering questions, solving problems and developing ideas.

(DCSF/QCA 2007a: 62)

Suggest a drama activity that you might set up in an English lesson to stimulate the types of creative response described. Further scope for drama can be found in the multi-modal approach to text highlighted in the 'Range and content' sections of the programmes of study for Key Stage 3 and 4. Here a much broader definition of text, and indeed of reading, emerges, which moves beyond the literary, beyond the written. Thus an intertextual approach to film, script and dramatic enactment can enhance the work of the English classroom. A viewing of the scene from James Cameron's *Titanic*, which shows the dining rituals in first class as witnessed by a third-class passenger, can, for example, guide students towards an informed representation of the class hierarchy in their own dramatised scenes from Sheila Birling's engagement party (*An Inspector Calls*). It is also appropriate for students to employ technology as a means of analysing and commenting upon key events in a play. For example, by filming their own news reports of the Scottish army's victory against the Norwegians in *Macbeth*, they will

---

consider the differences in political perspective and the consequent reporting style of Scottish, Norwegian and English television stations.

While it may not be immediately apparent how ICT contributes to learning through drama, Neelands (1993) demonstrates that ICT can be both a tool for developing the drama and an integral part of it. With the former, research using specific Internet websites might inform students' knowledge of places and historical events that are relevant to a particular character or dramatic situation. In the case of the latter he describes a project in which students developed characters from newspaper stories of young offenders. ICT was used to create their criminal records, alongside taped interviews, 'surveillance' videos and other 'evidence'. In this instance the technology itself, through the key themes of freedom of information and the surveillance society, became a focus of the drama. Even when ICT is used for research tasks, it may be helpful to root this within a dramatic context. As part of the drama, the information gleaned from the research is interpreted by students adopting a range of different roles. This offers opportunities to explore ideas around point of view, bias, propaganda and vested interest.

ICT: ICT in drama

While observing in a range of English lessons during your teaching practices note how ICT is used creatively in English lessons to engage students. How do teachers and students make use of ICT during drama-based activities in English? Speak to a drama teacher about the ways in which he or she uses ICT to support learning. Arrange to shadow a student for a day, focusing your observations on the ways in which teachers and students use ICT to enhance learning in different subject areas. Consider how you might adapt some of the techniques and applications observed for use in drama-based activities in English.

'Activating' text

The place of drama in English is still most often understood in terms of its usefulness in activating a literary or play text, or in exploring language in simulated or imagined situations, or a combination of both.

Into practice: planning for drama

Think of a particular play that you know well and that could be studied in English at Key Stage 3 – it might be a contemporary play or perhaps one by Shakespeare (for example, *Romeo and Juliet* or *Macbeth*). Suggest some ways in which drama could be used to activate this play text. Although 'bringing a text to life' is an accepted purpose of drama in English there are some dangers to be considered in terms of how the activity is conceived.

Byron (1986: 67–8), in his discussion of the role of active approaches to teaching literature in English, suggests that:

> behind the use of drama to animate or enliven the text is the idea that reading is somehow passive and drama active ... One can be actively learning without much or any physical activity. And it is quite possible for students to be physically active, yet passive as learners.

In a similar vein, Coles warns of 'a false dichotomy between "desk-bound" teaching (bad) and "active" teaching (good)' (Coles 2009: 34). In spite of these concerns there is clearly value in melding both literary and practical approaches to teaching texts. She also suggests that the high-stakes testing regime at Key Stage 3, particularly the Shakespeare paper, has even co-opted drama to the end of providing an 'acceptable' answer:

> Affording access to a reified text becomes drama's prime objective. Consequently the notion of 'active Shakespeare' draws attention away from the socio-cultural role of students as readers.
>
> (Coles 2009: 35)

When under pressure in a 'teaching to the test' situation it may seem expedient to 'tell' students what their interpretation should be. However, from a pedagogical perspective Vygotsky has questioned such an approach to concept development, which relies entirely on 'transmission' of knowledge by the teacher. The scaffold that will support students in arriving at new insights is informed by and arises from their prior learning and may take many forms. It should not be a 'very rigid instrument of support' (Williams 2005: 28), with an 'off the peg' design. Thus, in addition to the teacher's input, through drama students will provide the scaffold for each other's development of individual and collaborative interpretations.

Speaking and listening

The revised National Curriculum for English still maintains a focus on the importance of drama in this area of English. Kempe and Holroyd (2004) make a case for co-ordination between English and drama departments to support student progression in S&L, although such curriculum collaboration may in reality be somewhat patchy (Pitfield 2006).

EAL: EAL learners and drama

Look at the following exchange from a focus group interview with drama PGCE student teachers. At this point they are finding ways to describe their understanding of the contribution of drama to S&L.

Drama student-teacher 2: The ability to access the language and use it in imaginative ways. That's probably the point of it.

Drama student-teacher 1: Using language in real live terms.

Drama student-teacher 2: It goes to communication …

Drama student-teacher 3: Starting to take on board the nuances of the language you're speaking, whether it's your native language or not, knowing the appropriate usage.

Drama student-teacher 2: Understanding verbal communication on a level of confidence.

Write your own statement explaining the purposes of using drama to support EAL students' development in S&L. Kempe and Holroyd identify two dimensions to oral work: 'It can be the focus of the learning or the frame in which learning occurs' (2004: 3). Thus students learn through talk and/or learn about talk in the English classroom. Drama in English also serves this dual purpose – it is the focus of the learning, as delineated by specific National Curriculum S&L requirements, but it can be utilised as a learning medium in all areas of the English curriculum.

With regard to the former dimension, S&L in the English classroom should not be viewed merely as a set of speech skills that exist outside of meaningful contexts (real or imagined), but neither is it conversation that has no discernible learning purpose. Clearly there is a place for drama in developing 'dialogic conversation', described as 'conversation that has the overriding objective of playing with ways of articulating ideas and that, by doing so, generates and explores new ones' (Kempe and Holroyd 2004: 5). (For a fuller consideration of dialogic teaching, see Chapter 11.)

In conveying meaning the 'embodied and active semiotic representation of social relations' (Franks 2010: 242) through drama is also significant. Drama contributes what Winston (2004: 27) refers to as the 'language of drama', making 'use not only of words but also of visual and other types of aural signal'. He emphasises 'the importance of drama … where visual communication and issues of cultural value and social critique have always been of central concern' (2004: 29).

Drama and inclusion

'Communication' as well as 'Probing, questioning and challenging' are among the identifying features of 'Gifted learners in English' (Dean 2008: 22), as proposed by the National Academy of Gifted and Talented Youth (NAGTY). It is therefore not unreasonable to assume that drama can provide an appropriate context for developing the higher-order communication skills that denote a gifted learner. While it might be somewhat surprising to find the word 'tentative' included in the NAGTY definition of communication – 'tentative and/or confident communication of ideas and responses to and in a broad range of ideas/language/situations and roles' (Dean 2008: 22) – this has more to do with exploration and experimentation than with hesitancy or lack of confidence.

Jarrett (2010: 32), bringing together the findings from schools deemed by Ofsted to be good or outstanding in English, supports this exploratory approach. The experience of these schools suggests that learner independence is fostered by 'regular opportunities for students to exercise choice over topic and approach'; an emphasis on teamwork, discussion and decision-making; and risk-taking and 'experimenting without the fear of assessment' (2010: 33). Such a curriculum is therefore inclusive as it recognises that all learners, whether identified as having special educational needs or as gifted in the subject, benefit from an appropriate degree of challenge. As Thomas (2010: 16) states, 'My aim has been to establish a teaching repertoire to develop Gifts and Talents in all … devising activities that allow all to work at the top of their ability and above.'

Dean (2008: 21) issues a timely warning that written communication should not be privileged above other aspects in any judgements about giftedness in English, making it clear that learners need to be given opportunities to express their insights in other ways. For example, he highlights 'the confidence and skill' required 'to take on a role' and to become 'keen observers of the lives of others, and quickly able to discern how a character in a play should be portrayed'.

Inclusion

Consider the range of learner needs in one classroom where you have observed drama used. In what ways did the teacher use drama activity to meet the range of individual needs? Were these methods effective? How might you seek to develop these methods in your own teaching? Think of practical contexts.

For EAL learners it is widely accepted that they 'need an environment rich in talk', although Scott suggests that many teachers, 'especially those of us that believe that learning is created through dialogue' (Scott 2010: 38), would argue in favour of such an environment for all learners. Drama activities in English, particularly role play, can help EAL learners move from informal language use, which they may develop quite quickly through out-of-class social situations, to more formal applications. Drama in English is also instrumental in elevating modes of representation other than writing, for example a story told interpretatively through pictures (tableaux).

A great deal can be achieved through more advanced dual language work in drama. Hulson (2006: 45), as part of her *Refuge* scheme of work, describes the power and benefits of students working together in different languages:

I have watched scenes where one student speaks English and the other Kurdish, and all the Kurdish speaking children in the audience are laughing (with delight, not spite) … When the scene is replayed with an interpreter the humour can be shared with the whole class, and the scene is used to demonstrate, 'the use of comic timing, and the narrator/interpreter's use of bathos'.

M level

The following excerpts are taken from subject studies assignments at Masters level.

Title of assignment 1: What model do we have? And what model do we need? Considering the past, present and future of drama in English

> I would argue that working in role provides particular scope for learning in English – by working in 'now-time', students are encouraged to negotiate unfamiliar linguistic convention and codes with no prior preparation – hence they are given first-hand experience of language as a living entity. As such, language becomes not just the means of communication but the subject to be interpreted.

Title of assignment 2: Can drama contribute to literacy at KS3, and what is its place in the English curriculum?

(The discussion in this section of the assignment is of an English lesson which explores the idea of our 'surveillance society' and the introduction of ID cards, supported by the reading of extracts from a novel.)

> Students need to have the opportunity to role play and 'act out' situations in a safe 'make believe' environment in order to understand what should or should not be said, or written; students need to have behaviour modelled, perhaps by the teacher, perhaps through the use of forum theatre by their peers – especially at KS3 as they begin to encounter real social and moral dilemmas in their own lives … drama does not necessarily just have to be an outlet in support of other drama (such as Shakespeare) or literature, but it could be the key to unlock 'functional' literacy.

1. For what reasons should students be given opportunities to participate in structured role play activities as part of their S&L programme of study?
2. In what ways can drama support the learning of the full ability range of students in English?
3. How do drama pedagogical practices support spoken language development within the English classroom?
4. How can drama practices specifically support EAL learners in the English classroom?

Drama, the National Curriculum for English and assessment

To locate the discussion in the National Curriculum requirements, it is through drama-based activity that students can, for example, learn to: infer, analyse, and understand explicit and implicit meanings in spoken language; plan, organise, sustain and adapt their talk depending on situation and/or audience; make judgements about a speaker's intentions; work purposefully; and negotiate in groups. These are all highlighted within the 'key processes' sections for S&L. Also identified are 'different dramatic approaches', 'different dramatic techniques' and, explicitly at Key Stage 4, evaluation of the drama from the point of view of both participant and audience.

Into practice

Examples given for dramatic approaches are:

- tableaux
- hot-seating
- teacher in role
- thought tracking
- forum theatre

Think about your own experience of drama in English either as a student or student-teacher and select one of the above approaches. How have you seen this approach used in English *or* how have you employed it yourself *or* how might you use it 'to explore ideas, texts and issues' DCSF/QCA (2007a)? The terminology can be confusing because in other contexts dramatic approaches are sometimes referred to as dramatic techniques or conventions.

According to Neelands (2000: 49–50), within drama as a discrete subject:

> The emphasis in the conventions approach has been on giving students the means to make their own dramatic representations by introducing them to increasingly wide and complex choices of 'means' for depicting the world.

Thus exploration of the relevance of conventions to particular cultural, historical and contemporary theatrical settings is also important, and use of a conventions approach is woven into a coherent curriculum plan: what Neelands (2000: 53) refers to as 'some sort of temporal map that will ensure progression and continuity and which presumes that the child will want and can expect to "get better" at drama'.

As far as drama in English is concerned, it is likely that conventions will be employed in a more haphazard and restricted manner if they are viewed as a means to an end. However, such an approach does not do justice to the part they can play in providing students 'with the knowledge to make more effective and complex relationships between "means" and "meanings" in their own drama-making' (Neelands 2000: 58). Therefore, being able to suggest the appropriate convention to use in any given situation while ensuring that it is 'not too challenging to the student's personal boundaries' (Neelands 2000: 59) requires no little skill on the part of the teacher.

The 'temporal map' for English includes drama in S&L as one focus of the learning, which therefore presumes that students can 'get better' at this aspect. Thus the processes for measuring progression must necessarily include the assessment of drama within S&L. The 'lines of progression', as identified in the renewed *Framework for Secondary English* (DCSF/QCA 2007b) which now covers both Key Stages 3 and 4, are presented as strands and substrands. The two substrands for drama in S&L are:

- using different dramatic approaches to explore ideas, texts and issues; and
- developing, adapting and responding to dramatic techniques, conventions and styles.

For each substrand specific objectives for Years 7 to 11 are described.

At Key Stage 3, via the APP process, teachers use assessment focuses (AF) to reach decisions about students' achievements in meeting the objectives. At Key Stage 4, S&L is assessed in the English GCSE and the English language GCSE, and a drama task, again focusing on role playing and creating and sustaining roles, contributes to this assessment. As well as formal assessments which confer National Curriculum 'levels of attainment' at Key Stage 3 and GCSE grades at Key Stage 4, the English teacher also engages in ongoing formative assessment of student progress. The requirement in the 'curriculum opportunities' sections of the National Curriculum for English for students to 'evaluate and respond constructively to their own and others' performances' signals the importance of student self- and peer-assessment in informing this formative assessment process.

Into practice: assessment

Arrange to speak to an English teacher while on one of your teaching practice placements to find out about the ways in which self- and peer-assessment activities as part of S&L and drama work at Key Stage 3 are structured and used. Also speak to a drama teacher to find out more about self- and peer-assessment opportunities for students in drama at Key Stage 3.

Joining the discussion

In researching the views of teachers and student teachers about the contribution that drama makes to teaching and learning in English I have conducted focus group interviews utilising a 'diamond twelve', a teaching activity which stimulates and focuses discussion (see Figure 9.1).

The participants were given the following statements, developed and categorised by investigating a range of views about drama in English represented in key policy documents and the writings of well-known theorists and practitioners in the specific and related fields. Drama-based learning in English:

- allows students through role play to inhabit the patterns of action and the language of the adult world;
- draws on elements of child play to enhance learning in English;
- is a tool for literacy and social transformation in young people's lives;
- makes meaning beyond language, through signs, gesture, movement, action and use of dramatic space;
- involves students in representing 'virtual worlds' which relate to but are distanced from the everyday;

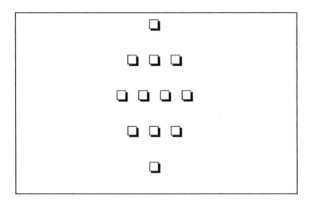

Figure 9.1 Diamond twelve

- models the skills required for employment and the world of work;
- is an immediate and physical means of getting to grips with texts and textual representation;
- stimulates and provides opportunities for students to write genuinely and purposefully;
- offers a set of techniques or conventions for exploring (English-specific) ideas, situations, issues and texts;
- is about the freedom to imagine, experiment and take risks;
- helps students to appreciate great works of literature, particularly plays such as those by Shakespeare;
- other … (own statement).

Participants discussed the statements, then placed the statement to which they ascribed the most importance at the top of the diamond shape, the second and third most important on the second row, and so on. A statement in a line containing three (or four) is considered to be roughly on a par with others in the same line. Participants were also asked to add their own statements (the 'other' category), to identify perspectives they felt were missing from the existing statements.

Professional reflection

Here are the 'other' statements agreed among the student teachers taking part in the two focus groups. Drama-based learning in English…

English student teachers
- … allows students to critically and creatively respond to texts and ideas with confidence and independence.

Drama student teachers

- · ... helps students to achieve confidence in effective verbal and non-verbal communication.

English teachers

- · ... encourages creativity.
- · ... helps students to appreciate *all* literature and to develop understanding of the relevance to their lives of studying these texts.
- · ... encourages students to work in groups they would not always choose themselves and encourages teamwork.
- · ... helps students appreciate/explore a play in the way that the playwright intended.

Which of the 'other' statements above most closely represents your view? Alternatively, you could write your own 'other' statement. Create your own diamond twelve using the eleven given statements and your 'other' statement. Give your reasons for choosing as the most important the statement that sits at the pinnacle of your diamond. As the statements demonstrate, there are different understandings and philosophical positions that relate to the role of drama in the secondary curriculum and its relationship to the subject English. Therefore, when following up some of the ideas suggested by the statements, the readings below will help you to develop your understanding of the contribution that drama makes to the curriculum and to teaching and learning in English.

M level: reading

- · Drama as art and aesthetic activity: Franks 2010.
- · Drama as a tool for literacy and social transformation in young people's lives: Freire and Macedo 1987.
- · Theories of child play that underpin approaches to drama in English: 'Drama, more than any other form of creation, is closely and directly linked to play, which is the root of all creativity in children' (Vygotsky 2004 [1967]: 71). See also Abbott 2010.
- · Development of critical reading skills: Neelands 2008.
- · Approaches to connecting drama and writing: Cremin *et al.* 2006.

Recommended reading

- · Byron, K. (1986) *Drama in the English Classroom*. London: Methuen. A text which offers ideas specifically for drama within English lessons, and links theoretical and practical perspectives through an imagined discussion between teachers.
- · DfES (2003). *Key Stage 3 National Strategy: Drama Objectives Bank*. London: DfES Publications. For further practical teaching ideas and a glossary of approaches and conventions.

- Fleming, M. (2003). *Starting Teaching Drama*, 2nd edition. London: David Fulton. This is just one of the many texts available which give guidance on strategies for teaching drama.
- Hulson, M. (2006) *Schemes for Classroom Drama*. Stoke on Trent: Trentham Books. Although aimed primarily at drama teachers, this offers detailed schemes of work and a theoretical underpinning for the practice the author espouses.
- Kempe, A. and Holroyd, J. (2004) *Speaking, Listening and Drama*. London: David Fulton. A consideration of issues around teaching and assessing S&L through drama, with some practical examples.
- www.ite.org.uk/ite_topics/drama_secondary/008.html entries written by Jonathan Neelands.
- www.mantleoftheexpert.com 'Mantle of the expert' is an advanced application of drama across the curriculum developed by Dorothy Heathcote.

You might also consider the National Association for the Teaching of English (NATE) Drama Packs by Ruth Moore and Paul Bunyan.

In summary

- Historically the subjects drama and English can claim strong links.
- Drama is a popular subject in its own right with its own curriculum and discourse.
- Within English drama serves a dual purpose: it is one focus of the learning in S&L, and it can be utilised as a learning medium across all areas of the English curriculum.
- An understanding of the importance of drama-based learning in English can overcome perceived barriers to its more widespread application in the English classroom.

References

Abbott, L. (2010) 'Mantle of the Expert in New Zealand', *The Journal for Drama in Education* 26:2: 42–9.

Arts Council England (2003) *Drama in Schools*, 2nd edition. London: Arts Council England.

Bunyan, P. and Moore, R. (2005) 'Tracks in the sand: developing critical thinking through drama', *EnglishDramaMedia* 3: 28–31.

Byron, K. (1986) *Drama in the English Classroom*. London: Methuen.

Coles, J. (2009) 'Testing Shakespeare to the limit: teaching *Macbeth* in a Year 9 classroom', *English in Education* 43:1: 32–49.

Cremin, T., Goouch, K., Blakemore, L., Goff, E. and Macdonald, R. (2006) 'Connecting drama and writing: seizing the moment to write', *Research in Drama Education* 11:3: 273–91.

DCSF/QCA (2007a) *The National Curriculum: English Programmes of Study for Key Stages 3 and 4*, www.qcda.org.uk/key-stages–3-and–4/subjects/english/programme-of-study/ (accessed on 28 July 2010).

DCFS/QCA (2007b) *The Framework for Secondary English*, www.standards.dcfs.gov.uk/secondaryframeworks (accessed on 28 July 2010).

Dean, G. (2008) *English for Gifted and Talented Students*. London: Sage.

DES (1989) *English for Ages 5 to 16 (The Cox Report)*. London: HMSO.

DfE (2010) *The National Strategies Secondary. Developing Drama in English: A Handbook for English Subject Leaders and Teachers*. London: DfE Publications.

DfEE (2001) *Key Stage 3 National Strategy Framework for Teaching English: Years 7, 8 and 9*. London. DfEE Publications.

DfES (2003) *Key Stage 3 National Strategy: Drama Objectives Bank*. London: DfES Publications.

DfES (2004) 'Unit 11: active engagement techniques', *Pedagogy and Practice: Teaching and Learning in Secondary Schools*. London: DfES Publications.

Dixon, J. (2009) 'English renewed: visions of English among teachers of 1966', *English in Education* 43:3: 241–50.

Franks, A. (2010) 'Drama in teaching and learning language and literacy', in D. Wyse, R. Andrews and J. Hoffman (eds) (2010) *The Routledge International Handbook of English, Language, and Literacy Teaching*. London and New York: Routledge, 242–53.

Freire, P. and Macedo, D. (1987) *Literacy: Reading the Word and the World*. London: Routledge and Kegan Paul.

Hulson, M. (2006) *Schemes for Classroom Drama*. Stoke on Trent: Trentham Books.

Jarrett, P. (2010) 'Beyond the crossroads (part two)', *Classroom: The Magazine of the National Association for the Teaching of English* 12: 32–3.

Kempe, A. and Holroyd, J. (2004) *Speaking, Listening and Drama*. London: David Fulton.

NACCCE (National Advisory Committee on Creative and Cultural Education) (1999) *All Our Futures: Creativity, Culture and Education*. London: DfEE.

NATE (National Association for the Teaching of English) (2006) *Revised NATE Position Paper: Drama*, www.nate.org.uk (accessed on 19 August 2010).

Neelands, J. (1993) *Drama and IT: Discovering the Human Dimension*. Coventry and Sheffield: NCET and NATE.

Neelands, J. (2000) 'In the hands of living people', *Drama Research* 1: 47–59.

Neelands, J. (2008) 'Drama: the subject that dare not speak its name', *ITE Readings for Discussion*, www.ite.org.uk/ite_readings/drama_180108.pdf (accessed on 7 March 2011).

Ofsted (2005) *English 2000–2005: A Review of Inspection Evidence*, www.ofsted.gov.uk/Ofsted-home/Publications-and-research/Browse-all-by/Education/Curriculum/English/Primary/English (accessed on 28 July 2010).

Ofsted (2009) *English at the Crossroads*. London: HMSO.

Pitfield, M. (2006) 'Making a crisis out of a drama: the relationship between English and Drama within the English curriculum for ages 11–14', *Changing English* 13:1: 97–109.

QCA (2005) *English 21 Playback: A National Conversation on the Future of the Subject English*. London: Qualifications and Curriculum Authority.

Scott, S. (2010) 'EAL advice "off the peg"', *Classroom: The Magazine of the National Association for the Teaching of English* 12: 36–8.

Thomas, P. (2010) 'Developing gifts and talents in English (part one)', *Classroom: The Magazine of the National Association for the Teaching of English*, 12: 16–19.

Vygotsky, L.S. (2004) 'Imagination and creativity in childhood', *Journal of Russian and East European Psychology* 42:1: 7–97.

Williams, G. (2005) 'Through the glasses of human culture', *The Journal for Drama in Education*, 21:1: 24–31.

Winston, J. (2004) 'Integrating drama and English: literacy and oracy in action', *English Drama Media* 1: 25–9.

Yandell, J. (2010) 'New Labour, old school tie: what is education For?', *Changing English* 17:2: 113–27.

10

JENNY GRAHAME AND ANDREW GREEN
Media in English

In this chapter you will consider

- the relationship between media studies and English;
- what constitutes the study of media;
- the meaning of media 'literacies';
- key concepts underpinning the study of media texts;
- a range of practical strategies for teaching media.

Introduction

Since its contentious birth in the late 1980s, the English curriculum has been frequently misrepresented in public discourse as a cultural battleground, invested with
the competing ideologies of successive governments, and nowhere are these debates
more visible than in its changing approaches to the role and study of media texts.
This complex history involves the consistent intervention of Conservative, Labour
and Coalition governments in the nature of subject English, from the 'Back to Basics'
campaigns of the early 1990s and subsequent brutal curriculum revisions, through
the New Labour Literacy Strategy and Framework years, the development of new
and contentious assessment practices, the 2007 'opening up' of the Revised 'Big
Picture' National Curriculum, and the current (January 2011) uncertain future of
the Coalition's next steps in the reframing of the core curriculum. At the same time,
the qualification regulators, and the examination awarding bodies in particular, have
experienced a growth in status and the acquisition of enormous power in the shaping
and assessment of young people's experience of English, in which media study as a
school subject has come to occupy the role of 'scapegoat' for declining standards.

The story has also been complicated since the early 1990s by the extraordinary
changes within the media landscape itself, in terms of its products, the technologies
and platforms through which they are accessed, and the opportunities for audiences
to interact with and generate them. As a result, there has been a major shift in the

perceived significance of the media and cultural industries to the British economy, which in turn raises questions about the extent to which an increasingly 'mediatised' English curriculum can enable young people to understand and fully participate in the changing digital world of the twenty-first century.

In this chapter we want to explore how these changes are experienced by young people studying English in schools at Key Stages 3 and 4, starting with a broad over-view of the historical development of media study both within the English curriculum and as a specialist subject, and its relationship to previous curriculum models: the conceptual differences and overlaps between the study of media texts, institutions and practices in English and in media studies.

At the time of writing, the introduction of a radical new suite of English GCSE specifications is already impacting dramatically on classroom practice, and may ulti-mately transform the ways in which communicative practices and media texts are inte-grated into programmes of study. What new opportunities are opening up for media study, and how can they be strategically exploited to develop the teaching and learning of media skills both within and despite the constraints of the English curriculum at Key Stages 3 and 4? We will explore a variety of approaches drawn from current prac-tice, consider the longer-term impact of new technologies on teaching and learning in English, and briefly suggest some classroom activities that may offer ways of integrat-ing engaging and creative perspectives into an English curriculum fit for twenty-first-century learners.

ICT: what's available?

English teachers are expected to deal with the constantly developing field of media technologies. Spend some time researching and using the hardware, applications and software currently available and consider how you might use them in your teaching.

Media and English: snapshots from an uneasy history?

The continuing story of media in English – which some media educators have char-acterised as a soap opera – hinges on the relationship between language, communi-cation and technology, and raises challenging debates about the nature of texts and their cultural value. And, like all good soap operas, there are key characters and family groupings, each with their own discourses, vested interests and conflicts, in the form of ministers, curriculum regulators, theorists, awarding bodies, and schools of teach-ing and learning; spin-offs into other curriculum areas, disciplines and qualification frameworks; cliff-hangers (how will each successive version of English accommodate new texts, concepts and forms of communication?); and, most importantly, a lack of closure: this is a narrative without an ending, susceptible to extreme plot twists, economic constraints and editorial volte-faces under the executive production of the Minister for Education.

The development of a body of conceptual understanding about the media, and its relationship to the English curriculum, has a long and much debated history dating back to the early 1940s (Barratt 1998; Hart and Hicks 2002; Buckingham 2003; Kirwan *et al.* 2003). In many ways the struggle to establish its academic validity parallels early twentieth-century scepticism about the value of literary study, explored in Chapter 2. In the 1930s early advocates of the classroom study of media texts, who included Leavis, focused on the moral dimensions of mass media culture as opposed to the great traditions of the literary canon, and the need to 'inoculate' students against the dangers of advertising and popular cinema. Twenty years later, anxieties about the advent of commercial American media and its possible erosion of British working-class culture were embraced by the National Union of Teachers in the light of Cold War moral panics about the subversive influence of American horror comics and the arrival of rock and roll in the 1950s. A hugely influential flowering of critical and creative study in higher education in the late 1960s and 1970s marked the first growth of media studies as an interdisciplinary area of study at university level, and its subsequent introduction into schools as part of a liberal arts agenda, focusing on self-expression, creativity and deconstruction. By the early 1980s, structural analysis of the language of newspapers and advertising – for many years the vehicle for the teaching of language, bias and viewpoint – was supplemented by the regular use of film, popular television and advertising. Variety of and engagement with popular media forms were acknowledged features of good practice in English teaching, and student-centred optional media studies courses developed and moderated by teachers themselves proliferated in successful comprehensive schools.

But with the advent of the National Curriculum, the incorporation of media into the English programmes of study, and its development as a GCSE subject in the mid-1980s effectively neutralised its transformative potential as an agent of political and pedagogic change. Despite strong grassroots advocacy and government rhetoric arguing for learners' entitlement to a varied and inclusive curriculum, the limited references to media forms required to satisfy National Curriculum requirements failed to encourage moving image study; indeed, the focus on prescribed authors and specific literary forms led in practice to polarised perspectives, setting popular genres and forms in direct opposition to the canon of English literature. By the early 1990s the Tory government was explicitly exhorting teachers to reject the cultural relativism of a 'Chaucer and chips/Milton and MacDonalds' English curriculum that might span both literary heritage and popular culture. Subsequent developments within the National Strategy further marginalised mandatory requirements for media study to the status of conveniently avoidable and non-assessed tick-boxes.

By the dawn of the new millennium, the massive impact of emergent new digital technologies, New Labour's emphasis on the potential of ICT, and the economic demands of different stakeholders in the school curriculum could no longer be ignored. Since that time, the terms of debate have shifted to acknowledge the significance not only of the cultural and moral implications of the vast spectrum of multi-platform media and practices now on offer, but also of exploiting the increasingly complex technologies used to 'deliver' knowledge in schools.

The study of media texts within English has been shaped by a series of contradictory rationales which until recently have promoted a defensive attitude to media study. Crudely summarised, late twentieth-century English aimed (often reluctantly) to develop critical media reading skills as a way of protecting young learners from manipulation, bias and misinformation. It implied a range of ideas about discrimination, notions of value and quality, and often a focus on media effects and influences exemplified in 'dumbing down' discourses. While most teachers of early twenty-first-century English would now challenge these views, they still inform some assessment practice in English, particularly in the unimaginative and restrictive pairing of non-fiction and media texts in the new GCSE examinations, and the limited opportunities to create assesment tasks in media other than writing. They are also, perhaps, residual in the curiously abstract term 'multimodal texts' used across awarding bodies to signal the embrace of new digital and communicative technologies.

Studying texts: the same but different?

One of the defining features of the study of media in schools, both in the familiar location of English and as a specialised subject, is an explicit concern with an inclusive definition of literacy and the significance of all forms of text. This was drawn initially from academic models of media studies in higher education since the mid-1980s, and starts from four key assumptions which are partially shared, but not synonymous, with those underpinning English study.

1. *In its broadest sense, literacy encompasses all communicative texts – and they are all equally worthy of study*, whether in print, words, still or moving images, sound, or online form, across the entire spectrum of analogue and digital forms and genres. This inclusiveness has always been a central principle of media education, but has only been formally acknowledged in English since the 2003 publication of *English 21*, a discussion document designed to promote the development of a curriculum fit for the digital demands of the twenty-first century (www.literacytrust.org.uk/resources/practical_resources_info/1130_english_21-the_future_direction_of_the_curriculum_2005–2015). Questions of value are harder to address, but it is worth emphasising that media teaching at both GCSE and A level avoids prescribed texts or the notion of a textual canon of individual great works, and focuses instead on the language, conventions, representations and impact on audiences of broader genres.

2. *Texts are polysemic* – they can be read in multiple ways, and readers or audiences bring to them a range of different meanings. There is no one fixed 'right answer'; the act of reading is an active and social process. While best practice English teaching has always acknowledged this, the demands of the National Strategy and GCSE assessment have often tended to privilege specific linguistic meanings and interpretations; media studies, on the other hand, approaches meaning as the outcome of a triangular relationship between the text, its audiences/readers, and the producers and industries that created it.

3. Whatever form, genre, mode or platform, all texts are *constructs* that *represent* particular points of view; there is no such thing as a value-free or 'transparent' text. This idea is of course central to much of the English curriculum, in particular its traditional analytic focus on non-fiction, fact and opinion, the language of persuasion, and issues of bias. The emphasis for media studies has been to look

beyond the text itself to explore not only the technical ways in which points of view are constructed and the social and cultural factors influencing them, but also the economic and industrial forces at play. Thus the study of meaning in a news story across different news media might in conventional English explore the specific language and editorial conventions of each medium, while a media-focused approach would also question the visual impact of design, layout, sound and image, in the context of the broad political affiliation of the owner(s) of the text, the financial and regulatory constraints of the marketplace, and so on.

4. To become fully literate – the ultimate aim of both English and Media teaching – students need to become *both readers and writers* in the widest possible range of modes and text types; the writing or production of texts is as important, and as essential to understanding, as reading or analysis. This has to date marked perhaps the most significant variation between the ways media texts have been studied in English and in media studies. The English curriculum has since its inception consistently located understanding of the ways in which media texts produce meaning within programmes of study for reading; students are required to understand 'how meaning is created through the combination of words, images and sounds in multimodal texts' and 'how writers structure and organise different texts, including non-linear and multimodal'. However, apart from small-print exemplification of a range of text types, the programme of study for writing excludes any requirement for the creative production of media texts, whereas in media studies production skills and the ability to research, plan, construct and evaluate 'real' texts for 'real' audiences constitutes at least 50 per cent of the assessment process. There are of course historical and resourcing reasons for this difference, and many English departments – particularly those in specialist media arts schools or where media studies is already well-established as a Key Stage 4 option – offer students engaging and creative opportunities for simulations, paper-based work and production work. The revised curriculum of 2007, and the development of technology and the media as a cross-curricular dimension, apparently endorses such opportunities.

A question of concepts

While English draws on a range of literary concepts – genre, narrative, language, readership, and so on – these have tended to be implicit, and have only recently been addressed formally at A level within the structure of the newest specifications. Media studies approaches, however, have since the 1980s been explicitly constructed around an adaptable theoretical framework of key concepts, which inform all aspects of classroom practice and have been refined over time, albeit contentiously, to embrace the advent of digitisation, enormous changes in media technologies, and the ways audiences consume, produce and interact with them.

Specialist media studies courses at GCSE and A level are organised around a framework of four major concepts. The version of these reproduced below is one of many, and may already be familiar, but it is framed in questions that English teachers have found particularly helpful.

Media language

- *Meanings*. How do the media use different forms of language to convey ideas or meanings?
- *Conventions*. How do these uses of language become familiar and generally accepted?
- *Codes*. How are the grammatical 'rules' of the media established? What happens when they are broken?
- *Genres*. How do these conventions and codes operate in different types of media, such as news or horror?
- *Choices*. What are the effects of choosing certain forms of language, such as a particular type of camera shot?
- *Combinations*. How is meaning conveyed through the combination or sequencing of images, sounds or words?
- *Technologies*. How do technologies affect the meanings that can be created?

Media audiences

- *Targeting*. How are the media aimed at particular audiences? How do they try to appeal to them?
- *Address*. How do the media speak to audiences? What assumptions do media producers make about audiences?
- *Circulation*. How do media reach audiences? How do audiences know what is available?
- *Uses*. How do audiences use the media in their everyday lives? What are their habits and patterns of use?
- *Making sense*. How do audiences interpret media? What different meanings do they make?
- *Pleasures*. What pleasures do audiences gain from the media? What do they like or dislike?
- *Social differences*. What is the role of gender, social class, age and ethnic background in audience behaviour?

Media producers, industries, institutions

- *Technologies*. What technologies are used to produce and distribute media texts? What difference do they make to the product?
- *Professional practices*. Who makes media texts? Who does what, and how do they work together?
- *The industry*. Who owns the companies that buy and sell media? How do they make a profit?
- *Connections between media*. How do companies sell the same products across different media?

- *Regulation.* Who controls the production and distribution of media? Are there laws about this, and how effective are they?
- *Circulation and distribution.* How do texts reach their audiences? How much choice and control do audiences have?
- *Access and participation.* Whose voices are heard in the media? Whose are excluded, and why?

Media representations

- *Realism.* Is this text intended to be realistic? Why do some texts seem more realistic than others?
- *Truthfulness, accuracy.* How do the media claim to tell the truth about the world? How do they try to seem authentic?
- *Presence and absence.* What is included and excluded from the media world? Who speaks, and who is silenced?
- *Bias and objectivity.* Do media texts support particular views about the world? Do they suggest moral or political values?
- *Stereotyping.* How do the media represent particular social groups? Are those representations accurate?
- *Interpretations.* Why do audiences accept some media representations as true, or reject others as false?
- *Influences and effects.* Do media representations affect our views of particular social groups and issues? Do they influence our behaviour?

Adapted from Buckingham (2003)

M level: media concepts

Apply these concepts to a range of media and non-media texts, including moving image, online media and hand-held media. What different issues emerge and how can these be addressed in the classroom?

Joining up the concepts

There are, of course, limitations to this linear account of the key concepts and their key questions.

- These key concepts are interlinked and inseparable. To fully understand any media text, readers need to ask how its language, narrative, genre and effects have been constructed technically, by whom, under what constraints and for which audiences.
- Some concepts are easier to address – and more familiar to English teachers – than others. For example: exploring the institutional context of a media text and

evaluating its impact draws on cross-disciplinary approaches from sociology or economics; a hands-on exercise in constructing meaning through a web-based activity may require skills and confidence in ICT.

- There is no agreed hierarchy of knowledge about the key concepts. The general consensus is that media learning is recursive – a spiral curriculum. This makes planning for progression a particular issue.

There is increasing debate among media educators as to whether and how far these concepts remain fit for purpose when the role of the 'reader' or audience is changing so rapidly. Texts are now rarely read in isolation, but as part of a complex network of platforms and formats, which in turn are increasingly inseparable from the politics of media ownership. In the academic arena of media studies, the implications of Web 2.0 and beyond suggest a move away from the textual study of media language towards a greater focus on audiences, the ways they access, make sense of and interact with texts, and the social, cultural and economic contexts of these interactions. This may ultimately mark a real divergence from the text-focused and skills-based approaches of the traditional English curriculum.

However, what is clear is that until recently the concepts have proved a useful framework for the study of any text across any media form, and that they have been applied productively across all strands of the English programmes of study to enrich classroom activity and enhance student engagement and voice. This view is embodied in the increasing encouragement for multimodal study in the new GCSE specifications, which actively endorse cross-media work and in some cases actually require the comparison of texts across media in their assessment process. The following snapshots of classroom approaches, organised around the English programmes of study illustrate some of the ways in which this can happen.

Media and reading

By far the most common form of media activity used in most English classrooms is the use of film and television literary adaptations as light-touch introduction to difficult set texts, to whet the appetite, to provide short cuts through the narrative, and as the 'carrot' at the end of the reading process. All such approaches are valid and useful, but have a relatively narrow analytic function and focus predominantly on the use of media to access close study of language, characterisation and theme. Nevertheless, the space exists to make more of the media language and production values of literary adaptations, and increasingly teachers have learned to exploit them by:

- varying their use, alternating between different extracts from different eras and production styles;
- coupling them with modern re-versions of the text, including popular cinematic re-tellings such as *O* or *10 Things I Hate About You*;
- investigating them via ICT processes such as re-editing, annotation or using still frames to create photo-story sequences; and

- creating alternative soundtracks such as demotic translation of dialogue, subjective voice-overs or inner thoughts, or directors' commentaries justifying media techniques such as editing styles and shot-types.

Professional reflection: using adaptations

Adaptations for both TV and the big screen can be used at various points in the teaching of literary texts: before reading, after reading or alongside reading. What is your view of using such adaptations? What are the advantages and disadvantages of each of these? How are they likely to impact on student learning? How are they likely to affect students' engagement with both texts?

The summarised activities which follow incorporate strategies adapted from media studies practice to actively address some of the demands of the progammes of study for reading and of the English literature GCSE specifications.

What's so great about the great British literary heritage?

This sequence of work fulfils a wide range of reading objectives, with opportunities for lively group or individual speaking and listening assessment, and for the development of practical media skills. However, it also addresses wider issues such as the function of the literary heritage for the media, publishing, broadcasting and other cultural industries, and the impact of developments in media technologies on the ways in which audiences receive and interpret them.

Aims

To develop close reading skills around an extract from a set literary text and to explore:

- its meanings and interpretation over time and across media;
- the impact on the original text of adaptation from print to moving image; and
- the reasons for its relevance and cultural significance over time.

Activities

1. In small groups, students in role become researchers for a TV production company commissioning new drama adaptations from the English literary heritage. Using one or two accessible newspaper articles, they conduct simple research into recent adaptations in film and TV, and ideally some (very limited) audience research into the appeals of 'braces and bonnets' drama. Students can be prompted to think about why canonical literature is so frequently recycled, and what might be at stake for the media, cultural and tourist industries.

2. Groups are briefed, in role, to produce a new updated adaptation of the text, and a sample storyboard or camera script for one key moment or scene – preferably

one around which they may be writing as a controlled assessment task. Following a close reading of the original text, they produce a treatment and storyboard for the sequence, including consideration of camerawork, soundtrack, mise-en-scène, editing, appropriate casting and performance; these are presented to the class, with a rationale for their choices and interpretations of theme and characterisation. Versions are compared and evaluated, exploring close references to the language and structure of the original scene; they could go on to produce their extract digitally.

3. Students watch and critique several clips of the scene from a range of screen adaptations, preferably from silent cinema to the present day. Different groups in the class can compare different versions with their own treatments, and evaluate them in various ways, tracking such aspects as the media language of camera, sound and lighting; variations in mise-en-scène; and casting and performance, and its impact on the representation of themes and characterisation in the novel. Equally importantly, comparison of mise-en-scène and production style can help students 'read' the social and cultural context of the adaptation and its meanings for contemporary audiences

---

Inclusion: media production

In what ways does this kind of media production activity advantage a wide variety of learners? How does it help them engage with speaking and listening, reading and writing, for example?

Transforming Shakespeare

- To support the close study of a difficult Shakespeare scene, the text is poured into a word-cloud or similar software application which collapses it to identify key adjectives and recurrent nouns.

- On the basis of the outcome, you devise one or more fictitious products which are linked to the language and imagery specific to the scene.

- Students are now put in role as creative teams in an advertising agency, with a structured brief to produce an advertisement for the product, based on the original text.

- They storyboard an appropriately edited version of the text, construct a pack-shot which exemplifies the symbolic nature of the original imagery, select an appropriate music track and pitch their treatment in a persuasive presentation to their classmates, who will take on the role of account manager.

This very flexible and pleasurable activity can be adapted to use with a wide range of language-rich or difficult extracts including prose, poetry and non-fiction (newspaper features and editorials work particularly well). It can either form a 'light-touch' starter-type activity, or extend across one or more lessons for a more in-depth approach. It also offers a motivating and lively context for a speaking and listening assessment. And while the 'media' aspect of this role play is secondary to its analytic function, the process of adaptation from print to a visual moving image text invariably raises interesting questions of point of view and narrative structure.

Digital poetry activities

Creating a graphic poster-poem

In an ICT room or using laptops, students re-present the text of a poem in Word, using choice of size and style of font, colour, layout and use of white space to construct a visual representation of the significant elements of structure, rhythm, metre and imagery. These can then be printed out as A3 posters or A5 postcards, annotated, or wall-mounted for comparison and as study texts for other classes.

Creating a digital poem from a sequence of 'found' images

Students are provided with a diverse range of images – as hard copies, or in digital form – which reference literal or symbolic imagery in the poem. In pairs, students create their own audio reading of the poem, and select a synchronised sequence of images to illustrate their interpretation, as a slide-show of images using software such as Photo Story or iPhoto; if this is not possible, a cut-and paste storyboard will do. In comparing each different selection of images, students will actively engage in quite sophisticated analyses of their differing interpretations, and evaluate different readings. The process of anchoring the meaning of the verbal language with different types of image can also make concrete the differences between, say, metaphor or simile, and other techniques such as rhyme and metre. Equally importantly, the analytic experience will be active and therefore memorable.

Do-it-yourself digi-poems

Students can create their own digital image-bank, or, if resources are available, construct and edit a moving image video poem from scratch.

Creativity: try it yourself

Many of these ideas may be unfamiliar to you. Try out a selection of them for yourself. For each one, try to summarise the learning you believe students will be engaged in and the practical issues (or difficulties) you as a teacher will face. What issues does this raise in terms of developing your subject knowledge for teaching?

A TV or radio debate

- Students analyse clips from a current reality or factual entertainment show – preferably one which has provoked controversy in the press, for example on grounds of duty of care to participants, misleading editing, ethical issues, celebrity behaviour, intrusion, and so on. Talent TV shows or teen reality programmes are particularly useful examples.

- Students read and discuss a range of perspectives from the show's production team and psychologists, and blogs and chatroom responses from experts, former participants and viewers of various ages.

- In role as various interested parties (participants, parents, counsellors, critics, producers), they prepare and take part in a 'live' debate representing a range of different points of view on the issue.

- Hosted by the teacher, the debate is recorded, allowing students then to evaluate their own and others' performance and responses.

A public health campaign simulation

- Students study and evaluate a range of appropriate public information campaign material, including slogans, copy, imagery and construction of core health messages, drawing on skills of reading and image analysis.

- They analyse TV, print and online examples from a single topical controversial campaign – ideally one which has provoked outrage or a ruling from the Advertising Standards Authority – focusing on the representation of specific health appeals to different audiences, and the techniques used to create impact. They explore media coverage of the campaign and evidence of its effectiveness.

- Small groups each develop a treatment for a new campaign targeting particular audience demographics, in a range of online and terrestrial media.

- Each group formally presents its treatment, together with a rationale, visual aids, and evidence from an audience sample. They then compare their research, planning and branding strategies with a case study from the agency whose campaign they have previously analysed, thus relating their own experiences to those of the real world.

Into practice

How could some of these suggested approaches be adapted and applied in relation to a range of other issues and/or media text types? Spend some time playing with ideas for what you might do.

How real is reality TV talk?

- Students annotate a transcript of a very short extract from a presenter's introduction to a TV reality or talent show, and comment on its language features, tone and register.

- They listen to the extract from which it was transcribed, and evaluate the impact of voice, register, dialect, additional sound, and timing. They then watch the full extract, to see how the meaning of the spoken words is reinforced by body language, mise-en-scène, framing and camera shots, insert and cutaway extracts, and visual edits.

- They compare this scripted dialogue with further extracts of unscripted (but of course highly edited) talk from the participants in the show. They use their findings as the basis for a study of the various ways in which spoken language varies according to the range, demographic and functions of the speakers, and how it is mediated by the format of the show and its editing processes.

Writing and media

Despite increasing acknowledgement of the value of practical media production and its huge popularity with students, opportunities for large groups to 'write' in media in the English classroom are still rare. However, the cumulative use of low-tech activities such as storyboarding, developing treatments, screenplays, or sequences of 'found' images can act as powerful aide-memoires and prompts for structured writing activities which can help learners with more visual learning styles – and in particular boys – focus on issues such as point of view, creating a sense of place and atmosphere, and characterisation.

- *One-lesson production of short moving image texts, slide-shows or graphic texts, using ICT software*: these are good starting points for narrative and genre writing, particularly around perennially popular themes of horror, suspense or romance.
- *Extracts and themes from topical recent media genres* can act as the starting point for creative writing – for example extracts from *Criminal Justice* or *Skins*; soap storylines; dilemmas posed by TV news, reality or documentary coverage; screenplays; current media campaigns.
- *Ideas and narratives prompted by media technologies or genres* – include the mobile phone as deus ex machina; the virtual worlds of games; a science-fiction, historical, medical or crime narrative; a story told in text or chatroom-speak.

Making a still-image documentary

- Students analyse the impact and meanings created by a range of still digital images which represent different aspects of a contentious issue (e.g. fox-hunting, environmental issues, climate change or pollution).
- Using software such as PicturePower 3 or Photo Story, they sequence, crop and edit their images and draft a voice-over commentary which develops their argument; this is recorded, and evaluated by the class.
- The still-image movies they have produced become the scaffolding for a piece of creative or argument writing, depending on context.
- Using different banks of images, the same process can be used as the stimulus for poetry writing, or for narrative.

EAL: media and writing
Think carefully about the suggested writing activities. In what ways do you believe these could particularly assist the learning and engagement of students with EAL needs? Be as specific as possible in your thinking.

Writing from a short film

Students watch and deconstruct a short film narrative with an unexpected twist, told visually with limited dialogue. Using the visual images, themes and narrative structure of the film as a starting point, they can:

- create and refine their own narrative re-telling, told from the viewpoint of the protagonist, developing their own take on atmosphere, mood, tension and sense of place;
- script an alternative soundtrack for the film which amplifies or changes its meanings;
- construct a director's commentary;
- recreate the narrative in an entirely different format – for example as a factual news report, a poem, or a screenplay for another media genre;
- devise their own narrative with a twist, either in prose, as a treatment, or in script format;
- compare the film with another short on a similar theme, focusing on the film techniques of camera language, sound and editing, and on their different representations of character and voice; or
- re-edit the film to create an alternative narrative, and produce an evaluative commentary explaining their rationale and the impact of their decisions.

The way ahead: putting media at the heart of English?

The teaching approaches outlined in this chapter are based on the assumption that teaching and learning with and about the media are currently likely to be undertaken in most classrooms in a spirit of pragmatism; in the past, there has been little explicit reference to the media in assessment frameworks, and therefore limited encouragement for hard-pressed or sceptical teachers to develop innovative media approaches. Nevertheless, those committed to media education will continue to work within the limited openings afforded to offer their students a range of interesting texts and writing experiences across media. It has been argued that the most recent English curriculum has drawn extensively on concepts and practices adapted from media studies, and that a truly twenty-first-century curriculum should not only extend this relationship but indeed collapse the boundaries between the two subjects. Thus, just as the centrality of 'the text' as the core object of study is giving way in media studies to a greater focus on audiences and the processes of consumption and production, so too the skills and practices of English should perhaps place a greater premium on the reader, the institutional and cultural context of reading, and the ways meanings are circulated across media. David Buckingham (2003) proposes an inclusive concept-based English curriculum which addresses the economic operations and integration of the publishing industries; the 'branding' and marketing of writers and producers; the representation of social groups, themes, characterisation and ideas across different media; and the reading and writing habits of different audience groups – ideas similar to those outlined in the literary heritage simulation outlined earlier.

What might happen, however, if a media issue, debate or even technological plat-form was integrated horizontally as the focus of an entire course of English study over a term? Take the smartphone, for example – the perfect convergence of technology, communication, consumption, creativity and play. It yields opportunities to explore the key processes of reading and writing, and the different multi-modal functions of spoken language via text, email and social networking. It supports skills of informa-tion retrieval, Internet research, access to literature, news, institutional understand-ing, entertainment, shopping and any and every media genre. And it incorporates the creative possibilities of image capture, short-film-making, animation and game-play. It has generated rainforests of press coverage, news stories from celebrity scandals to phone-hacking, user-generated content documenting iconic moments of change, and controversies about its impact on the English language, on social behaviour, even on classroom practices. An entire English curriculum addressed through the explora-tion of a single hand-held device? Unlikely in the short-term future perhaps – but an interesting taste of the ways in which our currently compartmentalised programmes of study might need to adapt to the digital world in which our students communicate.

M level: further reading

- British Film Institute (2000) *Moving Images in the Classroom*. London: BFI.
- Burn, A. (n.d.) 'Media'. Available at www.ite.org.uk/ite_topics/media/001.html (accessed on 7 March 2011).
- Burn, A. and Durran, J. (2007) *Media Literacy in Schools: Practice, Production and Progression*. London: Paul Chapman.
- Burn, A. and Durrant, C. (2008) *Media Teaching*. Sheffield: NATE.

In summary

- Media studies is not the 'dumbed down' enemy of educational standards it is often portrayed to be.
- Media studies offers a highly theorised and conceptually challenging subject for study.
- Detailed study of the media sits logically within the English curriculum and enhances it.
- Students should be given a range of opportunities both to respond to and to produce media texts.

References

Barratt, A.J.B. (1998) *Audit of Media in English: A BFI Education Research Report*. London: BFI Publishing.

Buckingham, D. (2003) *Media Education: Literacy, Learning and Contemporary Culture*. Cambridge: Polity Press.

Hart, A. and Hicks, A. (2002) *Teaching Media in the English Curriculum*. London: Trentham Books.

Kirwan, T., Learmonth, A., Sayer, M. and Williams, R. (2003), *Mapping Media Literacy*. London: British Film Institute, BSC and ITC.

11

VICKY OBIED

Knowledge about language and multi-literacies

In this chapter you will consider

- theories of language development and what is meant by knowledge about language;
- the position of teaching and learning about language in English;
- ongoing discussions around Standard and non-Standard English usage in the English classroom;
- knowledge about language and pedagogical practices, particularly in relation to teaching grammar; and
- a pedagogy of multi-literacies and the kind of pedagogical practices that can support the language development of students with EAL.

Introduction

This area of English enters a highly contested arena because language(s) is part of our identity and reflects our shared cultures and histories (see Chapter 12 for an exploration of some of the other dimensions of culture and history). A teacher of English will have to grapple not only with complex questions of how individuals relate to language, but also with how language is learned and taught within mainstream classes. The initial question to raise is what is meant by knowledge about language.

You can start by exploring your own understanding of language and then conceptualise your ideas with a word or phrase. These metaphors could act as a stepping-off point for further discussion and reflection about language.

Creativity: metaphors to describe language

David Crystal (2009: 13) suggests a range of metaphors for language:

- a tool
- an instrument

- a mouthful of air
- an art
- a symphony
- a game
- a social force
- the autobiography of the human mind
- the house of being

Explore in as much detail as you can the elements of language that each metaphor suggests. Then invent your own metaphor for language and justify your choice of imagery. A central and complex question is where English language teaching positions itself in the curriculum. There has been an ongoing debate about how language should be studied in the classroom, and concerns have been raised about the separation of language and literature in English. Carter and McRae (1996) see such a separation as problematic, as this can tend to atomise learning, and advocate the interconnectedness of pedagogic practices at the interface between language and literature, and yet in many ways the curriculum separates the two.

Thinking about language

In developing knowledge about language at a deeper, more reflective level, it is useful to return to the principles of language development expounded by Vygotsky in *Thought and Language* (1986). Vygotsky drew on examples and analysis of literature to illustrate his understandings of the relationship between speech and thought. He put forward the very important premise that word meanings evolve and that the relation between thought and language is a living, dynamic process. His work helps teachers to understand that:

> the structure of speech does not simply mirror the structure of thought; that is why words cannot be put on thought like a ready-made garment. Thought undergoes many changes as it turns into speech. It does not merely find expression in speech; it finds its reality and form.
>
> (Vygotsky 1986: 219)

As a teacher of language, you will need to start exploring the subtleties of language usage and the thoughts that are hidden behind the words.

In continuing to explore the interconnectedness between language and literature pedagogies, you could reflect on the way that Patrick Ness has played with language in his young person's novel *The Knife of Never Letting Go* (2008). The characters can hear the inner speech or thoughts of all the other characters in the novel.

Into practice: *The Knife of Never Letting Go* (Patrick Ness)

Extract 1

There's just no such thing as silence. Not here, not nowhere. Not when yer asleep, not when yer by yerself, never.

I am Todd Hewitt, I think to myself with my eyes closed. *I am twelve years and twelve months old. I live in Prentisstown on New World. I will be a man in one month's time exactly.*

It's a trick Ben taught me to help settle my Noise. You close yer eyes and as clearly and calmly as you can you tell yerself who you are, cuz that's what gets lost in all that Noise.

(Ness 2008: 17)

Extract 2

Cuz as me the almost-man looks up into that town, I can hear the 146 men who remain. I can hear every ruddy last one of them. Their Noise washes down the hill like a flood let loose right at me, like a fire, like a monster the size of the sky come to get you cuz there's nowhere to run.

Here's what it's like. Here's what every minute of every day of my stupid, stinking life in this stupid, stinking town is like. Never mind plugging yer ears, it don't help at all.

(Ness 2008: 20)

Extract 3

And them's just the words, the voices talking and moaning and singing and crying. There's pictures, too, pictures that come to yer mind in a rush, no matter how much you don't want 'em, pictures of memories and fantasies and secrets and plans and lies, lies, lies.

(Ness 2008: 22)

Discuss the way Patrick Ness presents the inner speech or thoughts of the characters. How could you use this novel in the classroom to discuss some of the ways that language works? Arguably, the study of prose is an integral part of language learning, as the 'art of prose is close to a conception of languages as historically concrete and living things' (Bakhtin 1981: 331). Bakhtin argues that the novelist works with the living heteroglossia of language in a novel, its deep speech diversity, and talks about the multi-languagedness surrounding a novelist's own consciousness. Again, it is important to bear these arguments in mind when looking at how language is taught in the classroom.

M level: suggested readings

- Bakhtin, M. (1981) 'Heteroglossia in the novel', in *The Dialogic Imagination*. Austin, TX: University of Texas Press, 301–31.
- Vygotsky, L. (1986) 'Thought and word', in A. Kozulin (ed.), *Thought and Language*. Cambridge, MA: The MIT Press, 210–56.

How do you think Vygotsky's argument that 'the relation between thought and word is a living process' relates to the English classroom? How can Bakhtin's views on 'heteroglossia in the novel' inform your own teaching of the language of prose in the classroom?

The use of language

If we start to broaden the debate further to the study of living language, then as teachers of English you will be expected to develop students' understanding of spoken language in society and the range of new writing forms that is continually evolving. A useful starting point is to understand your own language habits and reflect on particular attitudes that you have towards language usage.

Professional reflection: your idiolect

Think about your own personal dialect and language habits:

- Do you have a favourite filler that you often use, e.g. 'well'?
- Do you have particular words for good and/or bad?
- Do you have particular words for feeling tired?
- Do you have words and phrases that you particularly like, and often use?
- Are there certain words and phrases that you avoid because you dislike or are offended by them?
- Are there certain words that you always have trouble pronouncing, or whose meaning you have trouble remembering?
- Do you have particular habits in conversation? (e.g. interrupting)
- What are your common body gestures when speaking or listening to someone?
- Do you have particular words for a local landmark or place you know well?
- Are there any family words or phrases that you use that wouldn't mean much to others?

Adapted from EMC 2010

What further areas of language use would you include in your idiolect? What influences on your language usage can you identify?

Historical perspectives

In reflecting on the learning and teaching of language within the English curriculum it will be important for you to further explore historical perspectives and understand the impact of particular government reports and policies on pedagogical practices in the classroom. It was the Bullock Report, significantly entitled *A Language for Life* (DES 1975), that first really emphasised the role of language in learning and viewed this relationship as a central concern for all teachers. PGCE students, particularly specialists in English, would all study aspects of language including:

- some knowledge of the nature of language;
- the functions of language;
- the relationship of language to thought;
- the relationship of language to learning;
- the acquisition of language;
- the development of language; and
- reading.

The report also focused on the needs of students with English as an additional language (EAL) who were learning to live in two or more languages or dialects. The Bullock Report (DES 1975: 285) insisted that:

> No child should be expected to cast off the language and culture of the home as he crosses the school threshold, nor to live and act as though school and home represent two totally separate and different cultures which have to be kept firmly apart.

This had a profound impact on the work of many teachers.

Standard and non-Standard dialects in the classroom

Support for language development of EAL learners will be considered later in this chapter, but the debate around the position of Standard and non-Standard dialects of English in the classroom is an important one to consider. Labov (1972) wrote about the logic of non-Standard English and hit out against the fallacies of the verbal deprivation theory. He counters the myth that most speech is ungrammatical by stating 'the highest percentage of well-formed sentences are found in casual speech, and working-class speakers use more well-formed sentences than middle-class speakers', and attacks the verbosity of Standard English where 'words take the place of thought, and nothing can be found behind them' (Labov 1972: 206). The linguist Randolph Quirk (1972) looked at the grammar, vocabulary and transmission of Standard English and talked about 'standards' rather than *a* standard. As you begin your career as a teacher, you should analyse a range of views on Standard English, dialects and accents, as well as the differences between them and the pedagogic demands they place on teachers.

The Standard dialect is often treated as the norm in schools because of its connection with literacy and the written form of the language. However, in the English classroom students will come across many examples of non-Standard English within literary texts and a variety of other language contexts. For example, writers use different varieties of English to identify their characters and locate them within particular places and cultures. Or, in exploring the new emphasis on spoken language (see Chapter 12), teachers of English may also consider the spoken word in the entertainment industry and in the political arena, analysing oral text to understand how language is adapted according to the method of communication. The National Curriculum (2007) also states that students should be taught about dialect differences, and this provides space within English to look critically at attitudes towards language varieties: 'if they know something about the history, structure and uses of English dialects, students as well as teachers can make up their own minds' (Cameron 2007: 113).

Implicit and explicit language knowledge

In developing your knowledge about language and pedagogical practices, it is also important to think about the distinction made between implicit and explicit conditions, processes and knowledge in language acquisition. Student teachers may be familiar with the debates around a generative perspective of language in which syntax cannot be learned explicitly; it can only be developed implicitly from the interaction of universal grammar – a central set of grammatical rules according to which language functions. This theoretical syntactical theory of universal grammar was at the heart of Chomsky's ideas on language and created a revolution in linguistics. However, these views of grammar have been challenged, and Reber (2009: 14) argues that 'the search for Universal Grammar has been a search for a will-o'-the-wisp. The models of generative grammar that have been produced are largely irrelevant to language as it is spoken and understood'. His argument is that we should focus on language as a communication system rather than sequences of words that follow some abstract 'grammar'. Nevertheless, it is important that English teachers are able to engage students in some explicit discussion of the components and functions of language.

This brings us to the debate around teaching grammar in the classroom and the kinds of knowledge that teachers of English need to acquire. Deborah Cameron in *The Teacher's Guide to Grammar* (2007) returns to the distinction between explicit and implicit knowledge about grammar. She argues convincingly that prescriptive grammar is not the best basis for understanding how language works, and that 'the descriptive study of grammar is about bringing the "real" rules to consciousness, so that they can be described systematically' (Cameron 2007: 8).

Professional reflection

- What is grammatical knowledge good for?
- What is the purpose of teaching grammar? Cameron (2007: 14) talks about the blurring of boundaries between descriptive and prescriptive approaches to language in the classroom, 'but for English teachers, exploiting the potential of the National Curriculum and making it their own is a challenge, which not infrequently they feel ill-equipped to meet because of their own lack of experience studying language'.

This is a frequently voiced concern raised by student teachers of English who enter the course with the typical preparation of an undergraduate degree in English literature and feel underprepared for teaching language in the English classroom, particularly grammar. Blake and Shortis (2010) report the majority of English literature graduates and ITE tutors citing the study of language, including grammatical description, as a major cause of anxiety, but also identify an inexplicable perception that English language graduates are unprepared in many ways to teach English.

Into practice: language knowledge

You may find it helpful at this point to explore your own knowledge of English language in order to (re)familiarise yourself with any gaps in your understanding.

The two main components of grammar are morphology and syntax, and teachers of English are often worried about developing a clear understanding of how to teach about the form and internal structure of words, and sentence structure. Attempts to teach grammar in isolation have a history of failure and most English teachers advocate an integrated approach to the study of language.

This veers back to the ideas of the anthropological linguist Dell Hymes, who focused on the importance of studying real-life examples of language, and language in context. Another influential voice in the development of pedagogical practices and approaches to language study in the mainstream English classroom has been Michael Halliday. He is particularly interested in the concept of functional grammar, studying language interaction in educational settings, and focusing on the critical discourse analysis of different text types. Norman Fairclough was also highly critical of linguists who studied language isolated from variations within communities and over time. He brought into sharp focus the relationship between language, power and ideology.

The teaching of language is intensely political, and teachers of English have to tread a careful path through the many misconceptions and beliefs about how language should be taught. Cameron (1995: 215) argues that

> Language-using is a social practice: what people think language is, or should be, makes a difference to the way they use it, and therefore to what it becomes.

The notion of language as a 'living thing', with teachers and students as active agents in a dynamic process, became lost in the moral panic for standards in the late 1980s. Advocating a prescriptive approach to teaching grammar ran against all educational research and practice, but this approach became metaphorically linked with tradition, authority and rules and started to gain false credence. The 'great grammar crusade' reached an unfathomable point when the teacher training materials, Language in the National Curriculum (LINC) – a set of innovative and contextually located language teaching resources – were stopped at publication and refused copyright.

According to Carter (1990), the aim of the LINC project was to enhance teachers' understanding and knowledge about language in relation to processes of teaching and learning. The assumption was that explicit knowledge about language can sharpen teachers' understanding of children's achievements and help them broaden language experiences for children in the classroom.

M level: knowledge about language

Consider each of the following views carefully.

- There can be no return to formalist, decontextualised classroom analysis of language, nor to the deficiency pedagogies on which such teaching is founded.
- Language study should start from what children can do, from their positive achievements with language and from the remarkable resources of implicit knowledge about language which all children possess.
- A rich experience of using language should generally *precede* conscious reflection on or analysis of language. Language study can influence use but development of the relationship between learning about language and learning how to use it is not a linear one but rather a recursive, cyclical and mutually informing relationship.
- Being more explicitly informed about the sources of attitudes to language, about its uses and misuses, about how language is used to manipulate and incapacitate, can *empower* students to see through language to the ways in which messages are mediated and ideologies encoded.
- Metalanguage should be introduced where appropriate to facilitate talking and thinking about language but children should be allowed to come to specialist terms as needed and in context.
- Teaching methodologies for KAL [knowledge about language] should promote experiential, exploratory and reflective encounters with language; transmissive methods are usually inappropriate for the study of language in schools.

(Carter 1990: 4)

Discuss the points made about language study and start to reflect on your own views of teaching knowledge about language. Think about your own experience of acquiring knowledge about language and how this has affected your own confidence and ability to teach grammar. After twenty years of a more prescriptive approach to teaching grammar, those who advocate an experiential view of language may once again be able to focus on some of the tenets put forward by Carter and his LINC project team. In the revised National Curriculum (2007) for England and Wales some space has been opened up for looking at social and cultural aspects of language structure and variation. Students need to learn about the ways in which language reflects identity, and consider language as a dynamic process that changes and develops over time. In the new English Language GCSE (2010), for example, the spoken language study creates opportunities for teachers and students to develop original resources and materials to study aspects of everyday speech and analyse language with reference to class, ethnicity and gender.

However, the 'grammar crusade' still lingers in the background, and there is a danger that the new 'functional skills' agenda will revert to prescriptive approaches to teaching grammar. The focus is once again on correctness, standards and levels of literacy, when there is far more to becoming a confident and effective language-user. In looking at students' writing and the progress that they make to become confident writers, to illustrate the point, Cameron (2007: 6) argues:

> weak writers do make grammar and spelling errors, but when these are corrected the result is often not much better, because the writer's real problem goes deeper: s/he has problems conveying meaning in written language or designing text to meet the needs of a reader.

Effective language use in speaking and writing is about more than simple functional accuracy; it is about communication.

M level: what is functional literacy?

Some key questions:

- How do we decide on an objective set of functional skills? Can language ever be socially neutral?
- How does one stipulate the parameters for functional literacy?
- How does one decide on a uniform set of standards?
- Is the ability to read a newspaper a functional task, or is it extra-/supra-functional? If we do decide that one must be able to read a newspaper in order to classify as functionally literate, which newspapers define the standard?
- Which social groups will the government consider as templates to decide what proficiencies are required for meaningful participation in social contexts?
- How does a policy maker create a uniform functional literacy programme considering disparate communities, workplaces and educational settings: the very different 'everyday life' of students?

Consider your response to each of these questions. Is the term 'functional' neutral? What do you think is the baseline for acceptable knowledge of English language?

Multi-literacies and EAL learners

In developing knowledge about language and pedagogical practices, teachers of English need to consider wider views of literacy. This was recognised by researchers in the field of language who introduced the term *multi-literacies* to represent both multi-modal and multi-lingual texts. A pedagogy of multi-literacies extends the idea and scope of literacy pedagogy to account for 'the multifarious cultures that interrelate and the plurality of texts that circulate' (Cazden *et al.* 1996: 61).

Multi-literacies pedagogy builds on the cultural and linguistic capital that students bring to schools and recognises the role of new technologies in developing students' language(s). Cummins (2006: 57) argues that a multi-literacies approach that attempts to incorporate students' language and culture into the curriculum is much more capable of including all students productively within the learning community.

This brings us to the question of teaching EAL students within mainstream English classes.

Many teachers at the end of their ITE course still feel underprepared for teaching EAL learners (TDA 2008a), and this has become a pressing concern now that most teachers of English encounter bilingual and even multi-lingual students within their classes. All the research now points to the beneficial effects of bi- and multilingualism and the interdependency between languages, but there is a lack of expertise within schools to implement inclusive language policies. There is a shortage of EAL specialists in schools and EAL training is viewed as a national priority (TDA 2008b).

EAL learners are a diverse and multi-faceted group of students who bring many rich and varied experiences to the English classroom. This again points to the importance of considering the cognitive, linguistic and cultural aspects of learning language(s), so that EAL students are challenged in the classroom and can draw on their personal resources as learners of other languages. There are certain misconceptions surrounding how the first-language needs of EAL learners can be met in mainstream classes. An interesting example is of an English ITE student on her first teaching practice who, when faced with a student newly arrived from Portugal, asked if she now needed to learn Portuguese to support him in the English classroom. This would probably prove an insurmountable task for even the most able linguist, as schools in inner-city areas could have over 240 different languages spoken by their students.

Into practice: preparing to work with EAL learners

- Arrange to shadow an EAL learner for the day and focus on the specific language demands of the curriculum.
- Meet the EAL co-ordinator in the school and find out about EAL support in English, partnership teaching, and first-language development.
- In developing differentiation strategies for EAL learners reflect on the central role of talk in learning and developing a language. In planning for working within such linguistically wealthy and diverse environments, teachers of English have a particular responsibility for language development, and it is therefore vital to have an understanding of EAL learners' progression in their first language. A very real danger for EAL learners is language attrition of their first language as they become immersed in English, thus losing the cognitive, linguistic and cultural benefits of bilingualism. English has many cognitive dimensions, many of which students can access in any language. Why, for example, should an EAL student not read *Macbeth* in translation in order to engage with the concepts of the play? And why should English teachers not, in their classrooms, work with the class on looking at ways in which different cultures present argument or debate?

In secondary schools, there has been a traditional divide between mainstream English teachers, EAL teachers, and modern foreign language (MFL) teachers in approaches to teaching language(s), and these artificial boundaries have prevented meaningful dialogues which could have significantly informed classroom practices. In creating conversations across these disciplines, teachers may be able to develop a more comprehensive language pedagogy for all students, but particularly EAL learners. In recent research in bilingualism and language pedagogy, Valdés (2004: 33) argues that EAL specialists need to 'open the discussions about academic language and discourse to the voices of the mainstream English profession and to invite them to solve the problem with us'. English teachers can also look at ways that MFL and EAL teachers support first-language development in languages other than English, and start to collaborate and work in tandem with colleagues to create possibilities for intercultural learning and a more creative and inclusive curriculum.

EAL: observing teaching and learning

Observe a range of colleagues working in a variety of subject areas, including specialist EAL lessons and MFL lessons. How do they create a rich language environment? How do they seek to support EAL learners in their use of English? In what ways and on which occasions do they allow EAL learners to use their first language?

Strategies for working with EAL learners

At this point it is interesting to reflect on strategies that have proved effective in developing the language of EAL learners. Pauline Gibbons in *Scaffolding Language, Scaffolding Learning* (2002) provides the most comprehensive guidance to teaching EAL learners in the mainstream classroom. Again, she draws on a theory of language which is based on the work of Michael Halliday, and the notion of a context of culture and context of situation. She talks about integrating language and content so that language abilities are developed in tandem with new curriculum knowledge. Promoting opportunities for structured classroom talk has been proven to be important for all students in the development of language, but it is essential for EAL learners.

In reflecting further on a multi-literacies approach in the English classroom, EAL learners at very different stages of language development can be given access to multi-modal and multi-lingual texts to develop their literacy. Creative ICT usage can extend learning environments beyond the physical constraints of the classroom and build bridges between languages and cultures (Becta 2004). ICT provides a rich array of resources that enables EAL learners to draw on their prior learning. However, as English teachers, you will need to ensure that ICT is not used as a substitute for classroom talk and that EAL learners are encouraged to work collaboratively with new technology.

ICT: EAL and ICT

- Access the National Association for Language Development in the Curriculum website www.naldic.org.uk/docs/resources/ICT.cfm and investigate how ICT is being used for EAL learners. Look at practice in your own school and find out how new multi-lingual technologies are being used to support English language learning.
- How can ICT be used creatively and collaboratively to support isolated EAL learners?

Although EAL learners could have exceptional linguistic talent and considerable cognitive ability, their skills may go unnoticed, particularly if they are placed in bottom sets in schools. This is both demotivating and unsatisfactory. In discussing English for gifted and talented students, Dean (2008: 84) explores an holistic view of identification and claims that a reasonable expectation of more able language users should be that they have an interest in language and a fascination about the ways it works in the many different circumstances it is employed.

London Gifted & Talented led a project, *Realising Equality and Achievement for Learners* (2006–09), which considered how to enable schools to develop identification processes that are more inclusive of gifted and talented EAL learners and to recognise students who use effective language learning strategies. Within English, advanced EAL learners who are identified as gifted and talented may show a particular responsiveness to language, but will require additional support in understanding and constructing texts where there are cultural differences. Many teachers in mainstream schools may themselves be advanced EAL learners and we can learn from their experiences as successful language learners and confident users of English as an additional language.

Inclusion: working with advanced EAL learners

The following excerpts are from interviews with two advanced EAL learners who both recently qualified as English teachers in London schools.

Italian-English bilingual student-teacher – four years in London

Interviewer: How can your bilingualism help you when you teach emergent bilinguals English?

Student-teacher: Well, it can definitely help me understand the way they structure sentences and also maybe translate in their own languages, but also think in their mentality, like culture-wise. For me, when I think in Italian I think in a completely different way. It mainly has to do with the structure of the sentence and associations of words.

Interviewer: What areas of English do you feel you still want to develop?

Student-teacher: Vocabulary. I just keep hearing people saying words that I know the meaning of, relating to that context, but I don't really use as much, not at all, so that's why I'm writing down one word every day I want to learn and I've got this book of words.

Spanish-English bilingual student-teacher – eleven years in London

Interviewer: How can your bilingualism help you when you teach emergent bilinguals English?

Student-teacher: It's probably, I'm more aware of how language is actually put together because I've had to, in my mind, formulate it. I've got a better grasp of grammar and I think I've probably found it easier than someone else when I was doing grammar, lexis, semantics and all that.

Interviewer: What areas of English do you feel you still want to develop?

Student-teacher: Well, I think my vocabulary, big time, that's probably my main area … I think vocabulary is the main issue.

Think about your own attitudes to and/or experience of bilingualism. Discuss the advanced EAL learners' knowledge about language. Reflect on the areas of language study that advanced EAL learners felt most anxious about in English. This debate around advanced EAL learners points to the metalinguistic awareness that these learners possess, and they are not concerned or anxious about English grammar (on the contrary they see this as one of their strengths), but it is a deeper knowledge of vocabulary that they wish to develop. Vasquez (2010) raises this issue of developing deep word knowledge for EAL learners, particularly those wanting to continue their academic study post-16. Valdés (2004: 33), working with EAL learners, argues that we must move beyond the acquisition of grammar and lexis, and contextualised and decontextualised language, and 'continue to struggle to make accessible to our second language students the textual worlds that are now beyond their reach'.

Conclusions

These reflections take us back to where we started – the argument about the fractious divide between decontextualised language study and the study of language rooted in a variety of texts, literary and non-literary – and how as English teachers you can help to bridge the divide or widen the chasm. You are in a position to observe and reflect on current practices of teaching language within your subject and develop your knowledge about teaching language in situated contexts. As Carter (1996: 15) argues:

the extent to which teachers choose to look both ways, and to encourage their students to do the same, may be the factor in determining how many students cross the road to linguistic and literary competence.

In summary

- Knowledge about language can be an exciting and creative area of study if language is viewed as a living dynamic process.
- Teaching language can be enriched through its interconnectedness with literature and other languages.
- Language is not neutral and needs to be studied in its social, political and cultural contexts.
- English teachers can develop ways to foster bi-dialectalism and bilingualism within the subject of English.
- It is essential to harness, not suppress, students' first language skills.

Recommended reading

- Cameron, D. (2007) *The Teacher's Guide to Grammar*. Oxford: Oxford University Press.
- Carter, R. (ed.) (1990) *Knowledge About Language and the Curriculum*. London: Hodder and Stoughton.
- Cazden, C., Cope, B., Fairclough, N., Gee, J., Kalantzis, M., Kress, G., Luke, A., Luke, C., Michaels, S. and Nakata, M. (1996) 'A pedagogy of multiliteracies: designing social futures', *Harvard Educational Review* 66:1: 60–92.
- Davies, N. and Lama, D. (2007) '"It's too slow. It doesn't make sense. I'll ask my friend to help – it's better!": Using e-translation in the classroom', *NALDIC Quarterly* 4:2: 33–8.
- Leung, C. and Creese, A. (2010) *English as an Additional Language*. London: Sage.
- Rassool, N. (2004) 'Sustaining linguistic diversity within the global cultural economy: issues of language rights and linguistic possibilities', *Comparative Education* 40:2: 199–214.
- www.coe.int/t/dg4/linguistic/langeduc/LE_PlatformIntro_en.asp – Council of Europe website: Language Policy Division, Languages in Education, Languages for Education.
- www.englishandmedia.co.uk – English & Media Centre.
- www.naldic.org.uk – National Association for Language Development in the Curriculum.

References

Bakhtin, M. (1981) *The Dialogic Imagination*. Austin, TX: University of Texas Press.

Becta (2004) 'Using ICT to support students who have English as an additional language: general guide for managers and all teachers', *Becta*, Version 1.0, 17 June 2004.

Blake, J. and Shortis, T. (2010). *Who's Prepared to Teach School English?* London: Committee for Linguistics in Education, King's College London.

Cameron, D. (1995) *Verbal Hygiene*. London and New York: Routledge.

Cameron, D. (2007) *The Teacher's Guide to Grammar*. Oxford: Oxford University Press.

Carter, R. (ed.) (1990) *Knowledge About Language and the Curriculum*. London: Hodder and Stoughton.

Carter, R. (1996) 'Look both ways before crossing: developments in the language and literature classroom', in R. Carter and J. McRae (eds), *Language, Literature and the Learner*. London and New York: Longman.

Carter, R. and McRae, J. (1996) *Language, Literature and the Learner*. London and New York: Longman.

Crystal, D. (2009) *Just a Phrase I'm Going Through*. London and New York: Routledge.

Cummins, J. (2006) 'Identity texts: the imaginative construction of self through multiliteracies pedagogy', in O. Garcia *et al.* (eds), *Imagining Multilingual Schools: Languages in Education and Glocalisation*. Clevedon: Multilingual Matters.

Dean, G. (2008) *English for Gifted and Talented Students*. London: Sage.

EMC (English and Media Centre) (2010) *Investigating Spoken Language*. London: English and Media Centre.

Gibbons, P. (2002) *Scaffolding Language, Scaffolding Learning*. Portsmouth, NH: Heinemann.

Labov, W. (1972) 'The logic of nonstandard English', in *Language in Education*. London: Routledge and Kegan Paul.

Leung, C. and Creese, A. (2010) *English as an Additional Language*. London: Sage.

Ness, P. (2008) *The Knife of Never Letting Go*. London: Walker Books.

Quirk, R. (1972) 'What is standard English?', in *Language in Education*. London: Routledge and Kegan Paul.

Reber, A. (2009) 'An epitaph for grammar', in *Implicit and Explicit Conditions, Processes, and Knowledge in SLA and Bilingualism*. Washington, DC: Georgetown University Press.

TDA (Training and Development Agency) (2008a) *Results of the Newly Qualified Teacher Survey 2008*, www.tda.gov.uk/training-provider/itt/data-surveys/~/media/resources/training-provider/data-surveys/nqt_survey_results_2008.pdf (accessed on 9 March 2011).

TDA (Training and Development Agency) (2008b) *TDA Business Plan*, www.tda.gov.uk/about/plans-policies-reports/policies/foi/~/media/resources/about/policies/business_plan_2008-13.pdf (accessed on 9 March 2011) .

Valdés, G. (2004) 'Between support and marginalisation: the development of academic language in linguistic minority children', in J. Brutt-Griffler and M. Varghese (eds), *Bilingualism and Language Pedagogy*. Clevedon: Multilingual Matters, 10–40.

Vasquez, M. (2010) 'Beyond key words', in C. Leung and A. Creese (eds), *English as an Additional Language*. London: Sage, 33–43.

Vygotsky, L. (1986) *Thought and Language*, ed. A. Kozulin. Cambridge, MA: The MIT Press.

12

RICHARD QUARSHIE
English and student diversity

In this chapter you will consider

- cultural diversity in its broad sense;
- the relationship between cultural diversity, teacher autonomy and student-centred learning;
- what your own 'culture' is; and
- a pedagogy that makes space for students' cultures in the classroom.

Introduction

In the final issue of *The English and Media Magazine* Jones (2002: 12) describes a project in which he was then engaged, looking at 'the production of school English' by English teachers. In his concluding remarks he mentions the 1993/94 boycott of national tests by English teachers, saying that:

> it provided a platform for an impassioned defence of 'good practice' against the Conservative government that was seen to be hostile towards *cultural diversity, teacher autonomy and student centred learning.* [My emphasis]

The three concepts he yokes together lie at the heart of what I want to write about here.

Cultural diversity

In 1948, 492 Jamaican migrants arrived on the *Empire Windrush*. I too am a colonial and a migrant, and arrived ten years later, from the Gold Coast Colony. In the sixty years or so since *Windrush*, this society has been transformed from one which saw itself as white and fundamentally monocultural to one which sees itself, with varying degrees of acceptance, as ethnically diverse. Given this transformation, it is not surprising that for many, 'cultural diversity' is more or less synonymous with 'ethnic diversity'. As I will discuss below, a common response, when trainee English teachers are asked to talk about their culture, is: I'm white and English so I don't have a culture. I want to use cultural diversity, however, in a broader sense.

Burns (2010: 21) proposes that

> diversity is a multi-faceted concept that can contain as many elements and levels of distinction as required. Work on the topic includes but is not limited to: age, ethnicity, class, gender, physical abilities/qualities, race, sexual orientation, religious status, educational background, geographical location, income, marital status, parental status and work experiences.

We need a view of diversity that is not rooted in the past but which allows us to embrace and accommodate fully the diversity to be encountered in the classroom. Tomlinson (2008) provides an authoritative and illuminating discussion of the complex and shifting perceptions of 'race' and differing educational responses to it during the period 1960–2007. There is not space here to do justice to her subtle and complex arguments. I will merely point to some key moments.

The 1960s emphasised 'assimilation', which was seen as absorption by the host society which would itself remain fundamentally unchanged, but with minorities abandoning their original cultures. In the 1970s, despite anti-immigrant legislation, there was a growing, if in some quarters grudging, acceptance of cultural pluralism. There was, however, no national consensus as to what education for such a society might be and there was often fierce debate between those who advocated teaching about different cultures and those who felt the emphasis should be on anti-racist education (Tomlinson 1990; Bonnett and Carrington 1996). The landmark Swann Report (DfES 1985) moved a step further in seeking to address the education of all children:

> We believe it is essential to change fundamentally the terms of the debate about the educational response to today's multiracial society and to look ahead to educating all children, from whatever ethnic group, to an understanding of the shared values of our society as a whole, as well as to an appreciation of the diversity of lifestyles and cultural, religious and linguistic backgrounds which make up the society and the wider world.
>
> (DfES 1985: para 1.4, 316 cited in Craft 1996: 3)

The murder of Stephen Lawrence in 1993 was a grim reminder of the persistence of virulent racism in some sectors of our society and the ensuing inquiry (the Macpherson Report, 1999) was an indictment of the mishandling of the investigation into his murder because of the institutional racism of the Metropolitan Police.

With particular regard to diversity and educational attainment, there has been a recent shifting of focus. In 2007 The Joseph Rowntree Foundation published *Tackling Low Educational Achievement* (Cassen and Kingdon 2007), which highlights a number of key points, the most important being:

- Nearly half of all low achievers are white British males.
- White British students on average – boys and girls – are more likely than other ethnic groups to persist in low achievement.

- Boys outnumber girls as low achievers by three to two.
- Chinese and Indian students are most successful in avoiding low achievement.
- Afro-Caribbean students are the least successful on average, though their results have been improving.
- Eligibility for free school meals is strongly associated with low achievement, but significantly more so for white British students than other ethnic groups.
- Not speaking English at home is typically a short-lived handicap: African and Asian students who experience it commonly recover by secondary school.

EAL: guidance on working with EAL students

While it is important to have a positive attitude to EAL learners, and the advantages that bilingualism can bring, it is also important to acknowledge the challenges that trying to meet the needs of all students can pose for the teacher, particularly in the absence of specialist in-class support.

Here are some excellent websites which deal clearly with the principles as well as the practicalities of teaching bilingual students.

- www.multiverse.ac.uk – Topics covered are: race and ethnicity, social class, religious diversity, bilingual and multi-lingual matters, refugees and asylum seekers, travellers and Roma. It also covers: key debates and ideas; legislation, policy and statistics; diverse communities; students' perceptions; ITE pedagogy; parents and communities. There is also an expanded glossary with definitions of commonly used terms in the field of diversity and achievement, articles and book chapters to download. (Sadly, the current contract for maintaining the site has ended and readers are strongly advised to download material, rather than read online.)
- www.naldic.org.uk – This is the site for the National Association for Language Development in the Curriculum. The association's aims are to provide a professional forum for the teaching and learning of EAL, raising the achievement of ethnic minority learners, and supporting bilingualism. The 'resources' link gives easy access to key documents. The ITTSEAL link takes you to the ITE section.
- www.emaonline.org.uk/ema – This site provides online support for ethnic minority attainment. There is a wonderful section on EAL and bilingual resources in nineteen languages.
- www.britkid.org – This site has a useful section on 'serious issues' which presents useful information very clearly, such as a chart of the main UK language and religious groups, the numbers of minority ethnic groups in Britain and where they live, and so on. And a section on 'teachers' stuff', which discusses how you might use Britkid as an educational tool.
- www.standards.dfes.gov.uk – This has links to work in the area of gender and achievement, ethnic minorities, and gifted and talented. The links and publications button under ethnic minorities brings up the important 'Aiming High' publications in pdf.

The need for schools to have effective practices and policies for teaching EAL students has not gone away, but while class, gender and ethnicity have a strong bearing on educational attainment, they cannot be seen in isolation from each other and interact in subtle and complex ways. We need a view of diversity, therefore, which does not limit itself to a focus just on gender or ethnicity or social class but allows the 'crosshatching' of all three.

M level: key reading

Read up on the differential effect of class, gender and ethnicity on student attainment.

- Cassen, R. and Kingdon, G. (2007) *Tackling Low Educational Achievement*. York: Joseph Rowntree Foundation. Available online at www.jrf.org.uk/publications/tackling-low-educational-achievement (accessed on 8 March 2011).
- Strand, S. (2010) 'Disadvantage, ethnicity, gender and attainment', in F. Demie and K. Lewis (eds), *White Working Class Achievement: A Study of Barriers to Learning in Schools*. London: Lambeth Children and Young People's Service, 11–32.
- Strand, S. (2011) 'The limits of social class in explaining ethnic gaps in educational attainment', *British Educational Research Journal* 37:2 (April), 197–229.

Teacher autonomy and students' culture

In 'Room of one's own: making space for English' (2002) Jones describes an initial investigation of the way in which English was 'enacted' or 'realised' in the classroom in the day-to-day work of teachers. He identifies two sets of related issues. One set of questions concerns English teachers' 'professional space' and the extent to which their autonomy has been diminished by government policy (see Chapter 4 for a fuller account of this). A second concerns the space for students' own cultures and how these connect to wider social movements. Jones (2002: 9) looks back to a time preceding the National Curriculum when, he suggests,

> 'culture' was not so much a management project as an uncertain space where the formal curriculum and procedures of the school encountered, and to varying extents negotiated with the cultures of students. The work of teachers, from this point of view, had an essentially cultural character and, to a significant – albeit minor – extent drew from the knowledge and identities created by social movements.

He cites as an example of this a conference on popular culture and education organised by the National Union of Teachers at the beginning of the 1960s. At this conference John Dixon had recommended work by teachers that was, Jones suggests, quite novel at the time, recognising that 'there exists not merely the sort of elite culture … but some different kind of culture which it is necessary to seek out by going into other people's experience' (2002: 11). Commemorating the work of the late Harold Rosen, Clements and Dixon (2009: 15) discuss the ground-breaking syllabus that Rosen wrote for the English department of Walworth School. They quote his opening statement of key principles:

The teaching of English at Walworth calls for a sympathetic understanding of the students' environment and temperament. Their language experience is acquired from their environment and from communication with the people who mean most to them. This highly localised language is likely to stand out in their own minds in strong contrast to the language experience being consciously presented in the framework of English lessons in particular, and school work in general. The contrast can too easily become a conflict; 'aversion to poshness' and affectation easily bedevils the teaching of English. Whatever language the students possess, it is this which must be built on rather than driven underground.

In order to start where the students are, and work, as it were, with the grain of their language and experience teachers had to 'set up a productive interaction between the language and experience of our students and a relevant selection of language and experience that we could progressively offer in response'.

(Clements and Dixon 2009: 15)

Clements and Dixon promote powerfully the principle of student-centred learning. But this is very far from the laissez-faire, anything-goes version that is often caricatured in the media. The teacher's role is to have a sympathetic understanding of where the students are coming from, literally and figuratively, and to build on their language and their experiences. The students' experiences and concerns are a guide to the teacher in choosing material that their students will find interesting, engaging and relevant to their experience. This material is offered, progressively, in response to what the students bring. A whole philosophy of education is encapsulated in these apparently simple words. The teacher will draw on her or his own experience of literature and language, as well as of life, to offer something that might engage the class.

The kind of happy match that can ensue between the students' interests and what the teacher selects to offer them is nicely illustrated by Burgess *et al.* (2002: 18):

a novel that imaginatively involves the readers and listeners acts as a powerful language model, and extends and refines their own use of language. The students are receptive to the structures and registers and conventions of the written language which will now be in the framework of their expectations in their own further reading; and their familiarity increases the range of possibilities for them to draw on in their own writing.

This is also part at least of what Jones means by 'improvisation' in which the teacher combines and orchestrates a wide range of resources (Jones 2002: 10). In order to be able to do this, two things are necessary:

• The teacher needs to know her or his students, and be genuinely interested in what interests them. As Clements and Dixon (2009: 16) put it, 'this meant we had to gain those students' trust in the quality of our interest and concern for the lives and neighbourhood – their culture'.

• Teachers need a measure of autonomy, pedagogic room for manoeuvre, to be able to exercise their judgement as to what they offer, progressively, in response to their students.

I am conscious of the fact that I am referring to ways of working that pre-date the launch of the National Curriculum, but I think that there is something valuable about these practices and about ways of working and interacting with students that risks being lost and that can perhaps be re-emphasised, certainly at Key Stage 3, now that the unlamented National Curriculum tests have been abolished. I pray in aid no less an authority than Ofsted. In June 2009 Ofsted published *English at the Crossroads*, a report based on evidence from inspections of English between 2005 and 2008 in 122 primary schools and 120 secondary schools. At a conference organised by LATE on 3 July 2010, Philip Jarrett, HMI, Subject Adviser for English, spoke to this report. What was striking in his discussion of what Ofsted considered an appropriate curriculum for English was his stress on distinctiveness. A department's curriculum, if it is to be judged 'outstanding', needs to have a particular stamp. In the best schools, students can see that English 'reaches out to them', that it relates to their lives. There is a negotiation of learning objectives, for example, with students involved in discussing and agreeing them. The reader will have noticed the similarity to the language used by Clements and Dixon earlier.

Making space for our cultures

Jones's article was the stimulus for work that I asked trainee teachers to undertake in October 2009. I wanted to explore with them how they might go about 'making a space' for children's own cultures within their classrooms. My normal way of working is to ask the trainees to do themselves what they might ask their students to do. I ask them to take on the role of students and to think themselves into their learners' minds. We then look critically and with a teacher's eye at the activities in which they have been engaged. After discussing the Jones article, I asked them each to make four PowerPoint slides representing their 'culture' in some way, and to present these. Some time later, they were asked to think back to their presentations and respond to two questions:

1. What did you think you were being asked to do? What sort of things did you decide to focus on?
2. What happened after you had heard and seen each other's presentations? In what ways, if any, did your views of your own culture, your colleagues' culture and your perception of the group as a whole change?

Professional reflection task: 'My culture'

Before reading on, in about four PowerPoint slides, try to represent your 'culture' in whatever ways seem best to you.

- What is the point of this activity?
- What sort of things did you decide to focus on?
- What did you learn in the course of doing this?

This was not designed in advance as a piece of research, but seeing the presentations one after the other, with their spoken commentaries, was fascinating and had a powerful effect on us all. I felt, in some way that I want to articulate, that something had happened to us as a group, and that our views of each other and of what we were about as tutor and trainee English teachers had changed. Drawing on some of the presentations and commentaries, I will attempt to explore and theorise what is involved in this kind of 'cultural making'. I want to explore the notion of culture not merely as something handed down but as something created and inclusive, with a transformative effect on the collective learning that goes on in the classroom.

The first point to be made is that all the presentations were listened to with rapt attention. There were differences in the formality with which they were presented – some were more tightly structured than others – but this was a collective experience that absorbed everyone. It seems invidious, therefore, to choose specific examples but I do this merely in order to illustrate some of the aspects of this collective experience.

Working out a cultural identity

Several students observed at the outset that they had not thought of having any particular culture. Nick says, 'My culture is non-existent, because Essex…'. He leaves his sentence trailing to good-humoured laughter but he is only half-joking, I think. John-Paul's opening slide states: 'I have never really thought of myself as having a culture but I suppose that I do'. Allison has found the task easier because she is from the USA and over here her difference is constantly reinforced:

> In my experiences, stepping out from your perceived culture and encountering the outside makes you appreciate the depth of your own culture. For instance, growing up in a largely Jewish area, I never thought there was anything special or different about being Jewish; I never thought about the culture tied to it … until I went to university in Baltimore, where very few people ever met anybody Jewish. Similarly, living in the UK has revealed my 'American-ness' to me. I never felt there was an American culture, and if I had to complete this project in New York, it certainly would have been much more self-conscious and apologetic that I didn't have a culture. Yet, friends here misinterpret my words and pronunciations; they don't know that a child's birthday party always involves pizza and that there are no school uniforms; they don't understand why food portions are so big or why we talk so fast or push so hard.

In other words, she defines herself through difference. Coming up against otherness invokes a kind of reflexive self-consciousness.

John-Paul has organised his presentation into four sections: one on his hometown, one on what being Irish meant to him, one on the culture that he was exposed to by his parents and finally one on the ambivalent and complicated relationship that Ireland has with British culture.

Lalage is English but grew up and went to school in France before attending university in the UK. Her presentation is organised according to the parts of the body:

'around my culture in various body parts'. She begins with an image of the Cerne Abbas giant (because her family originally came from Dorset), labelling hands, nose, mouth, feet, head and heart. The slides that follow illustrate a particular part of the body. For 'hands', for example, she is shown feeding a lamb on her parents' sheep farm in Normandy.

Matthew's, like many others, is organised according to places, people and passions. Images of Mull, Winchester, the Cotswolds and so on are succeeded by pictures of various doctors, missionaries, bishops and administrators, and the flags of the countries in which they served: Egypt, Sri Lanka, Pakistan, Nigeria, Tanzania: 'They served Britain abroad.' His passions include music from 'dead white European males' like Thomas Tallis and Richard Wagner, jazz, literary touchstones (not all dead, he notes) and art.

Orjan, who was born and brought up in Norway, has very little commentary in his presentation, which consists of montages of jazz musicians, books ranging from *Bleak House* to *Neuromancer* and Raymond Chandler, and a wide and eclectic range of films.

Many of the presenters say how difficult they found the task initially but how they enjoyed the process of trying to articulate and present their view of their own culture. The way in which Madalein has structured her presentation illustrates nicely this process of trying to answer a puzzling and difficult question and attempting a synthesis of disparate and sometimes conflicting influences. Madalein begins her presentation with a definition that draws a distinction between culture actions and conditioning elements of further action:

> culture consists of patterns, explicit and implicit, of and for behaviour ... ; culture systems may, on the one hand, be considered as products of action, and on the other as conditioning elements of further action.
>
> (Kroeber and Kluckhohn 1952)

The next slide shows 'culture actions' such as 'Hippies drinking wine; addressing The Issues'. The following slide shows 'conditioning elements': there are four images superimposed on a picture of a church, with a central quotation. The left-hand picture shows marchers on a demonstration, with one holding up the banner: Fight for London's services. The top right-hand corner has a poster of Rosie the Riveter, wearing her red and white dotted headscarf, with her sleeves rolled up, flexing her bicep, with the slogan: we can do it! Beneath this is a picture of Karl Marx and in the bottom left-hand corner is a picture of a young Madalein dressed in white at her first Communion. The quotation is from the introduction to Marx's *Critique of Hegel's Philosophy of Right*: 'religion is the sign of the oppressed creature, the sentiment of a heartless world, and the soul of soulless conditions. It is the opium of the people'.

Most people are familiar with the last sentence, which is generally taken as a contemptuous Marxist dismissal of religion. The longer quote, however, reveals a much more nuanced and sympathetic understanding of the role of religion in people's lives. One parent, she explains, is a Communist, the other a Catholic. Catholicism and Marxism have both had a strong influence in creating in her a sense of activism and service. By giving the quote in full, she creatively reconciles two very different family traditions.

Not everyone, however, is able to or wants to reconcile opposites in the way that Madalein does. John has called his presentation 'My cultural baggage'. His first slide sums this up:

> I was born and grew up in the Republic of Ireland ... 'the land of Saints and Scholars', a land of principled political and cultural independence ... or 'the old sow that eats her farrow', priest-ridden and depressed, where the best have always already left ... so my baggage felt pretty heavy to start with.

Thinking of travel, which has taken him to France, Aberdeen and the United States, leads him to the weight of the literal cultural baggage he carries with him, books: his favourite possessions. His final slide is a montage of shots of various bookcases in which three particular authors stand out: Milton's *Paradise Regained*, various texts by James Joyce and finally Albert Camus, on whom John has written a published book. His presentation has no spoken commentary by him at all, just the slides to a sound-track of 'Eclipse' from Pink Floyd's *Dark Side of the Moon*. My sense, though, is that while there may be 'confusions and complexities', as he puts it, in his metaphorical cultural baggage, he is happy with the literal baggage of the books he carries around with him, both physically and in his head. There is no need for him to have to choose between Milton, Camus or Joyce.

John-Paul, who is also Irish, has shown us images, among others, of Dundalk, Dromiskin, the H blocks, Patrick Kavanagh, a churchyard, place names and book titles in Gaelic, a game of hurling, *Where the Wild Things Are*, *The Hobbit*, Seamus Heaney, Marilyn Monroe reading James Joyce's *Ulysses*, the CND logo. His final slide, titled 'A "complicated relationship" with British culture', is particularly interesting. The BBC logo, covers of books by Roald Dahl and Enid Blyton, are juxtaposed to a Gaelic foot-ball player, a bowler hat (the headgear of Orangemen) painted with the colours of the Union Flag, and a photograph of a man protesting at Croke Park about 'foreign' games being played there. John-Paul points to this last picture and explains that Croke Park is the home of Irish sport, such as hurling and Gaelic football, as opposed to British and other foreign sport, such as rugby and association football, which are normally played at Lansdowne Road. While the Lansdowne Road stadium was being rebuilt, rugby and football were played at Croke Park, which gave rise to protests. 'The eagle-eyed among you will have noticed', he says with dry humour, 'that the man holding the placard "No to foreign games" is wearing a Celtic football shirt.' A complicated relationship to British culture, which, however, gives him insight into the complicated relationship that an English person may have with British culture also.

Matthew, to whose presentation I have already referred, on his final slide asks the question: Must these be mine? 'These' are: greed, under a picture of Margaret Thatcher; the Iraq war, under a picture of Tony Blair; utter, utter crassness above which is the front cover of some mindless celebrity magazine; the *Daily Mail*'s mast-head representing 'Middle England'; a photo of rioting football supporters and a pic-ture of someone sunbathing, above the caption 'The English Abroad'; and the BNP logo (crossed out). He answers his own question: 'I fear so ...'.

ICT: Multi-modal texts

- The original task merely asked for PowerPoint slides. How might you use other technologies – for example digital cameras, podcasts or film-editing software – to adapt the task to include other media, such as still or moving images, voice or music?
- The task was done individually. How might you approach this as a collective enterprise, to celebrate the cultures of the classroom, for example through the use of wikis?
- This activity also lends itself to reading as well as creating texts. When reading a comic or graphic novel, for example, how do the words and images interact? (Try reading a comic aloud for example!) A useful text here is: Kress and van Leeuwen 2006.

In the spoken commentary to accompany his slides, Matthew articulates this ambivalence. There is much about his cultural heritage and his family's traditions of which he feels justifiably proud. He is proud to be an Englishman whose family 'have served Britain abroad'. At the same time, to see himself as British is to be lumbered with a particular kind of 'cultural baggage' which he reviles but feels he cannot escape.

Another presentation is characterised by a similar ambivalence. Ellie stresses how difficult she found it to define her culture: 'I'm just English.' But there is real passion in what she says. She contrasts her pride in coming from Bradford, a city she finds beautiful, with her revulsion at the BNP, who in the popular mind are always linked with her home city. Her pride in her grandparents, who were born into great poverty, and the achievement of her brilliant, working-class father, who won a scholarship to Cambridge, is tempered by shame at the association of her home city with racist thuggery.

John-Paul comments sympathetically:

> I was particularly moved by the presentations that dealt with the difficulties faced by white English people in identifying a culture not tainted by jingoistic nationalism. It was a key moment in the group in that it helped us all to bond and resulted in an unspoken sense that we had collaborated on something special and unique.

Self-revelation

Pip, who has already worked out important things about her cultural identity, perhaps risked the most. She writes:

> For my culture presentation I decided to have a slide that 'commented' on my sexuality. I don't believe that you should be defined by your sexuality but I do believe that it has an impact. It certainly has had an impact on my politics, drinking venues, music and literary choices. This is why one of my slides had pictures of

Queer theory political texts, Soho bars, Tracy Chapman music and Sarah Waters'
books all set to the backdrop (just in case anyone missed the subtle clues) of a
rainbow.

I was particularly interested that she had chosen to 'comment' on her sexuality, as she
puts it. Her response is:

> Now I knew my class pretty well so I was comfortable with them and I knew that it
> wouldn't be a 'coming out' fest but a way of communicating an important piece of
> my culture. I never said (because I felt with the 'subtle clues' that I didn't need to)
> the words 'I am a lesbian'. I thought what I was projecting was pretty obvious. This
> is why it was particularly surprising when a fellow student and friend on viewing
> a later slide enquired if the young man on the photo that I was graduating with
> was my husband. Rather shocked but highly amused I replied '… I don't think
> you were concentrating on my presentation very well' which was met by a roar of
> laughter from the rest of the class.

The pre-condition, of course, for this kind of exploratory self-revelation is a safe environment. As a former PGCE trainee put it with pithy eloquence: 'I want my classroom
to be a place where it feels safe to think' (Hana Twebti, PGCE English, Institute of
Education 2001–02).

What all the presentations, of which these are a representative sample, have in
common is that each person is having to think of themselves as a cultural being, to
specify a cultural identity and to find a way of structuring and representing this to
themselves and to others in sound and images. This is a kind of autobiography, a process of self-definition, and the power of it lies in the fact that each person is starting, as it
were, from within rather than attempting to conform to some externally imposed label.
This is truly inclusive, therefore, because everyone has something to say about the
particular mix of influences that have helped make them who they are. We surprised
each other both in finding out things about each other but also in seeing unexpected
things we have in common.

This was also a collective enterprise. These multiple self-definitions helped define
the group as a whole and changed its sense of itself as a group. And, in so doing, this
led to a kind of reconfiguration of boundaries. For example Tas, a young woman of
Indian heritage, who wears a hijab, shares a passion for a certain kind of film with
Catherine, who is a young white woman from Essex. As Catherine says:

> I particularly found it interesting how myself and Tas found we have a shared love
> of extreme Asian cinema, mainly that of Korea. This was surprising and interest-
> ing as neither of us are from, or have any obvious cultural link to, Korea. Further,
> we are both of very different backgrounds on the surface, both religiously and cul-
> turally. This makes me pose the question as to how far we are born into a culture
> and how far we create our own culture?

The purpose of this activity, of course, was to explore in our tutor group what
would be involved in attempting such work with school students. John comments:

Even before seeing other presentations, I was struck by how valuable an exercise this might be in the classroom. This impression was confirmed when we met as a class to see one another's work. I feel that for it to be a really meaningful exercise in a classroom setting, it might require quite some time. As university graduates, we have had sufficient time and space to be able to untangle some of the confusions or complexities of our cultural identities, something our students, whose cultural identities are presumably similarly confused and complex, have not enjoyed. I can't say that viewing the presentations changed my perception of the group at all. It did, however, give me a sense of familiarity with the group which I think was of benefit in helping us to work together. This is also one of the reasons I think this exercise could be of great benefit in the classroom.

Into practice

- What do you currently do with your students that could lead into the exploration of the cultures of the class, for example work on identity or GCSE poetry?
- What guidance would you need to give in order to ensure that everyone feels that they have something to say?
- What preparatory work, if any, would you wish to do in order to 'untangle some of the confusions or complexities of our cultural identities', for example exploring the idea that an individual can belong to more than one cultural group?
- What pitfalls are there, for example inadvertently inviting students to promote a stereotype of their perceived culture?

The literature and other cultural artefacts to which the presentations make reference – whether it be Beckett, Shakespeare, science-fiction or lesbian vampire stories – exist 'out there', but in their varying ways the trainees had made them their own. Matthew quoted Dizzy Gillespie in his presentation – 'If you can hear it, it's yours' – and Matthew has indeed made Dizzy Gillespie his, along with Thomas Tallis and Wagner. The link between the music of these three is not any curriculum but Matthew's own tastes and experience – they reflect his particular personality. The task facing teachers is how to start with students' own experiences and to draw on the resources that our education and training have given us so that we can choose what to offer, progressively, in response in order to help them construct and shape their own identities. The last word goes to Swann (DfES 1985: 317):

all students should be given the knowledge and skills needed not only to contribute positively to shaping the future of British society, but also to determine their own individual identities, free from preconceived or imposed stereotypes of their 'place' in that society.

In summary

- Teachers can usefully spend time thinking about their own cultural history.
- Cultural history is a complex palimpsest of influences.
- Engaging with each others' personal cultures breeds understanding.
- Teachers should spend time engaging with students' cultural histories in order to think effectively about how best to work with them.

Further reading

- Jones, K. (2009) *Culture and Creative Learning: A Literature Review.* Newcastle: Creativity, Culture and Education. Available online at www.creativitycultureeducation. org (accessed on 8 March 2011).
- Kress, G. and van Leeuwen, T. (2006) *Reading Images: The Grammar of Visual Design.* London: Routledge.
- Williams, R. (2011) 'Culture is ordinary', in I. Szeman and T. Kaposy (eds), *Cultural Theory: An Anthology.* Oxford: Wiley-Blackwell.
- www.multiverse.ac.uk
- www.naldic.org.uk
- www.emaonline.org.uk/ema
- www.britkid.org
- www.standards.dfes.gov.uk

Acknowledgements

I want to thank all the members of my English tutor group at the University of East London 2009–10.

References

Bonnett, A. and Carrington, B. (1996) 'Construction of anti-racist education in Britain and Canada', *Comparative Education* 32:3: 271–88.

Burgess, T., Fox, C. and Goody, J. (2002) *'When the hurly burly's done': What's Worth Fighting for in English Education?* Sheffield: NATE.

Burns, T. (ed.) (2010) *Educating Teachers for Diversity: Meeting the Challenge.* Paris: OECD, Centre for Educational Research and Innovation.

Cassen, R. and Kingdon, G. (2007) *Tackling Low Educational Achievement.* York: Joseph Rowntree Foundation. Available online at www.jrf.org.uk/publications/tackling-low-educational-achievement (accessed on 8 March 2011).

Clements, S. and Dixon, J. (2009) 'Harold and Walworth', *Changing English* 16:1: 15– 23.

Craft, M. (ed.) (1996) *Teacher Education in Plural Societies.* London: Falmer Press.

DfES (1985) *Education for All (The Swann Report).* London: HMSO.

Jones, K. (2002) 'Room of one's own: making space for English', *The English & Media Magazine* 47: 8–12.

Kress, G. and van Leeuwen, T. (2006) *Reading Images: The Grammar of Visual Design*. London: Routledge.

Kroeber, A.L. and Kluckhohn, C. (1952) *Culture: A Critical Review of Concepts and Definitions*, Harvard University Peabody Museum of American Archeology and Ethnology Papers 47. Cambridge, MA: Harvard.

Tomlinson, S. (1990) *Multicultural Education in White Schools*. London: Batsford.

Tomlinson, S. (2008) *Race and Education: Policy and Politics in Britain*. Maidenhead: Open University Press.

13

GARY SNAPPER
Teaching post-16 English

In this chapter you will consider

- frameworks for the teaching of English in the sixth form;
- the relationships between English language and English literature in schools/ colleges and in universities;
- issues of progression from pre-16 to sixth form English and from sixth form to university English; and
- approaches to pedagogy, subject knowledge and curriculum design in sixth form English.

Introduction

The image of the inspirational teacher who fires up a class of students on the verge of adulthood with revolutionary and/or intellectual zeal, imbuing them with a passion for life and love of literature, is common currency; more often than not, it's an English teacher. The long-running *Times Educational Supplement* column 'My Best Teacher' testifies to this, and perhaps the most famous of all representations of teaching in popular culture – the film *Dead Poets Society* – provides a fictional analogue. Generations of English teachers have come to the profession – and many still do – motivated by the desire to pass on the love of literature which they developed in the sixth form, often through the offices of a particularly admired and charismatic A level English teacher (Goodwyn 2002).

Many students of English post-16 are (or quickly become) highly motivated, intellectually curious, and passionate about literature (and perhaps culture more generally), but teachers new to the subject at this level often express surprise that – given the element of subject and course choice that exists at this level – many do not seem to be; they quickly become aware that the relationship between teacher, student and subject can be more complex than that suggested by the popular scenario described above. Furthermore, radical developments in the discipline of literary studies, as well as the relatively recent introduction of the study of language post-16 as an alternative to literature, have challenged in different ways traditional notions of what it means to teach and learn English post-16.

This chapter, therefore, examines some of the issues facing students and teachers when engaging in English post-16 (whether A level, International Baccalaureate (IB) diploma or Scottish Highers), placing them particularly in the context of developments in thinking about post-16 English which have informed recent changes at A level (NATE 2007; Bleiman 2008). It also suggests a range of pedagogic approaches which might be employed to tackle some of those issues.

The landscape of post-16 English

The study of English literature has been at the heart of the English curriculum since the early days of the subject (Palmer 1965; Atherton 2005). The power of appropriately chosen literature to motivate young people, stimulate their imaginations, develop their linguistic skills, and act as a focus for them to consider significant personal, social and political issues is clear; for all these reasons, the study of literature remains one of the most enjoyable and rewarding aspects of the pre-16 English curriculum for most students and teachers. It is not surprising therefore that English literature is one of the most popular subjects at A level (in England, Wales and Northern Ireland) and remains central to Higher and Advanced Higher English (in Scotland). The particular value of literary study is also recognised in the IB, the post-16 programme which provides the most common alternative to A level and Highers; in the IB diploma, the literature of the student's first language is one of the six compulsory areas of study (Snapper 2008).

However, the landscape of post-16 English is more complex than such a sketch suggests. The most obvious complexity is that, at this stage, the English curriculum – at pre-16, a unified curriculum – splinters into two specialised fields – 'English literature' and 'English language' (as well as a third, hybrid, variation 'English language and literature'). The formal division of the discipline at this stage affirms the vital role that the study of English language has in the curriculum, despite the lack of provision for it in post-16 English until relatively recently (Scott 1989), and offers students alternative pathways in English – but also sets in motion a series of tensions relating to the nature of subject knowledge in English (NATE 2005). (Such tensions are not confined to post-16 English, of course: the nature and content of the pre-16 English curriculum has been hotly contested for many decades, and in particular the place of language study within it. However, this is the first point at which students have to choose which element of English to specialise in.)

Each of these pathways offers particular challenges to both teachers and students in terms of transition from secondary English. Post-16 English literature has at its centre explicit ideas about literary discourses, contexts and values which until this stage have mainly been only implicit in what 'English' is. The disjunction between secondary English and post-16 English language study is even greater, with A level English language constituting an almost entirely new subject – essentially a foundational linguistics course – quite different from the socio-textual study which dominates language work in pre-16 English (although it should be noted that, from 2010, a GCSE course in English language has been introduced – to complement the GCSE course in English literature – in an attempt to balance the language and literature elements of English pre-16). A level English language and literature, meanwhile, combines elements of both specialisms and might be seen as a foundational course in literary linguistics (Bleiman 1999).

Professional reflection: syllabuses and subject frameworks

A level, the IB and Scottish Highers offer separate and combined language and literature studies in a variety of ways. Research the various courses that are offered, and consider the implications of each for subject knowledge and content:

- A level offers three different courses – English literature, English language, and English language and literature (see subject criteria at www.ofqual.gov.uk).
- The IB will, from 2011, offer a language and literature course as an alternative to its literature course (further details of both courses at www.ibo.org).
- The Scottish Highers system (Higher and Advanced Higher) offers only one course – English – which combines elements of language and literature (further details at www.sqa.org.uk).

Additionally, consider to what extent drama, theatre studies and media studies post-16 courses might have common ground with English, and whether the frameworks of those subjects might provide useful reference points for English.

We see here signs that post-16 English is sandwiched, inevitably but not always comfortably, between secondary English – comprehensive, unified and generalist – and university English – largely fragmented into specialised sub-disciplines (in particular literary studies, linguistics, and cultural or media studies). This complex situation has implications not only for those involved in the transition between secondary and post-16 English, but also for those who go on to read English (in any of its guises) at university, and, in particular, for the crucial minority who complete the 'cycle' of English by training to become secondary English teachers and subsequently returning to school to teach tomorrow's teachers – transitions which raise further interesting questions about the relationship between the university discipline of English and its practice as a subject in schools and colleges.

During the 1960s and 1970s, radical changes took place in university English (though not uniformly across the whole sector) which challenged many of the principles upon which sixth form literary study in the twentieth century was based (Eaglestone 2000). The implications of those changes have only sporadically filtered through to schools and colleges since that time, but recent changes in post-16 English, at A level particularly, have recognised that this phase constitutes a vital bridge between school and university study, and that there is much to be gained if the model of the discipline which pertains in sixth forms and colleges is in step with that which pertains in universities.

M level: sixth form and university English

The question of the relationship between sixth form and university English has preoccupied several writers in recent years. The National Association for the Teaching of English (NATE), the English Subject Centre and the English Association have all published reports offering reflections and research on the transition (Barlow 2005; Green 2005a; Goddard and Beard 2007; Hodgson 2010), while a number of writers have argued for greater continuity between the phases (Atherton 2004; Green 2005b; Atherton 2006; Snapper 2006; Atherton 2007; Green 2007; Hodgson 2007; Snapper 2007a, 2007b; Snapper 2009; Green 2010; Jacobs 2010).

After reading some of this material, consider the following questions:

· What are the implications for pedagogy and curriculum in sixth form English of the issues raised?

· To what extent can sixth form English *both* prepare students effectively for assessment and certification *and* accommodate a broader conception of the subject that prepares students for university?

· How might your school make use of a local university to address some of these issues?

One of the most far-reaching changes in university English in the latter part of the twentieth century was the development of departments of English language, of linguistics and of cultural studies. These new disciplines did not only assert the value of language and culture (defined broadly) as fields of knowledge which could produce critical and cultural discourses as worthy as that associated with literary study, they also questioned conventional ideas about the nature of literary language and values, particularly dominant ideas about the moral-aesthetic superiority of the literary canon – establishing the fundamental discourses of literary theory, which, in their turn, began to transform the work of departments of English literature.

The earliest manifestation of these developments in sixth forms was the introduction of A levels in communication, and, later, English language. English literature has been slow to change, but we can trace, to a great extent, the origins of discourses about literary genre, narrative, representation, value, consumption, production, interpretation, and so on, to the influence of linguistics, cultural studies and literary theory – discourses which have only recently begun to shape post-16 literary study in any systematic way.

Teaching post-16 English literature

Defining the discipline

As suggested above, the thrust of recent developments in the teaching of literature post-16 is towards a model which prepares students for the kind of work they are likely to encounter at university (whether they are to read English or another subject). Such a model seeks to move, on the one hand, away from the atomistic study and assessment of set texts (which has often characterised A Level courses in the past) towards the study of literary genres, periods, themes, movements, concepts and theories, and, on the other hand, from naive personal or heavily teacher-directed response to informed, critical, personal response which shows awareness of the roles of reader and writer in the creation of meaning, of the significance of context in understanding those roles, and of the function of literary criticism in debating the meaning and value of literary representations. It also seeks to foster the ability of the student to apply certain principles of literary criticism and theory independently, through choosing their own texts and topics to read, research and write about.

This may sound like a tall order – more like the description of what a university student should be able to do, and in many ways radically different from the appreciative *explication* of literary texts generally produced at earlier stages. But it is worth bearing in mind certain key points:

- Many subjects in their post-16 manifestations – for instance, English language, history, psychology and sociology – have a sustained emphasis (arguably considerably more so than in English literature) on research, theories and concepts, supported by concentrated study of secondary as well as primary texts – so students are likely to be familiar with such approaches.

- All university study is predicated on developing a grasp of the discipline's epistemological frameworks and parameters, and applying those frameworks to a range of texts and topics – so students stand to benefit from such approaches at A level.

- Students are often helped by having a conceptual framework by which they can understand what they are encountering – for instance a knowledge of genre; an understanding of the function of criticism; awareness of debates about literary value. Without such frameworks, however crude, there is the possibility that their awareness of the parameters of the subject may be unhelpfully circumscribed.

- Many students at post-16 (at all levels of ability) are keen to engage in broad questions about the nature, purpose and applications of the study they are engaged in – a set of questions which has often in the past risked neglect in literary study. As Eaglestone (2000) points out, in many respects 18-year-olds are natural theorists, wanting to test the boundaries of what they encounter.

Creativity: concepts, theories and debates

Learning in English literature has traditionally been organised almost exclusively around the detailed study of set texts, rather than literary concepts and theories, or debates about literary purposes and values. Consider the following questions:

- If you were given free rein to design a literature syllabus, what would it include and how might it be structured?
- If you were given the task of designing a new style of literature syllabus, organised around concepts, theories and debates, what might it include? What might be the advantages and disadvantages of such a syllabus?
- To what extent can some of these concepts, theories and debates be addressed through existing syllabuses?

Managing transitions

Of course, it is vital to remember that a progressive and ambitious curriculum such as this must be supported by pedagogy which clarifies rather than mystifies, and engages rather than dictates, especially given the often very mixed classes (in terms of ability, cultural background and learning styles) which post-16 teachers are likely to encounter; most importantly, whatever the eventual aim of such a curriculum, its starting point must be what students already know and can do, and its route must build gradually on that starting point, enlisting the active comprehension of students at every stage (Green 2005a; Snapper 2009).

What students already know and can do when they start post-16 English varies, of course, but certain general principles are likely to pertain. First, in relation to coverage, they are likely to have studied:

- the text of at least one Shakespeare play in some detail, and at least one in less detail (in England, one play at Key Stage 3 and one at Key Stage 4 are compulsory);
- a range of relatively accessible modern and 'classic' short poems and stories, including texts (especially poems) from a number of 'different cultures and traditions';
- at least one 'classic' novel – nineteenth or twentieth century (often by a modern writer such as Steinbeck or Orwell) – and one modern play (perhaps by Arthur Miller or J.B. Priestley);
- a range of high-quality children's literature;
- if studying in Wales, Northern Ireland or Scotland, a range of national literature.

Second, in relation to response:

- In the earlier stages of the secondary school, they are likely to have had considerable experience of writing imaginative responses to the range of literature they have studied in the form of textual interventions (extra chapters or verses; letters, diaries, etc., in the voice of characters; and so on) and transformations (poem or prose fiction to film script, and so on), or in the form of their own original writing.
- Later, there is likely to have been a greater emphasis on analytical responses, in essay form, to works from the literary heritage.
- They may have been introduced to some aspects of poetic and dramatic verse form, and are likely to be to some extent familiar with aspects of figurative language (simile, metaphor, etc.) and rhetorical device (questions, exclamations, etc.).

Although this, in many respects, constitutes a rich experience, the demands of post-16 literary study are considerable, and will inevitably cause many students difficulties. The following are common problems encountered at the beginning of a post-16 literature course:

- The independent reading load is difficult for some – both the amount of reading, and the type of reading. Some students find the independent reading of long Victorian novels (Brontë, Dickens, etc.) or even contemporary classics (Atwood, McEwan, etc.) demanding. Where students are studying pre-twentieth-century literature, in particular, there are issues for many in relation to grasp of language and allusion. Some struggle with the demands of close textual analysis of a whole Shakespeare play where much has to be done without immediate teacher guidance.

- Many students lack a confident vocabulary for describing aspects of literary language, form and genre, and of the craft and motivation of the writer, as well as for understanding the relative roles of writer and reader in making meaning.

- Poetry often causes problems because of students' relative unfamiliarity with the form in their own personal reading lives, and the consequent difficulty many have in grasping the purposes and pleasures of literary verse. Where poems have been studied for exams in pre-16 courses, there is a tendency for students to have 'learned' interpretations mechanically without fully engaging in the nature of the text's ambiguities or aesthetic effects.

- In essay writing, many students need to develop more confidence (a) in establishing and structuring argument without teacher scaffolding and (b) in formulating responses which are individual and personal and yet informed and critical (in other words, responses which are not 'spoon-fed' in one way or another, but are the result of confident assimilation by the student).

Into practice: planning for progression in literature

For each of the following areas, what strategies might you advise a teacher to adopt early in a sixth form course to help students to progress from pre-16 study?

- independent reading of long novels
- understanding of Shakespeare's language
- development of critical terminology
- understanding the craft and motivation of the writer
- interpreting poetry
- developing independent essay writing skills

Whatever problems may arise, however, it's vital to keep in mind that connections can and must be made with what students do have: not only their rich experience of literature and language from pre-16 English, but also, crucially, a range of personal experiences and enthusiasms in reading and culture more generally – from 'airport' fiction to teenage novels, from pop lyrics to computer games, from blockbuster movies to soap opera, as well as, for many, more 'highbrow' drama, film, music and literature. All of these can provide a fund of resources to draw on in the teaching of literary concepts and methods.

ICT: using media and ICT in literature

As suggested above, students' own enthusiasms for a range of media and multi-modal texts, often (though not always) in the realm of popular culture, can be drawn on to engage them in literary study.

- Consider how ICT and media texts might be used to support the teaching of: poetry, drama, the novel, imagery, narrative, genre, argument.
- What uses might be made in post-16 literature teaching of: music, film, television, theatre, computer games, blockbuster novels, graphic novels, blogs?

Developing subject knowledge

Perhaps surprisingly, emerging – as most English teachers do – from the study of literature at university does not automatically equip one with all the subject knowledge required to teach literature at this level (see discussion of subject knowledge for teaching in Chapter 2). Indeed, many literature teachers testify to the fact that one of the pleasures of teaching post-16 literature is continuing to learn, and that learning through teaching can sometimes be more profound than learning through university study.

Of course, part of this additional learning is concerned with texts – teaching texts which one hasn't studied or even perhaps read previously before (contemporary drama, poetry and fiction, often, but also gaps in one's 'classic' reading); this increases confidence in one's ability to transfer the methods of literary analysis and investigation from one area of study to another, while broadening one's coverage. (The IB programme contains an additional challenge, and pleasure, in that one unit of the course is 'world literature' – literature in translation. It's also possible to teach some literature in translation in A level literature courses.)

Another area of additional learning, and perhaps a more profound one, is concerned with frameworks and concepts. University learning is by its nature (and like many other kinds of learning) often fragmented, non-linear, and one often has the sense that the bigger picture is elusive, perhaps only understood by the lecturer. Becoming a teacher forces one to get to grips with that bigger picture, to piece together the patchwork – poetic form, narrative voice and structure, literary genre and mode, the origins of verse and the rise of the novel, the nature of literary language, production and consumption, representation, processes of interpretation, and so on. The more one teaches, the more one learns how texts are connected – especially if one strives to teach about literature through set texts, rather than simply about set texts.

Thus, one can begin to mediate rather than simply deliver the syllabus, to shape it in ways that make it make sense both to oneself and one's students, both through one's subject knowledge and through one's ability to communicate that knowledge through appropriate pedagogy. And of course it's important to keep reading both primary and secondary texts oneself – though time is inevitably often limited for such preparation, and access to libraries often impossible. Nevertheless, there are many resources available to help – volumes of literary criticism, of course, but also the vast resources of the Internet and the many advanced level text books, study guides and introductions that are available – not to mention newspapers, journals, TV and radio.

Approaching pedagogy and curriculum

Above, I have spoken of the need to teach about literature rather than simply about set texts. This idea – although it has always been a feature of good post-16 literature teaching – has not always been clearly enshrined in the way that syllabuses and assessment programmes have been constructed, but now lies at the heart of the current A level specifications (which began to be taught in 2008), and has for a long time been central to some aspects of the IB literature programme. In these syllabuses, which have gone some way towards recognising the ways in which syllabuses have sometimes in the past tended to circumscribe or narrow learning, there is a strong element of comparative study, and an emphasis on understanding concepts such as form, genre and narrative, and their manifestations in different periods. An increased concern with context, interpretation and theory also signals the importance of enabling students to see texts as more than simply the content of literature courses – and poems in particular as puzzles to be solved in exams – but rather as works of art that have had (and still have) a life outside the classroom.

The crucial challenge of these syllabuses is to teach set texts in the context of broader literary concepts, frameworks and debates. For instance, the class might prepare (fairly succinctly, for there is rarely much leeway in terms of time) for each set text by reading a range of related short texts or extracts in order to introduce or rehearse some of the broader concepts which will be the focus of the set text study. As an example, one might prepare for a reading of selected poems by Auden by introducing students briefly to a range of modernist poetry and art designed to highlight the features and interpretive processes of modernism; students will then better be able to understand the ways in which Auden uses and adapts modernist principles in his verse.

A range of appropriate pedagogic devices enhances such a strategy further. For instance, groups of students could be given two or three poems by different modernist poets and asked to work in groups to decide what, if anything, connects these poems stylistically and/or thematically; each group could then be given responsibility for presenting ideas about one or more of the poems to the rest of the class. Such devices make learning active, building confidence and independence in students; they also help to confirm that the teacher is not the sole interpretive authority, while enabling the teacher to draw together and direct the discussion that takes place. Table 13.1 develops this point by suggesting a range of pedagogic strategies for stimulating broad ideas about literature and literary texts, and for building students' knowledge, confidence and independence in literary study.

Creativity: active and creative approaches to texts
Design an approach to teaching the poetry of Auden, or another modernist poet, using a range of text types, media, and classroom activities. Ensure that you make links between the poems set for study, Auden's life and work more generally, and broader literary or cultural concepts such as modernism and poetic form.

Table 13.1 Approaches to post-16 English literature

Text and context	• Set the study of individual texts in the context of the study of literature generally: teach about 'poetry', 'drama' and 'the novel'/'the short story' rather than just individual texts. • Combine the study of individual texts with the wider study of genre, form and theme. Use a wide variety of extracts from a range of periods, genres and forms to set individual texts in the context of literary and cultural history. • Draw on texts from popular culture as well as high culture, and use a variety of media and text types in teaching. • Stress the idea that all texts are context-bound *representations* of reality that can be challenged.
Values and theory	• Be aware of the cultural tensions surrounding notions of pleasure, appreciation, study, response and creativity: students engaged in literary study may not straightforwardly value, like or 'appreciate' the literature chosen for study, so they need to be engaged in, for example, socio-cultural and creative as well as aesthetic responses. • Choose some texts which raise interesting issues about the nature of literature, and which play with language and ideas in a challenging way. • Introduce aesthetic, social, political and cultural issues relating to literature – for instance the definition, value and status of literature in society, the relationship between *reading* and *studying* literature, the ways in which the value of literature can be questioned, the role of literature in education, the ways in which political positions can influence readings and values.
Production and consumption	• Build in students' own creative writing and/or transformation of or intervention into texts so that they experience the process of creativity from the point of view of the writer, and to increase understanding of form, style and genre. • Encourage students to understand the motivations of both writers and readers, and the processes of production, consumption, reception and interpretation. • Build students' awareness of the life that texts have *outside* the classroom and for readers other than themselves in different times and places. • Encourage students to experience and discuss current literary culture – theatre, book prizes, debates, poetry performance, reviews, and so on.
Reading and response	• Vary methods of reading and response. Encourage independent learning by trying to avoid 'ploughing through' texts chapter by chapter. Give students responsibility for reading set novels over a period of time, preparing poems for class discussion, or taking the role of director in the analysis of specific scenes of plays.

Table 13.1 *(continued)*

	• Sometimes discuss texts as whole entities, and then set assignments which allow students to apply what they have learnt about the text as a whole to sections of the text, moving from wide to close reading. At other times, work in detail on close reading before asking students to apply ideas covered to wider reading. • Introduce students regularly to accessible literary criticism, providing opportunities to discuss such secondary texts in class.
Course planning	• Plan the course carefully to make effective use of time: break up the study of individual texts with short introductory, synoptic or extension modules. • Keep study concentrated and dynamic so that knowledge gained can be transferred from one text or topic to another and does not merely 'stay' in one context. • Plan to bring together a range of issues about the relationship between literature and society, and the function of different genres, forms and styles within it.
Literature and English studies	• Make students aware of the broader network of studies of which literary studies is part by making connections with elements of linguistic and cultural studies.

Teaching post-16 English language

Defining the discipline

As suggested above, recent approaches to the post-16 literature curriculum, emphasising concepts such as narrative and genre, and production and reception, have been strongly influenced by the development of linguistic and literary theory in recent decades, and to some extent also by the subsequent development of A level English language.

A level English language, developing from a very different starting point from that of post-16 literary study, has always set out to teach students a set of foundational concepts and theories, and to apply these to a range of texts and situations. At the core of this approach has been the idea of the interrogation of language data taken from life and literature, with a strong emphasis on the nature of spoken and non-literary language, sometimes as part of independent language investigations by students, in which students themselves collect the data which they are to interrogate.

As with English literature, a major concern in the teaching of English language post-16 is to prepare students adequately for the kind of work they are likely to encounter at university. In many respects, with its emphasis on individual investigation and the application of concepts and frameworks to data, English language at this level provides an excellent preparation for university study in general, and a solid grounding for further language study specifically. Even so, debates take place about the extent to which the A level language course is adequately aligned with the specialist content of university language courses (Goddard and Beard 2007), and in particular with linguistics courses. At present, the chief routes to studying linguistics at university are English language and modern languages – neither of which prepares students particularly well for a broader scientific study of the phenomenon of language. A fascinating A level course in linguistics has been mooted and elements of it trialled, but it remains unclear whether such a project is viable (Hudson 2007).

Managing transitions

Once again, it's necessary to approach the development of such disciplinary knowledge and methods with adequate pedagogic care, always starting with what students already know and can do. The pre-16 English curriculum has never been as specific about the elements of language to be covered as about the elements of literature; nor has it generally ventured explicitly into elements of linguistics such as grammar or language acquisition. Pre-16 English language is largely concerned with the effective practice of reading and writing, rather than learning about language as a subject in its own right. Most students therefore start post-16 English language with only a very sketchy knowledge and awareness of the nature of the subject; indeed, it is not uncommon for students to believe that they are beginning something akin to a creative writing course rather than formal linguistic study.

The experience in English language study of most students starting post-16 English is likely to consist of:

- analysis and production of 'original writing' (fictional, poetic and/or personal), supported by some study of the elements that make such writing effective, such as description and imagery, rhetorical devices and structures, varied sentence lengths, or speech; and

- analysis and production of simple print media and/or non-literary texts (newspaper articles, advertisements, letters, etc.) supported by some study of the elements that make such writing effective, such as persuasion; use of fact and opinion; rhetorical devices and structures; speech; or headings, captions and other presentational devices.

In addition, many students will, at some point, have learned about:

- elements of dialect and idiolect, such as national, regional and class variation in speech; Standard English and the difference between spoken and written English; features such as slang and jargon. (From 2012, students entering post-16 study who have taken the new GCSE English language (first taught from 2010) will have studied some or all of these features as part of their study of aspects of spoken English. This is likely to apply to most students from GCSE schools intending to do post-16 English study.); and

- some basic grammatical concepts (such as tenses, or parts of speech).

Thus, it is essential for teachers to recognise that a foundational approach needs to be taken to post-16 language study, as many areas of the curriculum are likely to be completely unfamiliar to most students, for instance:

- aspects of grammar, syntax, morphology, phonology and semantics
- aspects of socio-linguistics, including language change, language variety, and language and gender
- aspects of the science of language – including language acquisition and development, and ideas about neurolinguistics and psycholinguistics
- ideas about the nature of creativity in language, and the features and values of literary and non-literary language
- the mechanics and paraphernalia of language investigation
- the writing of language commentary and analysis

Although pre-16 language study may not have prepared students formally for this, one of the delights of language study at this level is enabling students to draw on the vast range of personal and social experience of language they have, especially in the areas of socio-linguistics and language development, and on their knowledge of their own language practices in speaking, listening, reading and writing.

Into practice: planning for progression in English language

Design an introductory unit for an English language course, aiming to build on what students may already know about language from their study and personal experience. The unit should aim to introduce students to the main areas of language study and make links with their existing knowledge, for instance by asking them to categorise aspects of their knowledge under different areas of language study.

Developing subject knowledge

In fact, something similar may be said of teachers as well as students. Although the situation is slowly changing, the majority of English teachers initially see themselves primarily as teachers of English literature, having studied English literature in the sixth form and at university (Butcher 2003; Blake and Shortis 2010). A number of such teachers will have studied some element of English language at university, but many will not. Conversely, a minority of teachers see themselves primarily as teachers of English language, or as equally conversant with both subjects. It is still the case that most English degrees focus chiefly on English literature. Such degrees may be called 'English', 'English studies' or even 'English literature and language' but still often focus chiefly on literature – though some such courses offer a more equal balance or even the option of a central focus on language. More complete approaches to linguistic study, however, are generally found in 'English language' or 'linguistics' degrees.

For teachers who feel more confident in the realm of literature, the challenge of teaching a post-16 English language course can at first be considerable; however, the following key points are vital:

- As an English teacher, one is already an expert in language. Mastering the elements of English language for teaching at this level is in many senses simply an extension of one's own existing expertise.
- A solid grounding in elements of English language is invaluable not only for post-16 English language teaching but also for the development of one's subject knowledge in pre-16 English teaching, and can also be extremely useful in the teaching of literature.
- The subject of English language is fascinating, and reading and learning in preparation for teaching English language, though hard work at first, can be exciting. There are many highly accessible introductory texts available, as well as dedicated resources and websites, which provide a manageable route to the acquisition of the appropriate subject knowledge.

It is also important to bear in mind that there is, in general, not a great deal of continuity between an English degree and the teaching of English in schools, even if one has concentrated chiefly on English literature at university; such challenges are therefore a common experience, especially in the early years of teaching. For most English teachers, an English degree of *any* kind may seem only loosely connected with the teaching of the school curriculum, including basic literacy skills, media analysis, drama, knowledge about language, and so on.

Professional reflection: subject knowledge in English language

Writing a language autobiography is a common, and often very rewarding, task set for Key Stage 3 and 4 students in developing their knowledge about language. Audit your own knowledge by writing a language autobiography, reflecting on:

- your own language development as a child and adult;
- knowledge gained about language from family and community;
- knowledge gained about language from school and university;
- knowledge gained about language from professional activity; and
- the extent of your knowledge about the following: grammar, semantics, pragmatics; language acquisition, language learning, language and the mind, language and the body; language and power, language and gender, language and class, language and ethnicity; language variety, language change, language and literature.

Approaching pedagogy and curriculum

The emphasis on concepts and theories in language study, and the lack of long central set texts (which form the focus of literary study), means that some of the staples of the

English teacher's pedagogy are not always applicable here. English language is in part a science, in part a humanities subject, in part an arts subject – and it requires a range of appropriate approaches.

There are of course many opportunities for classes to work with texts of many kinds, and, as with literature classes, group work can here be invaluable for building students' confidence and their ability, for instance, to classify and analyse types of text and language use independently. As with many science subjects, there is a strong emphasis on learning and applying concepts, such as grammatical functions and terms; here, games and drama activities, for instance, can be valuable tools. There is also, as in science, an emphasis on the collection and investigation of data, and a set of methods and concepts which need to be taught in order for students to manage this. Group work is again invaluable here, enabling students to support each other, and also giving them the opportunity to present their findings to others.

ICT: using media and ICT in language

Media and ICT texts are invaluable in teaching language, both as primary and secondary material; students' own enthusiasms for a range of media and multi-modal texts, often (though not always) in the realm of popular culture, can be drawn on to engage them in study, as can some excellent dedicated websites such as the British Library learning site (www.bl.uk).

- Consider how ICT and media texts might be used to support the teaching of: language change, language variety, language acquisition, semantics and pragmatics, attitudes to language.
- What uses might be made in post-16 language teaching of: film, television, radio, computer games, blockbuster novels, graphic novels, blogs, tweets, text messages?

In a quite different vein, writing workshops (such as are common on creative writing courses) are an excellent way of developing students' abilities in creating, editing and transforming texts. As with literature, texts, sets of data and concepts can become classroom-bound objects which lose a sense of their dynamic connection with real social situations, and so it is important to anchor data and analysis in real-world contexts and applications, for instance by making use of the wide range of media resources which exist for language study, and which provide a rich source for data collection and investigation. Table 13.2 provides an outline of pedagogic strategies for stimulating broad ideas about language, and for building students' knowledge, confidence and independence in language study.

Conclusion: beyond the syllabus

This chapter has only been able to offer starting points for understanding the rich history and theory of post-16 English, and for developing subject knowledge and

Table 13.2 Approaches to post-16 English language

Text and context	• Engage students with a wide variety of texts, extracts and data sets of many types, from a range of periods, genres and forms, gradually enabling students to mobilise a range of concepts and knowledge sets (such as language and gender, language change, grammar) in understanding them.
	• Introduce students to, and encourage them to do their own research on, a variety of areas of language, including ones that the specification does *not* focus on.
	• Use websites, and audio-visual and other media resources to strengthen students' sense of language data as a real-world phenomenon with socio-cultural implications.
	• Use students' own language and experiences where possible.
Values and attitudes	• Sharpen students' understanding of linguistic frameworks by investigating social attitudes to language, as well as their own beliefs and values, weighing these up against linguistic fact.
	• Encourage them to access – and perhaps intervene in – media debates.
	• Investigate real-world applications of ideas about language, for instance in local communities, education, employment or broadcasting.
Investigation and experimentation	• Engage students actively in the methods of language investigation – interviewing, transcribing, analysing data, and so on – to encourage independent learning and ownership of concepts.
	• Intervening in and transforming texts can help students to understand the nature of creativity and gain ownership of ideas about production and consumption of texts.
	• Use games, drama activities and other active techniques to teach linguistic concepts.
	• Engage students with what they already know – their own experiences, and those of their friends, family and community – as a starting point for broader investigation.
Course planning	• Plan the course carefully to create a good balance between different modes of work – research and investigation, writing, learning linguistic concepts.
	• Keep study concentrated and dynamic so that knowledge gained can be transferred from one topic to another and does not merely 'stay' in one context.
Language and English studies	• Make students aware of the broader network of studies of which language study is part by making connections with elements of linguistic, literary and cultural studies.

pedagogy. I have tried to suggest here that, for English teachers, it can be both a challenge and a pleasure to maintain, develop and communicate our subject knowledge at this level, maintaining alertness to the relationships between the different pathways through the subject that open up at this point, and to the tensions that exist between and within them. Courses, syllabuses and assessment regimes offer many opportunities, but can also circumscribe learning in ways which inhibit broader understanding. By helping our students to see the wider picture of the discipline, while deploying a range of appropriate pedagogic and curricular strategies, we can ease transitions from secondary to tertiary education, and onwards, developing young people who have a critical approach to and dynamic sense of the richness of the subject that goes beyond the mere practicalities of the exam room.

In summary

You have considered:

- ways of defining, developing and communicating the subject knowledge required for teaching English in the sixth form;
- ways of understanding and managing the transitions between pre-16 and post-16 English and between sixth form and university English;
- ways of approaching post-16 English teaching in order to achieve breadth and depth of understanding in students;
- ways of making connections between students' own cultural and linguistic capital and their studies in post-16 English.

Recommended reading

- NATE's report *Text: Message* (NATE 2005) and the English Association's response *Second Reading* (Barlow 2005) make an excellent introduction to some of the issues discussed here.
- A particularly useful text book, aimed at undergraduates, is *The English Studies Book* (Pope 1998), as is Robert Eaglestone's *Doing English* (2000).
- NATE's professional journal *English Drama Media* and magazine *Classroom* regularly feature articles on aspects of post-16 English (www.nate.org.uk), as well as information about books, resources, events and curriculum developments.
- The HE English Subject Centre (www.english.heacademy.ac.uk) is a valuable resource for keeping up with developments in higher education English.
- The English and Media Centre (www.englishandmedia.co.uk) publishes excellent resources for post-16 teaching, including *emagazine*. Philip Allan (www.philipallan.co.uk) also publishes dedicated resources.
- The British Library learning website (www.bl.uk) is a mine of rich resources for language and literature teaching at this level.
- The following articles provide inspirational discussions of aspects of sixth form literature teaching: Daw 1996; Daw 1997; Blake 2006; Snapper 2006; Wright 2006; Gibbons 2010.
- The following articles provide inspirational discussions of aspects of sixth form language teaching: Blake and Shortis 2009; Blake 2010; Clayton 2010; Kinder 2010; Robinson 2010.

References

Atherton, C. (2004) 'Critical literature? Context and criticism in A level English literature', *English Drama Media* 1: 30–3.

Atherton, C. (2005) *Defining Literary Criticism*. Basingstoke: Palgrave.

Atherton, C. (2006) 'A level English literature and the problem of transition', *Arts and Humanities in Higher Education* 5:1: 65–75.

Atherton, C. (2007) 'Balancing acts: preparing students for university in the mixed-ability classroom', *International Journal of Adolescence and Youth* 14: 65–76.

Barlow, A. (2005) *Second Reading*. Leicester: English Association.

Blake, J. (2006) 'Burying literary treasure: developing inspirational approaches to A level literature', *English Drama Media* 6: 21–6.

Blake, J. (2010) 'A regular army of hippopotami', *English Drama Media* 16: 37–44.

Blake, J. and Shortis, T. (2009) 'Corpus in the classroom', *English Drama Media* 15: 19–28.

Blake, J. and Shortis, T. (2010) *Who's Prepared to Teach School English?* Committee for Linguistics in Education.

Bleiman, B. (1999) 'Integrating language and literature at A level', *English and Media Magazine* 40: 19–22.

Bleiman, B. (2008) 'The mew English A level: further thoughts on the new 2008 specifications', *English Drama Media* 10: 41–6.

Butcher, J. (2003) 'Exploring difficulties in learning to teach English post-16', *The Curriculum Journal* 14:2: 233–52.

Clayton, D. (2010) 'Students debating language change', *English Drama Media* 17: 15–18.

Daw, P. (1996) 'Achieving high grades at A level English literature: an investigation into factors that contribute to schools' successes', *English in Education* 30:3: 15–27.

Daw, P. (1997) 'Using literary criticism in A level English literature', *Use of English* 48:2 and 3: 144–57; 250–60.

Eaglestone, R. (2000) *Doing English*. London, Routledge.

Gibbons, S. (2010) *Literature Study Post-16 (2)*, www.ite.org.uk.

Goddard, A. and Beard, A. (2007) *As Simple as ABC?* London: English Subject Centre.

Goodwyn, A. (2002) 'Breaking up is hard to do: English teachers and that LOVE of reading', *English Teaching: Practice and Critique* 1:1: 66–78.

Green, A. (2005a) 'English literature: from sixth form to university', *International Journal of Adolescence and Youth* 12: 253–80.

Green, A. (2005b) *Four Perspectives on Transition: English Literature from Sixth Form to University*. London: English Subject Centre.

Green, A. (2007) 'A matter of expectation: the transition from school to university English', *Changing English* 14:2: 121–34.

Green, A. (2010) *Starting an English Literature Degree*. Basingstoke: Palgrave Macmillan.

Hodgson, J. (2007) 'Organised innocence: towards a reframing of the school–HE transition in English studies', *International Journal of Adolescence and Youth* 14: 53–64.

Hodgson, J. (2010) *The Experience of Studying English in Higher Education*. London: English Subject Centre.

Hudson, R. (2007) 'Language for its own sake: an A level in linguistics?', *English Drama Media* 7: 21–6.

Jacobs, R. (2010) *Literature Study Post-16 (1)*, www.ite.org.uk.

Kinder, D. (2010) 'The power of games', *English Drama Media* 17: 27–32.

NATE (2005) *Text : Message – The Future of A Level English*. Sheffield: NATE.

NATE (2007) 'The new A level English: a guide to the specifications', *English Drama Media* 9: 39–55.

Palmer, D.J. (1965) *The Rise of English Studies*. London: Oxford University Press.

Pope, R. (1998) *The English Studies Book*. London: Routledge.

Robinson, J. (2010) 'Voices from the library', *English Drama Media* 17: 19–26.

Scott, P. (1989) *Reconstructing A Level English*. Milton Keynes: Open University Press.

Snapper, G. (2006) 'Beyond *Dead Poets' Society*', *English Drama Media* 6: 28–32.

Snapper, G. (2007a) 'Beyond Curriculum 2000: some national and international perspectives on A level English literature', *International Journal of Adolescence and Youth* 14:1: 13–29.

Snapper, G. (2007b) 'A level revamped: English literature, the universities and the schools', *Changing English* 14:2: 107–20.

Snapper, G. (2008) 'Voices across borders', *English Drama Media* 11: 37–44.

Snapper, G. (2009) 'Beyond English literature A level: the silence of the seminar? A study of an undergraduate literary theory seminar', *English in Education* 43:3: 192–210.

Wright, C. (2006) 'Tongues for the tongueless: developing critical confidence in A level English literature', *English Drama Media* 6: 15–20.

14

LINDA VARLEY AND ANDREW GREEN
Academic writing at M level

In this chapter you will consider

- the pre-writing, writing and post-writing stages of the writing process;
- writing educational assignments;
- component parts of assignments (introduction, structure and conclusion);
- the demands of analytical writing; and
- requirements of presentation, language and style.

Introduction

As an English PGCE trainee you will probably have an English-based (or closely related) degree and consequently you are likely to be more familiar with the demands of writing sustained assignments than those training to teach science, mathematics or ICT. There will be differences from the writing you are familiar with from your degree, however. Education is a discipline within the humanities faculty studying the human condition (by investigating aspects of educational life), and this means that with a focus on people, and in some cases a focus on your role, your writing may tend to have a more personal style. This may require a mental adjustment, since personal opinion may not have been encouraged or considered acceptable in your undergraduate discipline. Also, you may well be expected to incorporate presentation and analysis of quantitative and statistical data – unfamiliar territory for English teachers.

Into practice: thinking about writing

1. 'Fetch me a pen, I need to think.' (Voltaire)
2. 'There's nothing to writing. All you do is sit down at a typewriter and open a vein.' (Walter Wellesley 'Red' Smith)

---

3. 'I'm not a very good writer, but I'm an excellent rewriter.' (James Michener)
4. 'Easy reading is damn hard writing.' (Nathaniel Hawthorne)
5. 'The difference between the right word and the almost right word is the difference between lightning and a lightning bug.' (Mark Twain)
6. 'Proofread carefully to see if you any words out.' (Anonymous)
7. 'Write down the thoughts of the moment. Those that come unsought for are commonly the most valuable.' (Francis Bacon)
8. 'Write your first draft with your heart. Re-write with your head.' (From the movie *Finding Forrester*)
9. 'How do I know what I think until I see what I say?' (E.M. Forster)

Consider each of the above quotations about writing.

· What does each of them suggest about the activity of writing?
· Which comes nearest to your own views of writing?

It is also important to consider what writing is about for you, and the reasons why you write. There may well be a range of reasons for this, and thinking here may lead to some useful insights into yourself as a writer.

Professional reflection: who do you write for?

· Who do you write for in university and school?
· Who do you write for outside of these contexts?
· What kinds of writing do you do?
· How often do you write in each of these contexts?
· Which types of writing do you most enjoy?
· What are the differing demands of each of these contexts for your writing?
· Do you approach them all in the same way?

The writing process

Effective processes lead to better writing (see Chapter 9), and it is important to settle into good and systematic processes as you approach your own written assignments, especially as these will probably have to be produced alongside the demands of school placement. The assignments of your course are probably designed to encourage you to make connections between the academic content of the course and your developing practice as a teacher. You should, therefore, think carefully about the kinds of writing you do in response to your teaching, as these can be used as preparation for your written assignments, and may well provide content for them. You will, for example, be expected to write evaluations of your work with individual classes (and maybe individual students) in school. By undertaking a programme of relevant academic reading, you can both enhance the quality of your evaluations and also routinely engage with concepts and materials that will enrich your written assignments.

The following are other ways in which you might set about developing your thinking about writing, so that you use a range of your work dynamically to feed into your academic writing:

- Ask to see examples of written work that your tutors consider to be good, or that illustrate competence at a variety of levels. Sometimes bad examples can be as instructive as good ones.
- Spend time planning and preparing for your writing.
- Talk about your writing with other students on your course and with colleagues in school. Discuss points for consideration and test out the arguments you are going to use.
- Talk about your writing with mentors and other colleagues in school, discussing how the ideas you are working with relate to the practical context of the classroom.
- Use seminars to test out and develop ideas for your writing.
- Make sure you leave ample time for proofreading your work.
- Make sure you read and re-read your own work, allowing time for redrafting, developing thought, use of evidence and so on.

These all locate quite naturally within the cycle for writing at Figure 14.1. Let us consider each of these stages in turn.

Pre-writing

Any written assignment will arise from or at least relate to lectures and seminars. The first stage of writing an assignment, therefore, is the notes you make in preparation for lectures and seminars and the notes you take during them. It is useful to familiarise yourself in advance with assessment tasks and requirements so that you can proactively develop your note-making and note-taking to deal with this.

Your reading is also very important in the pre-writing stage of the process. Thinking carefully about what you need to read in order to fulfil the requirements of an assessment and to extend your understanding in the field is an essential part of the process. You should gather appropriate quotations and references for use in the written assignment, making full and accurate reference to where these are to be found – there

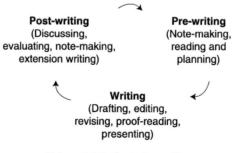

Figure 14.1 Cycle for writing

is nothing more frustrating and time-consuming than having to trawl back through large tranches of reading in order to find a carelessly jotted down reference.

Planning is also essential at the pre-writing stage. You should think very carefully about the content of your assignment, as well as its form and structure. This is especially important when you are working to strict time limits and word-length requirements. This stage of the process may also include undertaking some exploratory writing in which you try out certain concepts and ideas to see whether or not they will fit appropriately into the bigger picture of your assignment. Evaluations of your teaching can often prove very useful if carefully thought through.

Writing

The next stage is a sequence of drafting, editing and revising your writing. This can be a lengthy process, and may lead through a sequence of drafts as you compose, read and adapt your work. It is rare that the best exposition of your ideas comes out perfectly first time. Ideally you should leave some time between finishing a draft and going back to read and revise it. Obviously the amount of time you can leave will vary, depending on how long you have to complete the written task. However, as you are writing you become very close to a piece of work and easily blinded to shortcomings, inconsistencies and omissions. Time away from your work will help you to return to it with a fresh eye and will enable you to judge it in a more objectively critical way. It is also important to do a final proofreading and presentation check before submitting your work. Literal errors, weaknesses of expression, and incorrect and incomplete references should all be weeded out, and you should make sure that you have adhered to any presentational and referencing instructions provided by your lecturers.

Post-writing

Once an assignment has been completed and returned it is important that you do not see this as the end of your engagement with it. Assessed assignments have important formative value for you and can significantly help you in your further development as a writer. Discussing your work with your peers and your lecturers can provide all kinds of insights into how work – both in terms of content and in terms of writing – can be improved. Evaluating your work against published criteria for assessment can also be very useful, as it will enable you to see which aspects of the assignment you addressed effectively and which you did not. Careful evaluation like this will enable you to think proactively about how to plan and execute future written assignments.

Writing education assignments

The written assignments for your PGCE training are likely to comprise:

* generic educational or professional studies
* subject-specific planning and evaluation
* educational enquiry or action research
* reflective journal or reflective practice

This academic component of the PGCE is designed to develop reflective and analytical skills in addition to providing practical experience in planning effective lessons and learning strategies. Assignments are intended to encourage you to build bridges between current educational research, educational theory and the practice of English in the classroom. It is essential, therefore, to consider in specific detail the main functions of the assignment and the form your response is to take before commencing planning, reading and writing; bear in mind that you will probably need to incorporate:

- *description* – describing a particular situation or practice;
- *narration* – sometimes used to present a point or inform the reader;
- *argumentation* – persuading others of your point of view using sufficient support with which to do so (and any issue which has more than one viewpoint is a potential argument); and
- *exposition* – informing and explaining.

In terms of academic assignments there is no 'pure' genre, because very often an assignment will be written in order to achieve several purposes. For example, if discussing the planning of a unit of work, this is largely expository based, but may involve some narration (e.g. recounting the previous learning experience of your students) and an element of argument, such as arguing that one theorist's perspective is better than another in informing the rationale for your work. In the end, it is the exact wording for your assignments that dictates the main purpose and subsequent genre. For example, consider this assignment question related to SEN:

> Describe how the learning of students with special educational needs is supported in your English classroom, focusing on a small sample of students.

Your assignment may contain three sections: background, description and reflections.

Background

This initial section may outline the policy and provision for SEN in your school, including the role of individual education plans, making reference to the Code of Practice and SEN Toolkit where appropriate. It will also be useful to make reference to current debates surrounding inclusion and how this differs from other models of working with students with SEN. You may also want to place the recent inclusion agenda in historical context, demonstrating how thinking about provision for students with SEN has developed over the years, and to debate whether inclusion is necessarily the best model for working with all such students. (This directive clearly indicates a personal focus and requires a combination of description and exposition.)

Description of learning support

In this section you will focus on a small number of students identified as having special educational needs and describe the support provided to them in a particular lesson or series of lessons. It is important to select the students you will focus on with care. If you are meaningfully to discuss the individual learning and support needs of these students you will need to read around the literature that deals specifically with their needs (e.g. autism, or hearing impairment, or dyspraxia). This may be extensive, and so you may need to be selective, but it is very important that you demonstrate recent thinking in the field of working with such students in order to contextualise and provide a rationale for the choices you make as a teacher. You should also take care not to generalise, as not all students with SEN are the same, nor is SEN synonymous with low achievement (as is often implied). Your discussion should be carefully tailored to reflect the nuances in your approach to individual needs. (This indicates a degree of narration as well as description.)

Reflections on your practice

In the final section, which may well be interwoven with the contents of the previous section, you should reflect on your experience of observing and working with SEN students. As suggested before, beware the temptation to make crass generalisations, which are neither accurate nor helpful. That is one danger that such an assignment title poses for you. Here it is also important to make reference to a range of relevant literature on working with students with SEN generally as well as literature specific to the needs of your chosen student. Reference to the major thinkers in the field of education (e.g. Piaget, Vygotsky, Skinner, Maslow or Bloom) is also important, as their work is often foundational. (This indicates exposition and possibly some argument.)

Overall, the instructions point towards an expository genre.

Components of an assignment

The introduction

Focus

Your assignment is likely to be up to 5,000 words in length and consequently you will need to present your thesis (the main point of your assignment) in a clear, summative form that will ensure that you have a unified focus throughout. This will be more than merely stating the subject under discussion; you will be offering the parameters and specific focuses of your assignment. You may also use this section to identify any significant issues you have deliberately chosen to exclude and explain briefly why this is the case.

Background

In addition to a thesis, your introduction should also contain background information, in order to acquaint the reader better with the context of your writing. One possible way of constructing your introduction is to consider it from the perspective of an inverted triangle; in other words, consider beginning with broad background information and then make your focus progressively narrower, culminating with your thesis.

Assignment map

This indicates the order in which you will discuss the various aspects – known as topics – of your thesis. This map is usually accomplished within just one sentence and it makes it clear what the topics of your essay are and in what order they will be presented. Though an assignment map is not a requirement for an introductory paragraph and can be rather mechanical (e.g. the uninspiring and generally unhelpful: 'In this essay I will … then … then … then … and finally'), if carefully written it will guide your reader effectively and can demonstrate careful organisation and thought.

The body

Cohesion

You are aiming for a linear development from the thesis to the conclusion. In order to maintain this cohesive structure, ensure that you do not 'detour' in your writing by introducing new subjects which are not related to your thesis. A 'writing detour' is when a new subject comes up for discussion which does not fit with the thesis outlined within your introduction and/or describes a topic which, while related to your thesis, is too broad. Once you have made sure that all the topics relate to, connect with and illustrate your thesis, you then need to arrange them in a logical sequence:

- *Introduction thesis*: The impact of dyslexia on students' learning; discussion of the issues involved in diagnosing and an overview of key associated areas.
- *Topic 1*: Self-esteem: the experience of the students themselves as poor readers; dealing with perceptions of teachers that they are lazy or struggling with academic work.
- *Topic 2*: Reading skills: what skills are needed for reading, specifically reading strategies; making assessment judgements at the end of a Key Stage.
- *Topic 3*: Website support: resources available to support the teacher, the parent or carer, and the students themselves. (Google gives 3,230,000 results for 'dyslexia'; 2,280,000 results for 'dyslexia in children'.)
- *Topic 4*: Theories related to dyslexia: government-supported information on theories and approaches to dyslexia and dyscalculia.
- *Topic 5*: Case studies: related to specific students within your school-based experience.

For each body paragraph, a good structure is generally achieved by focusing on only one new topic per paragraph. The word 'generally' is to be emphasised. You may feel that a particular topic is so important in developing your thesis that it needs to be dealt with over a sequence of paragraphs. It is useful to remember that individual body paragraphs usually begin with a topic sentence and this topic sentence announces a topic which itself relates to the overall thesis; it is not a brand new topic which has no connection with your thesis.

The conclusion

Summary

This is a restatement of your thesis and/or the major points of your assignment. Such statements, however, are most effective if they are forward-looking rather than a simple rewording of what has already been said.

Implications

Important findings that have emerged from your work. For example, if you have discovered that the key factor for supporting students with dyslexia is the need to address their low self-esteem and that this will inevitably have an impact on your interactions within the classroom, then you need to reinforce this, making clear its implications for future practice. You could give a brief overview of where you will take these issues in the future by providing some speculative examples. It is expected that in academic educational study theory will inform future practice, so make sure you also tie this section back into the academic reading you have done where appropriate.

Effective ending

A 'closing thought', which is usually a sentence long, to give the reader something to remember and to make the assignment sound complete and finished. It could be a rhetorical question (don't overuse this device), a quotation from an academic source or from a case study student or a prediction for the future, based on the results of your research. Avoid trite, 'mission statement' endings, however, as these almost always sound hollow and lack any real meaning.

Use of sources

You are likely to be expected to use the Harvard system when citing quotations. Advice on usage is available (and clearly explained) on the web. Any search engine will produce a range of links, although it may be better to use the home page of your university and type in 'the Harvard System'. This will take you to links that are endorsed (and have been written) by academics to develop skills that you will need to improve your academic style. In addition, your training provider should also give clear guidance. Such requirements may seem pedantic, but accurate referencing is an important part of honest academic practice and is expected at Masters level. Your tutors will also see it as part of your academic development, an important element of your subject knowledge as educationists developing within the practices of the discipline.

It is important to choose the best quotations and put them in the best place within your assignment, but you must also consider carefully how your sources (and particularly any direct quotations you make) interact with your own writing. One of the major distinguishing features of effective work at Masters level is criticality. It is not sufficient simply to report what a particular author or authors have said on a topic; you must engage with their ideas, challenge them if this seems appropriate, and bring them into relation with one another (e.g. how do Piaget's ideas on any given topic relate to

Vygotsky's, and why is this significant in the terms of your discussion?). Consider the following excerpt from an assignment in terms of its use of quotation:

> All schools should ... use commonly agreed classroom management and behaviour strategies; such as a formal way to start lessons. In secondary schools this could include: all students being greeted by the door, brought into the classroom, stood behind chairs, formally welcomed, asked to sit and the teacher explaining the purpose of the lesson.
>
> (Steer 2009: 77)

This is good practical advice from the Steer Report. Although an organised beginning to a lesson may seem like a rudimentary aspect to classroom management, it is a key process in establishing routine in the classroom. In relation to Maslow's hierarchy of needs (1970), establishing routine is an important part in creating a sense of psychological security. This establishes an important level in the hierarchy of needs.

References

Maslow, A.H. (1970) *Motivation and Personality*, 2nd ed. New York: Harper & Row.

Steer, Sir Alan (2009) *Learning Behaviour: Lessons Learned* (PDF accessed 26 August 2010 DCSF-00453-2009, www.teachernet.gov.uk/publications).

While the quotation from the Steer Report and the reference to educational theory are well chosen, they drown out the writer's voice; in effect, the paragraph is too dependent on sources. The opposite of course is not to have enough. Deciding how much is too much or too little is not an exact science. Your tutors may advise you on the number of references they expect you to use (which will refer to the total number of sources you must show in your references page) but not to the number of actual quotations you should use within your assignment, simply because each assignment is unique. The important thing is to hear more of your voice in comparison with the voices of others through your use of quotations.

You may want to consider how this would work in terms of evaluations you make of your own teaching. Clearly you want your personal voice to direct your reflections, but you will also want to support your comments with academic input. Think about evaluations you are required to make of lessons you have taught. Description of the context and aim of the lesson are important, but reflective analysis is better supported if you focus these evaluations on specific areas that allow reference to theory. Hence you may write your evaluation on the following framework:

1. Comment on the effectiveness of classroom management.
2. How successful were the learning activities in achieving learning objectives?
3. How effective were the teaching strategies used in the lesson?
4. What will you do differently next time to improve the learning?

This will allow you to cite findings of the Steer Report; to reflect on the interconnection between learning objectives and learning activities; to reference theory of learning; to consider teaching strategies used; and to reflect on the use of formative assessment, both for students and for you as a beginning teacher. Integrating theoretical and pedagogical reading into your regular classroom evaluations will help you develop robust connections between theory and practice and will help you to build solid rationales into your planning and evaluation (see Chapter 3). It will also serve the purpose of assisting you in the preparation and writing of your assignments.

An example of good use of support occurs when a relevant quotation is used to introduce your own argument; in addition, do not be afraid to take on, and challenge, the theories of others. The following example offers a skilled introduction to the Opening Minds debate and uses a pertinent quotation:

> In his 2003 article in the RSA Journal, Bayliss wrote about the RSA's new curriculum, Opening Minds, saying that it 'sprang from the conviction that there was a growing gap between the way young people were being educated and their real needs, as well as the needs of the country' (p.30). His conclusions were that a curriculum that was driven by information, or content, was neglecting the development of competencies that young people would need in future employment and adult life. This article was to accompany the launch of the RSA's new curriculum, and so was, perhaps necessarily, positive about the concept, but it did reflect earlier thinking from educational theorists.

> Reference

> Bayliss, V. (2003) 'Opening Minds', *RSA Journal* (June 2003), 30–3.

There is a sense, here, that theory has been assimilated into a clear understanding of the issues (and agenda) behind the movement for an integrated curriculum.

Analysis

Analysis as a concept should be clear in meaning already and it is not something that any handbook can necessarily teach. Analysis is a skill that comes with practice. The more you look closely, the more you can see. Using the example of watching a favourite film, you could probably remember a few quotations (but perhaps not accurately), chronological detail, costume and the composition of some scenes. But if you analyse this film, you would be able to talk about the camera angles used, editing style and use of lighting, and how that all combines to affect viewers' perceptions and understanding of the characters. You might also pick out a theme, so that after analysing *Titanic* (1998), you could say that the theme is 'love is blind' or the theme focuses on class relations; nothing to do with a sinking ship at this point!

Or consider how you might analyse a football match; you would do more than simply say 'Jones passed the ball to Smith, who then scored a goal'. You might go 'beneath the surface' and say, 'Jones kicked the ball to Smith because Smith had run into space, waiting for the pass; he'd anticipated Jones' play. He knew he did not have time to control the ball properly and hit a left-footed volley; a beautifully floated ball gave the keeper no chance – Smith scored.'

These two examples involve the writer offering an opinion and, in part, speculating about the subject under analysis, be it directing style or football tactics. This is analysis: looking closely and discovering what the deeper meaning is, or implications might be, for the subject under study. If you do not analyse the subject within your essay, and merely describe it (i.e. discuss the basics of what it is and what it is about, but no more), then this indicates to the reader a lack of knowledge, understanding and criticality, because a lack of analysis tends to imply that the writer does not know much about the subject, and hence cannot analyse something which is not clearly understood.

If, for example, you write 'Cross-curricular planning is becoming more commonplace in schools and it allows different disciplines to collaborate' then you are merely describing the practice. This is acceptable as a means of introducing the subject, but if you continue in such general terms (e.g. cross-curricular integration draws upon a range of subject disciplines; it is used as a means of supporting broader learning; it has been promoted as part of the curriculum), although all these points are valid, you are demonstrating neither genuine understanding of the issues, nor any sense of how this could impact upon your work as a teacher. There is no critical analysis. In other words, it is necessary to explain more about the ideas and philosophy underpinning cross-curricular learning and offer an evaluation of how this can work in practice. For example:

> Cross-curricular planning allows different disciplines to collaborate as a means of encouraging an understanding of the similarities (and differences) of key content and key processes in different subjects. The aim articulated in the 2008 Curriculum, to develop successful learners, confident individuals and responsible citizens, can result in those practitioners who collaborate evaluating their own practice, and this process can help them develop a holistic approach to planning. It can be argued that the opportunity to work with colleagues outside your subject area improves thinking and creates different ideas and approaches.

In this example, the basic information about how cross-curricular planning involves different disciplines is followed by an explanation of the purpose underpinning its introduction, and opinions have been summarised to offer discussion of the implications of collaboration within a school-based context. This is what analysis is all about.

Presentation and language

Presentation and language combine to refer to correct use of Standard English grammar and appropriate academic style. As an English trainee teacher, it is likely that you will only need to check aspects of Standard English grammar, rather than undertake a crash course in correct usage. There are a range of textbooks available to support you, and your tutor will recommend preferred texts. You may, however, want to check your own grammatical understanding in the task given in the box opposite.

Into practice: grammar task box

Identify the grammatical issues in each of the following:

1. Writing on the board, a student started talking.
2. I can access the Internet effectively. Although I can't program.
3. It has been noted by Ofsted that a high percentage of students attend school every day, they like the supportive environment.
4. The school suspended it's students prior to carrying out a full enquiry.
5. An ethical researcher should always authenticate their sources before publication.

Example 1 is known as a dangling modifier and refers to sentences in which the 'ing' form of the verb has nothing or no one to connect to. In other words, who is writing on the board – the student or someone else? Since our expectation is that this is the role of the teacher, we can assume that this is the intended referent of the verb writing. By making explicit the subject to the sentence, the verb writing no longer 'dangles'; it now has someone to connect to. 'While the teacher was writing on the board, a student started talking.'

Example 2: The second sentence in example 2 is a sentence fragment; an incomplete sentence punctuated as though it were complete (hence the use of the full stop after 'effectively'). When you begin a sentence with 'although', you need to have 'two parts' as it were: one before the comma and one after the comma, such as: 'Although I can't program, I'd like to learn.' The issue with the second sentence in example 2 is that it only gives us one half of the puzzle; we need a second half to complete it and create a grammatically perfect sentence.

Example 3 places two sentences together. You can separate two sentences with a conjunction; this use of the comma is known as a 'comma splice'. This is simply two complete sentences separated by a comma, which is not grammatical in Standard English. Therefore, avoid placing two complete thoughts – and sentences – together if separated only by a comma. Instead, use a conjunction, a semicolon (as demonstrated in the second sentence of this explanation) or a full stop.

Example 4 is a contraction for 'it is', so the example would literally mean 'the school suspended it is students', which makes no sense. It is a common mistake, and it may seem incorrect to use possession without the apostrophe, but learn to use 'its' without the apostrophe when you are showing possession rather than omission.

Example 5 is common in speech and has therefore been transferred into writing. Basically, a researcher is a singular noun. However, when referring to this individual's sources, why use the plural form of their instead of his or her? This is perhaps due to the tendency for individuals (rightly so) to avoid designating an unknown person automatically as 'he'. However, rather than saying 'he or she', it is perhaps easier to default to 'they' (and there is some debate about whether this will become accepted practice in the future). In your assignments, however, wherever possible, use the plural form of the people you are referring to (e.g. students, teachers, researchers) in which case the pronoun 'they' will make grammatical sense and will also avoid unintentional sexism in your writing.

Style

Style within academic writing in general refers to a clear focus in your assignment and a coherent structure. Although it would be a mistake to believe that you have to extinguish your individual voice entirely, you need to consider the effect your expression will have on those assessing your work. Consider this example as an introduction to an assignment on inclusion:

> Years ago there was a three year old child who couldn't learn to talk. At eight he still couldn't read. His teachers thought he was retarded. He wasn't. Albert Einstein had a learning disability.
>
> (Poster 1994)

This very informal quotation (which has dubious academic validity) has a written style which replicates spoken English, appropriate for the targeted audience of the media campaign. However, in an academic assignment this is not appropriate, and the tone set for the assignment would be too superficial. It is important to adopt a more formal word choice (and more rigorous academic sources) since it is essentially a poor style in academic writing to use words and expressions which are broad or vague. Though stylistic choices are not strictly 'right' or 'wrong', there are certain ways of expressing your ideas which need to be avoided in academic writing, such as the use of constructions which are used to assert what you need to argue first. For example:

> *Many researchers believe* that this is a serious issue.

The problem with this construction (i.e. the italicised portion of the sentence) is that it suggests that the writer is trying to win his or her argument by making an assertion which may not have sufficient support. The example raises a number of questions: which researchers? Who believes this? If there are researchers' names available, then you must include them. For example:

> Many researchers (Jones 1999; Smith 2000; Higgins 2003) believe that this is a serious issue.

Other constructions to avoid are seen in the examples below:

> *It has been proven that* this is the best way forward. The school is *massively over-subscribed*.

Unless you can demonstrate in an absolute sense that something really has been proven (i.e. it is a fact which will not change and is predictable), or can quantify the term 'massively', then avoid such usage; the expressions above are examples of hyperbole. Exaggeration is tolerated in speech and informal writing, but such expressions and emotive terms in academic writing should be removed, especially as a means of arguing a point; it can convey an immature writing style. Therefore, avoid phrases and even individual words which are hyperbolic. You should tone down assertive statements, especially when trying to argue a point. This is a practice called 'hedging', and essentially involves using expressions such as the following:

> *It has been suggested that* this is the best way forward …
> My research indicates that *there may be evidence* for this issue …
> *There is reason to believe* that my findings indicate a relationship between …

These three examples do not convey a lack of confidence simply because they have been qualified. In the absence of absolute proof for your argument, the best you can do is simply present what you believe.

Given that you will often, in education assignments, be writing about and reflecting upon your own personal practice, use of the first person will on occasions be appropriate. To refer to yourself as 'the teacher' would seem stilted and unnatural. However, this does not mean that you should use first person repeatedly, since even in personal reflective writing this can become anecdotal and repetitive and this should be avoided in academic writing. Nonetheless, first-person usage is not prohibited and allows the development of a more active voice. For example:

> I undertook an Action Research Project to improve teaching and learning and, having evidenced the effectiveness of the pilot within one unit of work, I will ensure that all learning styles, as well as an interactive drama element, will be incorporated into my future planning.

Finally, it is best to avoid contractions in academic writing; their usage is viewed as too informal.

Conclusion

Writing is a process; it takes time to develop a good assignment and involves planning, writing, rewriting, revising, editing and fine-tuning. It will be important to remember as you go through your training year that all the written assignments have to be started well before the hand-in date, will involve reference reading, and may require some action research or case study. Consequently, it is very unlikely that a sudden emergency immediately before the submission date would actually prevent you from handing work in on time, and you are unlikely to be granted a deadline extension, except in extenuating circumstances.

Once you have composed the finished assignment and before you submit it, a good piece of advice is to read your essay out loud. If you read your essay out loud as opposed to just silent reading (i.e. reading in your head), you will train your eyes and ears to detect problems in your writing. For example, you will learn to detect grammatical problems with sentences that simply 'don't sound right' – maybe because you have a sentence fragment or a run-on sentence; you will be able to detect lexical repetition; you may even reconsider lexical choice or the examples you have cited. You are training your ears to listen carefully to each and every nuance of your writing and your eyes to scan for mistakes. Using this approach helps the process of becoming a better writer. Figure 14.2 provides some key issues for you to consider when evaluating your work before submission.

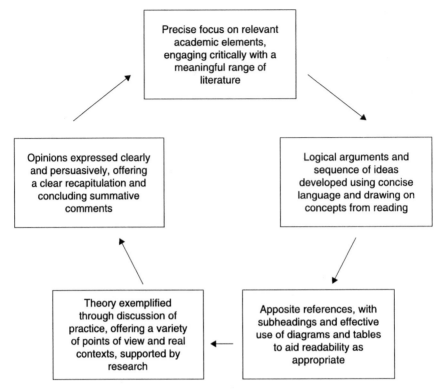

Figure 14.2 Effective writing checklist

In summary

- Good academic writing is clear, objective, formal and cautious.
- Use unambiguous vocabulary, even when discussing complex ideas.
- Try to avoid the use of jargon and explain any technical terms you use.
- Use active rather than passive sentences.
- Approach your topic in an objective way.
- Avoid the use of statements that include bias.
- Avoid making assumptions that have not been tested or challenged.
- It is better to use a cautious tone in your writing because in education you are discussing issues where there are no obviously right and wrong answers.
- Avoid definitive statements for which you do not have evidence.

Recommended reading

- Wallace, M. and Poulson, L. (2004) *Learning to Read Critically in Teaching and Learning*. London: Sage.

- Wyse, Dominic (2007) *The Good Writing Guide for Education Students*. London: Sage.
- *Oxford Advanced Learner's Dictionary*: www.oup.com/elt/oald – an online advanced learner's dictionary that you can use to look up new English vocabulary

Study skills
- www.palgrave.com/skills4study/studyskills – some useful information and tips on how to develop your study skills

Reading skills
- www.uefap.co.uk/reading/readfram.htm – useful information and practice in various reading skills for academic purposes

The following texts are particularly useful for assignments with an education, rather than subject-specific, focus:

- Burton, N., Brundrett, M. and Jones, M. (2008) *Doing Your Education Research Project*. London: Sage.
- Walliman, N. and Buckler, S. (2008) *Your Dissertation in Education*. London: Sage.

Reference

Poster (1994) 'Some Kids with Learning Disabilities do Okay for Themselves' [Poster], Connecticut Association for Children with Learning Disabilities, www.learninginfo.org/einstein-learning-disability.htm (accessed 26 August 2010).

Index

MASTER'S LEVEL STUDY IN EDUCATION
A Guide for Success for PGCE Students

Neil Denby, Robert Butroyd, Helen Swift,
Jayne Price and Jonathan Glazzard

9780335234141 (Paperback)
2008

eBook also available

This book offers an insight into the knowledge, tools and skills that
need to be developed for a successful outcome in a Master's in an
educational context. Using detailed – and real – exemplars, the
authors cover the conventions that need to be followed and consider
the different elements of Master's level work..

The book will enable you to:

- Understand how to prepare, carry out and write a literature
  review
- Consider the different methodologies and approaches that are
  inherent in Master's level work
- Understand the nature of Master's level work within education as
  a research/evidence based profession
- Appreciate the importance of ethical underpinning when working
  at this level

www.openup.co.uk

OPEN UNIVERSITY PRESS
McGraw - Hill Education